The
Surprising
Imagination of
C. S. Lewis

Praise for *The Surprising Imagination of C. S. Lewis*

"When I read the introduction, I could tell I was in for something special. How can one understand Lewis without understanding his conception of the imagination? And, as always, Lewis seems to have thought more deeply with more originality about the imagination than anyone else. Jerry Root and Mark Neal have done us a favor by digging thoroughly into the imagination of C. S. Lewis. As a result, we are better at imagining, better at reading, better at understanding."
— **Joel D. Heck**, Professor of Theology, Concordia University Texas

"Jerry Root has read, several times, absolutely everything C. S. Lewis has written. He has also made it his goal to read everything C. S. Lewis himself read. I can't think of anyone more qualified to contribute to this in-depth study of the many varieties of imagination that Lewis identified and employed in his writings. Resources on the imagination in Christian thought are all too scarce, so this valuable contribution from Root and Neal on the different types of imagination as exemplified in Lewis's work is welcome indeed. Lewis argued that reason is the natural organ of truth, but imagination is the organ of meaning. We don't understand the meaning of anything without an imaginative picture, story, or metaphor to make it clear! Understanding the place of imagination can increase your ability to communicate, write, or enhance your view of the world."
— **Art Lindsley**, Vice President of Theological Initiatives; Institute for Faith, Work & Economics; former President and Senior Fellow at the C. S. Lewis Institute

"Readers of C. S. Lewis's works cannot but stand in awe of his far-reaching and capacious imagination. Root and Neal's insightful work makes an indispensable contribution to our appreciation of the writings of perhaps the twentieth century's leading Christian apologist."
— **Rolland Hein**, Emeritus Professor of English, Wheaton College

"Recent studies have noted that one of the enduring contributions of C. S. Lewis was his reintegration of theology and the imagination. Jerry Root and Mark Neal have been able to particularize this observation to great benefit. Using a matrix of a dozen distinct descriptions for the imagination used by Lewis, they illuminate works both familiar and obscure with fresh clarity. Their introduction surprises and delights as well as informs. Whether you are an experienced reader of C. S. Lewis or just starting out, their efforts will add depth to your reception, contemplation, and enjoyment of the Lewis corpus."
— **Bruce R. Johnson**, General Editor, *Sehnsucht: The C. S. Lewis Journal*

"C. S. Lewis was a towering intellect and brilliant Christian apologist, but it was his imaginative approach to life and thought that makes him home for warm hearts, active minds, and hungry souls. Every page of this magnificent book takes the reader 'further up and further in' to *The Surprising Imagination of C. S. Lewis!*"
— **Dick Staub**, award-winning broadcaster, writer, and founder of The Kindlings, a movement devoted to rekindling the creative, intellectual, and spiritual legacy of Christians in culture

"Professors Root and Neal look far and hard into the Lewisian cosmos and then, organically and persuasively, connect their points of light. The result is foundational. They so refresh a touchstone of Lewis's thought and work that the entire Lewisian landscape is brought into sharp relief, and (by way of Lewis's own brilliant and abiding emphasis and the authors' contextual authority) also manage to reconstitute our insight into a dispositive human faculty. Just so does this original book matter, and matter (as Lewis knew) well beyond the arts, including the master's own."
— **James Como**, Professor Emeritus of Rhetoric and Public Communication at York College (CUNY), Lewis author and commentator, and founding member of the New York C. S. Lewis Society

"At long last, Jerry Root and Mark Neal's *The Surprising Imagination of C. S. Lewis* offers a clear and thorough guide to both explore and apply the wide variety of Lewis's thoughts about imagination, which he called 'the organ of meaning.' This careful, powerful book focuses helpfully on twelve of Lewis's most important ideas about imagination and ties them to his most famous works, while also citing twenty-two more ways Lewis approached the difficult idea. In doing so, Root and Neal have meticulously crafted a rich and thoughtful roadmap that illuminates the largely undiscovered country of all Lewis thought about the imagination. Although one may 'never get to the bottom' (as J. R. R. Tolkien proclaimed) of C. S. Lewis, this invaluable book takes us very far indeed, and offers deeply effective aid toward understanding one of the most imaginative thinkers of our time. *The Surprising Imagination* masterfully meets a need we hardly knew we had and shines a very, very bright light."
— **Andrew Lazo**, sought-after speaker on C. S. Lewis and the Inklings, edited and published *Early Prose Joy*, Lewis's previously-unknown first autobiography

Jerry Root and Mark Neal

Foreword by Steven A. Beebe

The
Surprising
Imagination of
C. S. Lewis

An Introduction

Abingdon Press

Nashville

THE SURPRISING IMAGINATION OF C. S. LEWIS:
AN INTRODUCTION

Copyright © 2015 by Jerry Root and Mark Neal

All rights reserved.

This book is printed on acid-free paper.

Library of Congress Cataloging-in-Publication Data

Root, Jerry.
The surprising imagination of C. S. Lewis : an introduction / Jerry Root and Mark Neal ; foreword by Steven A. Beebe.—First [edition].
    pages cm
Includes bibliographical references and index.
ISBN 978-1-4267-9510-7 (binding: pbk.)   1. Lewis, C. S. (Clive Staples), 1898-1963—Criticism and interpretation.   I. Title.
    PR6023.E926Z863 2015
    8238.912—dc23

                                                                            2015021224

15 16 17 18 19 20 21 22 23 24—10 9 8 7 6 5 4 3 2 1
MANUFACTURED IN THE UNITED STATES OF AMERICA

In Memoriam Chris Mitchell (1951–2014)
A part of us still cannot accept that you are gone. We feel the weight of
your loss daily, and we'll miss your childlike faith, your ability to see good
everywhere, the way we felt whenever we left a conversation with you, the
nimbleness of your mind, the way a discussion with you helped to clarify our
thinking. Our only consolation is knowing we will see you again soon.
And for his Julie...

Contents

Part 2: Imagination and the Literature of the Heart

Acknowledgments

The authors express gratitude to their wives, Reba Neal and Claudia Root, who made great sacrifices of time while their husbands dedicated themselves to the production of this book. Without them, it never would have come to light. Mark says, "Thank you, Reba, for your endless patience in putting up with long, late hours of writing and for your love, encouragement, and support for this book; I love you."

No book of any substance can be produced without significant contributions by others. Thanks to Stan Guthrie, our agent and editor, for all of his editorial assistance, speed, efficiency, and advice about this manuscript, as well as his assistance with the orthography. Also, we express our gratitude to those at Abingdon Press, especially Dr. Kathryn Armistead, who first believed the idea for this book had merit and who first saw its potential as an introductory textbook for C. S. Lewis courses being developed in universities and colleges, both secular and religious. Thanks to David Teel, also at Abingdon, for his part in making sure the manuscript crossed the finish line.

Any work devoted to the study of C. S. Lewis must acknowledge a great debt to the Marion E. Wade Center at Wheaton College and to the associate director, Marjorie Lamp Mead; archivist Laura Schmidt, editorial and administrative assistant Kendra Juskus; and to the staff: Elaine Hooker, Carla Mayer, and Shawn Mrakovich. We must express a sense of gratitude coupled with deep loss to Chris Mitchell for the years of long talks over pipes and single malt at the Perch and a host of other places all over the world. His passing, to this day, is felt sorely.

Mark acknowledges Matthew Farrelly for valuing the imagination, listening to late-night musings, and offering suggestions and feedback; Justin Conrad for encouragement and reading the manuscript; David Haskins for all the conversations about art and creativity and vision; Adam Babarik for inspiration when the flow of ideas was running dry; Todd Kelsey for encouragement, both for this book and writing in general; and his parents and siblings for their love, support, and interest in this project.

At various stages of this book's development, Mark's manuscript chapters were read by Jerry and generously critiqued by Tim Tremblay and members of the *Mead Men* including Dr. Lon Allison, Dr. Walter Hansen, Dr. David Henderson, Dr. Chris Mitchell, and Dr. Rick Richardson. Both Mark and Jerry discussed the various chapters over pipes at *The Brotherhood of the Briar* with men such as Chris Grant, Matthew Farrelly, Ralph Walker, Greg Bunch, Matt Dominguez, Jeff Frazier, Bob Hadad, Chris Lanier, Andrew Lazo, Carl Knighton, Dr. Ward Kriegbaum, Jeremy Rios, Greg Schmidt, Bert Bunn, and Ryan Thill with occasional visits by Steve Beebe and Michael Ward. We are grateful for those Thursday nights around the blazing fire. Thanks also to all the members of the 1405s for supplying much-needed breaks from writing and for the oil of conversation that puts a song in the heart, laughter on the lips, and a warm glow of contentment in the eyes.

There are others still whose conversation and feedback about the manuscript was noteworthy and appreciated: Bob Bennett, Professor Robert Bishop, Dr. Den and Pat Conneen, Dr. Jeff Davis, Professor Bruce Edwards, Debby Edwards, Karen Erkel, Dr. Brett Foster, Nigel Goodwin, Dr. Matej Hajek, Professor Pavel Hosek, Jean Kliebhan, Professor Mark Lewis, Dr. Art and Connie Lindsley, Dr. Wayne Martindale, Dr. Matthew Milliner, Dick Staub, and Professor Peter Walters. We remain grateful to each of you, not only for your insight on various occasions but also for your friendship.

Foreword

C. S. Lewis loved Oxford. I write this foreword in Oxford, a place of both inspirational beauty and mysterious secrets. Lewis became a student here in 1917 and continued to reside in the city until his death forty-six years later in 1963. Even when he accepted a professorship at Cambridge in 1954, he did so on the condition that he could continue to keep his primary residence in Oxford.

Oxford is a city that lifts eyes upward to see dreaming spires, crenelated walls, and soaring towers. But it is also a centuries-old warren of hidden passageways, cloistered corridors, and doors that open only if you have the right key. The ancient architecture of Oxford continues to stimulate the imagination of all who visit.

What is it about Oxford that makes it the home of imaginative stories and storytellers? C. S. Lewis was not the only Oxford author whose works resonate with imagination. This ancient academic community has nurtured the creativity of many well-known authors, including Lewis Carroll (*Alice in Wonderland*), Kenneth Grahame (*The Wind in the Willows*), J. R. R. Tolkien (*The Hobbit* and *The Lord of the Rings*), and more recently Philip Pullman (His Dark Materials). These authors' classic stories include references to holes, doors, and passageways that make us wonder what surprises are in store as they transport the reader to imaginary new worlds.

Given Oxford's mystique, it's not surprising that many movies and TV programs have also used and continue to use Oxford as a setting for imaginative storytelling. Several scenes from the Harry Potter movies were filmed in this ancient city, where one can find remnants of the medieval city wall and a mound where a castle can still be seen in the mind's eye.

Oxford provokes both dreams and drama. Colin Dexter's inspired *Inspector Morse* mysteries and the prequel *Endeavor*, as well as the sequel *Lewis*, are additional examples of how the city has inspired memorable dramatic characters.

Max Beerbohm's *Zuleika Dobson* and Evelyn Waugh's *Brideshead Revisited* are other classic stories set partly or completely in Oxford. Mysteries are mysterious because we can't yet see what is on the other side of the door. But eventually the door is opened and the mystery is solved—or at least resolved until another closed door confronts us and we are left to wonder what is behind it.

Perhaps it is the presence of so many closed doors and private entrances in Oxford that inspired Lewis to use the door as a frequent metaphor of how our imaginations can transport us from one place to another. Whether it was opening a wardrobe door, closing the door of a spaceship, peering behind the doors of N.I.C.E., or seeing an image of a door in the air in *The Last Battle*, Lewis described portals that simultaneously served as both exits and entrances. A door symbolizes transformation. It signifies both moving away from the past and venturing into an unknown future. Doors keep harm at bay or open to new opportunities. Lewis understood our lives are a series of simultaneous comings and goings as we daily cross thresholds and transoms, even when we are not aware we are between rooms.

This book will help you open the door to Lewis's imagination and explore the work of C. S. Lewis in ways that will both nurture and surprise you. Jerry Root and Mark Neal have written a masterful book that will give the reader new insight into the imaginative mind of Lewis. It's not only Lewis's Narnia stories, space trilogy, or other fiction that evidence his imagination—Root and Neal remind us that imagination imbues *each* of Lewis's works in the multiple literary genres they chronicled.

Root and Neal's book provides a door into the *Surprising Imagination of C. S. Lewis*, offering a panoramic view of his key works. Chapter 1 describes Lewis's own path to Christianity in *Surprised by Joy*. Logically following the story of Lewis's conversion, chapter 2 is a review of *Mere Christianity* and its creative visual metaphors that describe the essence of Christian belief. In chapter 3, about *Letters to Malcolm: Chiefly on Prayer*, the last book Lewis wrote, Root and Neal help the reader understand how these letters to a fictional friend evidence a satisfied imagination. Two of Lewis's key literary criticism works, *An Experiment in Criticism* and *The Discarded Image*, are the focus of chapters 4 and 5; these books help us metaphorically break out of the dungeon and stand on the shoulders of giants offering fresh, new perspectives. Appropriately, at the heart of the book are two chapters that open the door to his children's (and also adults') stories. *The Horse and His Boy* and *The Voyage of the Dawn Treader* are discussed in chapters 6 and 7—central chapters that illustrate Lewis's imaginative story-telling prowess at its peak. The first and last of Lewis's science fiction works, *Out of the Silent Planet* and *That Hideous Strength*, are presented in chapters 8 and 9. These two books constitute the beginning and ending of a space trilogy that continues to have contemporary relevance. The door to Lewis's world of things both celestial and hellish is opened in chapters 10 and 11, where a bus ride to heaven is the central plot of *The Great Divorce*, and the devilish epistles of *The Screwtape Letters* are psychological probes that simultaneously makes us laugh at, wince, and ponder our own follies. What better place to end a book about C. S. Lewis and imagination than with a consideration of his collected poetry? Lewis's early vocational aspiration was to be a poet. Although he was a published poet, his poetic talents are best known for infusing his prose and lifting his writing to imaginative heights.

Lewis taught us that reason and imagination are the doors to truth and meaning, respectively. Going through only one of these doors does not provide a complete picture. But by employing *both* reason and imagination we are able to see the entire vista as we sometimes struggle to make sense out of what confronts us. What is surprising about Lewis's imagination is its ubiquity. What is also surprising is that it took so long for us to have this excellent, systematic guide to his imaginative gifts.

If you are not able to get to Oxford any time soon, this book can take you there in your imagination by evoking images of dreaming spires, as well as doors that lead to destinations yet to be explored. Open the door and enter *The Surprising Imagination of C. S. Lewis*.

Steven A. Beebe

Regents' and University Distinguished Professor

Texas State University

Past President, National Communication Association

Oxford, 2015

Introduction

Cultivating the Life of the Imagination

It has been said that Eskimos have more than thirty words for snow and more than seventy words to describe sea ice. Where snow is an ever-present reality, people will refine their language to be more definite and descriptive. There are words to distinguish wet snow and powdery snow. There are words for fresh snow and old, heavy, light, icy, and dirty snow. We might expect this range of vocabulary from those whose survival demands such clarity. Eskimos must be exact in their descriptions. So, too, C. S. Lewis, who inhabited the world of the imagination, had a more nuanced understanding of that world. Consequently, we can be surprised and pleased by his many uses of the imagination. We can discover in Lewis a refinement of our own understanding of the gift of the imagination.

Lewis and Imaginative Depiction

This book is an introduction to C. S. Lewis's published work. To understand Lewis well requires a grasp of his uses of the imagination. Lewis said so himself. In a letter written in 1955 he observed,

> The imaginative man in me is older, more continuously operative, and in that sense, more basic than either the religious writer or the critic. It was he who made me first attempt (with little success) to be a poet. It was he who, in response to the poetry of others, made me a critic, and in defense of that response, sometimes a critical controversialist. It was he who after my conversion led me to embody my religious beliefs in symbolical or mythopoeic forms, ranging from Screwtape to a kind of theologized science fiction. And it was of course he who has brought me, in the last few years to write the series of Narnian stories for children.[1]

There is no getting around the fact that his remarkable output of publications are pearls held together on the string of his very active imagination. Therefore any introduction to Lewis's writing should include reference to his uses of the imagination. And no clear grasp of Lewis as a writer could ever be complete without paying attention to the importance of the imagination across the wide range of his literary output. One could accurately say that each of his books, in one way or another, displays a robust use of imaginative depictions. This is evident in his nonfiction as well as his fiction. Significant propositions or points are often accompanied by just the right metaphor or analogy that awakens the reader's own imagination, enabling a fresh insight to be grasped, understood, and remembered.

Contemporaries of Lewis noted that whatever he wrote, this power of depiction made him so interesting to read, so persuasive in his judgments, and so memorable. Evelyn Underhill, having read Lewis's *Out of the Silent Planet*, the first of his science fiction novels, wrote to him, "It is so very seldom that one comes across a writer of sufficient imaginative power to give one a new slant on reality; and this is just what you seem to have achieved."[2] Two years later, after reading Lewis's *The Problem of Pain*, Underhill again writes, "It is this capacity for giving imaginative body to the fundamental doctrines of Christianity that seems to me one of the most remarkable things about your work."[3] Here is Underhill commenting on Lewis's imaginative power as expressed in both his fiction and nonfiction. Lewis's close friend and fellow Inkling Austin Farrer, the Oxford philosopher, observed of Lewis that "his real power was not in proof, it was depiction."[4]

Lewis continues to be appreciated for his use of the imagination. It is an appreciation that transcends cultures. Lewis scholar Pavel Hosek, of the Charles University in Prague, observes that

> the imagination is necessary if experience is to be structured into patterns by which generalization can be made and meaning discovered. Through the imagination we perceive and understand ourselves. It is by means of the imagination that we are able to make sense of the world around us and begin to encounter the very presence of transcendence.[5]

What others have noted about Lewis, while significant, is not nearly so convincing as actually reading him and seeing the reality in a firsthand encounter with the works themselves.

Imagination as a Way to See with Greater Clarity

In his autobiography, *Surprised by Joy*, Lewis recalls the part imagination played in his own development. He observes three senses of the imagination. The first was what he calls "reverie, day-dream, wish-fulfilling fantasy."[6] He sees this self-referential use of the imagination as unhealthy and narcissistic; it imagines oneself as the hero in all of its fantasizing. The second sense is in invention, that is, the creative power to craft images and depictions to try to grasp the world as it is, rather than for any utilitarian benefit. Third, Lewis noted the importance of imagination in his own intellectual development, helping him to understand horizons beyond his own experience. Lewis becomes a guide for us to grow in understanding of ourselves and our place in the world.

The Scheme of *The Surprising Imagination of C. S. Lewis*

The Surprising Imagination of C. S. Lewis provides a unique and helpful introduction to Lewis's work by exploring his various uses of the imagination. We aim to show through Lewis's autobiography, children's stories, science fiction, satire, poetry, religious work (both apologetic and devotional), and literary criticism that an intentional use of the imagination is always at work.

An appendix lists additional ways Lewis used the imagination. Our horizons are widened and our seeing extended by means of Lewis's vocabulary of the imagination. Certainly, examples of his imagination can be seen in its various forms across the corpus of his published work. Nevertheless, for the purposes of this introduction to Lewis, we seek to provide representative examples as they are embodied in particular books. We won't describe all the uses listed in the appendix, but we want to give you a helpful sample, equipping you for later exploration.

The scheme of this study focuses on one Lewis book in each chapter and discusses that book in light of a particular use of the imagination. These chapters act as guides to new readers of many of his books. They also reintroduce readers who are familiar with Lewis to a fresh approach to his work.

In Lewis's autobiography, *Surprised by Joy*, we will encounter what Lewis calls the baptized imagination. The baptized imagination is the imagination regenerated; it is the very beginning of longing and desire. It is what George MacDonald called "Waked enough to feel a woe" in *The Diary of an Old Soul*.[7] The process of spiritual development requires one to imagine stages of spiritual life beyond one's current stage of development and experience. The beginning of that process is what Lewis calls the baptized imagination.

The reader discovers an embodiment of the penetrating imagination in *The Horse and His Boy*. Lewis, drawing on both Dante and Shakespeare, notes that the imagination can be used to develop a deeper, more significant grasp of any given thing. Lewis comments about Dante's multiple uses of similes in a single canto and also of Shakespeare's multiple, and various, uses of metaphor in a single sonnet to describe one particular thing, and yet still never fully describe it. Finite minds will never fully know anything; nevertheless, the penetrating imagination is one way to gain deeper knowledge about a particular reality.

In *The Voyage of the Dawn Treader*, Lewis displays the material imagination. He draws his own understanding of this from the writings of Christopher Marlowe. The power of the material imagination is found in its clarity to describe material things. This use of the imagination may be compared to the artist's use of materials. As an artist's materials begin to shape and influence the work of art, so the material descriptions within a story work on the author's imagination in a similar way. When a boy, such as Eustace in *The Voyage of the Dawn Treader*, is turned into a dragon, the description of his attempt to write in the sand as a dragon helps the reader grasp how difficult this must be. Eustace no longer has the capacity to write cursive with a practiced hand. The very material of a dragon's muscles and sinews properly attended to will shape the telling of the story. The author's imagination is directed by means of his material.

Lewis's science fiction provides other examples of his imaginative clarity. In his extraterrestrial novels he displays uses of the primary imagination in *Out of the Silent Planet*, as well as the generous imagination in *That Hideous Strength*. When writing about the primary imagination, Lewis acknowledges his debt to the poet Samuel Taylor Coleridge. The empirical gates of eye, ear, nose, tongue, and touch provide much information, but the sorting of that information transcends the data itself. Information supplied by the sensations must be made sense of: we choose at some level what data we will listen to as we sort through the sensations and determine what the information means. Primary imagination speaks of the imaginative capacity to make sense of the data; it is what is known as common sense.

Lewis does not use the generous imagination, exemplified in *That Hideous Strength*, in a positive way. He recognizes in it the tendency to inflate and embellish beyond desert. "It invites us first to reify, then to personify, finally to deify."[8] This use of the imagination tends to overstate things. It directs attention to what it wants others to find and directs attention away from anything that would count against the embellishments. It is dishonest. When the fruit of this sort of imaginative endeavor is cultivated, its expressions tend to be manipulative. Lewis sees the generous imagination as one of the few types of imagination that can be employed to do evil.

We see examples of the transforming imagination in *The Great Divorce*, a work of satire. Lewis borrows from William Wordsworth to depict a use of the imagination that is similar to what the psychologists call projection. It occurs when the subject projects his or her assumptions onto someone or something, whether or not such projection is warranted. It is the tendency to rationalize or justify bad acts to the point of moral blindness. This use of the imagination reminds us that, like all human endeavors, people are capable of both acts of dignity or depravity. Again, we should not be surprised to discover that not all uses of the imagination are good. Some uses of the imagination can take us further up and further in. Other uses can take us further down and further out. Lewis reminded his readers of the aphorism, "Any road out of Jerusalem must also be a road into Jerusalem."[9] In *The Great Divorce* Lewis depicts this unfavorable use of the imagination through his characters.

In *The Screwtape Letters*, Lewis delineates the controlled imagination, which projects one's self-seeking desires onto others. It projects the self in order to gain ascendancy over the world, and even more, to devour it, as the devil, Screwtape, and his nephew, Wormwood, seek to do in this work. It is a negative type of imagination based on wish-fulfillment.

Lewis's poetry embodies what he called the absorbing imagination. Lewis draws the concept from John Milton and writes about how Milton's imagination absorbed like a sponge.[10] Milton borrowed traditions and images from a host of sources and synthesized them in his work. Similarly, Lewis borrows images and embellishes them in his poetry. His sources are taken from the Bible, medieval poetry, and classical myth. These images allowed him to express his own ideas through these familiar forms.

Lewis's religious writing provides rich examples of various uses of the imagination. His work in Christian apologetics, *Mere Christianity*, expresses the shared imagination, with its rhetorical sensitivity to the reading audience. This sensitivity may be due to the fact that the genesis of the book was as a series of BBC radio broadcasts. The shared imagination speaks of those elements that both author and audience hold in common in their imaginative grasp of the environment in which they live. The shared imagination utilizes commonly held ideas and beliefs. The author appeals to these shared beliefs while building new structures upon these shared foundations, seeking to connect with the reader or the audience. It is a tool best employed when the writer is aware of the rhetorical need of a given moment.

Lewis's religious work also includes devotional writing. *Reflections on the Psalms* supplies an example of the compelled imagination, which focuses attention on what can and must be talked about. It does not tell and then suggest the type of response; rather, it awakens, focuses attention, and presents its material to the reader's senses: the smell, the colors, the sounds, the textures, and the tastes of the described world. The author has given data to the reader that compel a necessary response. In a sense, the reader has entered into the artist's world full-bodied. The compelling is not one of coercion; it is a compelling made just by allowing the reader to render to the made-up or imagined world its proper due.

The last book Lewis wrote is also a work in religious devotion: *Letters to Malcolm: Chiefly on Prayer*. In this he outlines the satisfied imagination, which he discovered in Marcus Aurelius and many early poets. The satisfied imagination takes delight in the world. While it may be easy to complain about circumstances, the satisfied imagination seeks to find glory and joy, not so much in the world of one's making, but in the world one has inherited, the very world into which one is born. It is the imagination of the citizen of the world. It has a hint of love of the fatherland. It can see through suffering and sadness of a broken world to things yet profound and worthy of poetry.

In one of the most significant genres of Lewis's work, his literary criticism, readers will also see his robust imagination at work. We take examples from *An Experiment in Criticism* for a look at the awakened imagination and *The Discarded Image* for an exploration of the realizing imagination. Lewis, in one essay, asks, "How can an unchanging system [like Christianity] survive the continual increase of knowledge?"[11] Certainly growth requires a change, not of kind but of degree. Without continuity, there is no growth. Lewis observes, "Wherever there is real progress in knowledge, there is some knowledge that is not superseded. Indeed, the very possibility of progress demands that there should be an unchanging element."[12] Thus, the awakened imagination, as Lewis conceives it, attempts to make sense of continuity and change. Any system of thought not subject to ossification must be awakening constantly to deeper consciousness, the awareness of fresh applications of old ideas to new challenges.

The Discarded Image originally was the Prolegomena Lectures to Medieval Literature he gave at Oxford University. In this book he utilizes the realizing imagination, which he claimed was characteristically medieval. Lewis notes the capacity of the medieval mind to embellish the material received from earlier sources to the next generation. This realizing is like the bud that is opening up into full flower. Lewis helps his readers see that the views of the past have to give way to more robust understandings. And he warns his readers to remember that their own images of the universe will, in time, have to give way to certain kinds of revisions as well.

We hope that readers will make a lifelong study of Lewis so that they will grow in knowledge and character. But we don't want you to stop with Lewis. Lewis would not want that either. Lewis opened more than wardrobe doors. In opening the covers of this book, may you become thirsty to read more and more in order to cultivate a vigorous love of the life of the imagination.

Part 1

Imagination and the Literature of the Mind

Chapter 1

The Book in the Bookstall

Baptized Imagination in *Surprised by Joy*

C. S. Lewis read George MacDonald's book *Phantastes* in 1916. He said that after reading this book his imagination was baptized. He meant that regenerative processes began in him. When this occurred, though he still considered himself an atheist at the time, he started on the long road to faith in Christ. He chronicles this in his autobiography *Surprised by Joy*.

Lewis and the Choice to Write Autobiography

Lewis wrote autobiography on purpose. That is, he was as intentional about writing *Surprised by Joy* as he was writing in each of the literary forms he employed. Lewis wrote in at least seventeen literary genres: apologetics, autobiography, educational philosophy, essays, fairy stories, journal, letters, literary criticism, literary history, lyric poetry, narrative poetry, the novel, religious devotion, satire, science fiction, short story, and translation.

He chose a literary form that matched what he wanted to say. Lewis was always seeking how to properly adorn his words, ideas, and imaginative expressions. He said, "It is easy to forget that the man who writes a good love sonnet needs not only to be enamoured of a woman, but also enamoured of the Sonnet."[1] Similarly, Lewis said, "I wrote fairy tales because the Fairy Tale seemed the ideal Form for the stuff I had to say."[2] He wrote his science fiction novels because they enabled him to say what he wanted to say about the longing for another world.[3]

Lewis's point was clear: an author should select his or her literary genre as carefully as he or she selects the content. He or she should take the same care as a

– 03 –

sculptor who selects her marble or a painter selects his material. He wrote in the literary form that helped him best set forth a certain body of ideas.

Some critics make large assumptions as to why Lewis wrote his autobiography. Some have suggested that *Surprised by Joy* is a bad autobiography because he leaves so much out.[4] Others infer that Lewis used autobiography as a therapeutic exercise to cleanse his conscience before taking on his Narnian project. In other words, the autobiography was, at the end of the day, merely an exercise in confessional psychology.[5]

Another critic claims that Lewis fails to disclose his shortcomings and hides realities behind pretense, suggesting that the work should have been called *Suppressed by Jack* (Jack was Lewis's nickname) rather than *Surprised by Joy*.[6] Others say that the autobiography is similar in style to Augustine's *Confessions*.[7]

Lewis probably chose autobiography so he could shape his rhetoric along the lines of a testimonial apologetic for the Christian faith. Lewis says that his goal in writing the book was to tell the story of how he moved from atheism to Christianity.[8] And, relative to its matter, the purpose of the book determines the details he chose to both include and to leave out. This specific purpose also determined that the narrative should end at the point of his conversion at the age of thirty-three.

True, Lewis lived another thirty years after the events recounted in *Surprised by Joy*. During those years he became a noted public figure. His picture was published on the cover of *Time* magazine in 1947. He was a popular writer of science fiction and children's books. Lewis was also a recognized academic in medieval and Renaissance literature. Norman Cantor claims Lewis was the greatest scholar of medieval literature of his age.[9] Lewis was even a popular radio presenter on the BBC and a noted lecturer.

None of these points, however, are mentioned in his autobiography. His intent was clear: to tell of his pilgrimage to faith, noting those events important in that process. He does not include details unnecessary to the story he wanted his readers to know. The details he left out did not advance this narrative.

One author faults Lewis for giving mounds of information about his school experiences but hardly anything about his war years. To be sure, Lewis did not have a positive experience in the schools he attended. As the autobiography makes explicit, he was awkward and bookish. He was an easy target for bullying and hazing by the older students. Lewis devotes many pages to these formative yet difficult days.

This same critic even charges that Lewis "seems bent on securing revenge on those he believed to have tormented him as a schoolboy by ridiculing them."[10] This accusation seems unfair. Certainly other, more probable interpretations could be given. Lewis's preconversion days were marked by loneliness and estrangements. His mother died when he was only nine years old. His father sent him off to a boarding school in London across the Irish Sea, far from his Belfast home. The headmaster at the school eventually was institutionalized. In that school Lewis was underfed, beaten, and made to sleep in a room where the boys were not kept warm in winter.

Later, when he attended other schools, he constantly highlights his feelings of isolation and estrangement. These feelings exacerbated the deep longings for some object that seemed remote, distant, and ever elusive. As Lewis writes about his school years, he makes a strong case for the human story of isolation. Lewis's childhood is merely a particular example. Virtually everybody can describe their own feelings of abandonment and loneliness. And Lewis, telling his story, bonds with his readers. The apologetic possible in autobiography connects with some readers more deeply than would be possible through discursive argument. The number of pages given to his school years is appropriate, since this time made up the bulk of Lewis's early years. On the other hand, he says far less of his experiences as a soldier in France during World War I. The war years were certainly traumatic and undoubtedly left some scars. Nevertheless, whatever memories they may have embedded into the psyche of the soldier Lewis, they do not represent a very long period of his life. Nor did they figure deeply in his pilgrimage to faith. He made no battlefield promises to God in exchange for safekeeping. But Lewis did discover the writings of G. K. Chesterton during those days, and they goaded him in the direction of faith—something he notes in his narrative.[11]

Lewis also came to have high regard for the common person and the unsung heroes he met in the trenches. These experiences shaped his understanding about real life. He found himself constantly in the presence of inclusion and good will, things that were noteworthy and relevant to his overall theme.[12] Two years in the service contrasted by many years in school seems to justify the brevity of the military narrative and validate the length of the school story. The events he selects were deliberately chosen to support his story of a man on a quest that eventually led him to faith. Autobiography was the literary form that worked best for this purpose.

Further, the events Lewis records are best interpreted without psychological projection by the critic. Certainly everyone in this broken world carries the baggage of past hurts, pains, misunderstandings, and nurtured bitterness. That is, everyone has an interesting psychology. Charging that someone is freighted with these things is easy enough. But these traumas are not necessarily what a book such as *Surprised by Joy* is about. Such criticisms may miss completely the literary motives or intentions of the author.

Lewis warns against these feeble attempts to psychoanalyze an author, especially when the author is not present. This kind of analysis often takes the reader further from the text itself, and likely leads into a fiction or fantasy of the reader's own imagination. When psychoanalytic projections onto the text do occur, there is seldom any way to prove the analysis correct. But thoughtful critics who keep an actual text before them have a better chance of keeping their interpretations on track by simply returning to the text for clarification.

Big Themes in *Surprised by Joy*

Surprised by Joy: The Shape of My Early Life is the full title Lewis chose for his autobiography. As has been mentioned, he sought to fashion his story by choosing those elements, such as his baptized imagination, that would best explain his conversion to Christ. The process was as much an imaginative endeavor as it was a rational one. And the story is a good place to begin any study of Lewis's life and work, for in his autobiography his readers receive a structural unity for most of his other writing. In his book on medieval literature, *The Discarded Image* (discussed later in this book), Lewis remarks that any attempt to understand a literary work should seek to "save the appearances."[13] What does he mean? Any literary interpretation is less likely to go awry if it can account for all the facts while making the fewest number of assumptions. Assumptions often say more about the critic than the text and are often freighted with the interpreter's projections onto the text. We should expect that a critic's own values are revealed in any judgments he or she makes. Nevertheless, literary critic Terry Eagleton rightly notes, "The subjective is a matter of value, while the world is a matter of fact."[14]

A reader of Lewis's autobiography would do well to keep his or her judgments tethered to the text. Saving the appearances suggests that interpretations that account for the greatest number of textual facts while making the fewest assumptions have the best chance of success. Lewis keeps the reader on course by making many explicit comments throughout his autobiography.

Lewis gives his readers an account of his pilgrimage from atheism to Christianity and is explicit in marking the importance his imagination played in this process. He clearly experienced a moment where his imagination was baptized. His eventual coming to faith was to some degree an outcome of that experience.

All growth in understanding will require some use of the imagination. Even scientists begin their method of exploration with a hypothesis. A hypothesis is an imaginative exercise. After experimentation, the discoveries are explained through the use of models. Models are imaginative depictions. Similarly, Lewis records that from his earliest days, he had imaginative experiences. These were linked with an awakening sense of longing or desire that he called *longing joy*. As he recounts, much of his youth was occupied with a quest to find the object of this longing. Lewis also sought to make sense of these heartfelt, imaginative experiences rationally. And while he sought to understand the meaning of these experiences rationally, these imaginative experiences seemed to be matters of the heart. How could Lewis unite his reason and his longing heart?

The challenge of uniting head and heart in a holistic way was a lifelong interest for Lewis. His friend and fellow Inkling, Charles Williams, wrote a cycle of poems recounting the Arthurian legend through the eyes of Taliesin, the court poet of Camelot. The poems are flush with profound theological wisdom and insight, but they do not easily reveal their treasures to a first-time reader. After Williams died, Lewis honored his friend by writing a literary critique of the poems, making them more accessible. Lewis's work is called *The Arthurian Torso*. He notes an image in Williams, borrowed from *The Prelude*, a poem by William Wordsworth. The image is of a Bedouin shepherd carrying a stone and a shell. As he walks, he is trying to fit the stone into the shell. Lewis notes that the stone is an image for the life of the mind, while the shell is an image for the longings of the heart. Then Lewis observes that the *first* problem in life is trying to fit the stone in the shell.

This is the process Lewis is describing in *Surprised by Joy*. In fact, Lewis titled the first book he wrote after his conversion *The Pilgrim's Regress: An Allegorical Apology for Christianity, Reason and Romanticism*, again emphasizing the significance for him of uniting the head and the heart in a holistic way. Lewis believed his newly discovered faith was the thing that could link reason and longing. He used an allegory (the only allegory he ever wrote) as a literary form to make the point. This allegory was employed with apologetic ends in mind. Similarly, Lewis uses his autobiography to do the work of an apologist. This further underscores Lewis's intention for *Surprised by Joy*.

If God exists and created the universe, then nothing in life can be separated from the supernatural. Lewis certainly thought so, and writes, "We may ignore, but we can nowhere evade, the presence of God. The world is crowded with Him. He walks everywhere *incognito*. And the *incognito* is not always hard to penetrate. The real labour is to remember, to attend. In fact, to come awake. Still more, to remain awake."[15]

God is always breaking into God's world and making the divine self known. Such was the case for Lewis when his imagination was baptized. And, often, it is by means of the imagination that God is first apprehended. Why? The word *definition* literally means "of the finite." We define things by virtue of their limitations. To be defined, anything must be small enough to wrap words around it and distinguish it from other things. The question arises, how do you define God? If God is infinite, then God breaks common categories of definition. The medieval scholastic doctors of the church understood the difficulty and wrote about God using what they called the *Way of Analogy*. To talk about the One who is infinite requires such imaginative depictions.

Perhaps this is why Jesus used the imagination while discussing spiritual matters. He said, "The Kingdom of Heaven is *like…*" and taught using similes, figures of speech, metaphors, and parables. Lewis observed that reason is the organ of truth but imagination is the organ of meaning.[16] And he chronicles in his autobiography his own search for meaning. This required him to have significant respect for the uses of the imagination if he was to make progress in a pilgrimage to God.

Surprised by Joy and the Imaginative Impulse

In *Surprised by Joy* Lewis marks the places where imaginative experiences goaded him onward in his pilgrimage to God. Very early in Lewis's childhood, his brother, Warren, brought into their nursery a toy garden that he created on the lid of a biscuit tin. Lewis noted that what all other gardens failed to do for him, that garden did: it awakened in him a sense of longing for something more than a toy garden.[17] A few years later, standing beside a flowering currant bush, he remembered that toy garden—and, with it, an almost sickening desire for some object, but the nature of that object was not clear to him.[18]

A similar experience occurred when he read Beatrix Potter's *Squirrel Nutkin*. Lewis recounts that he was moved by the quality of autumn, and desire was once again rekindled.[19] This happened again when he began reading Norse mythology. He was lifted up in desire for huge regions of northern skies and longed for somewhere remote and distant.[20] Lewis then remarks that those who do not identify, at some level, with these imaginative experiences that set his heart to longing might as well put down the book, for they will never grasp its central message. He writes of this longing, triggered by these imaginative experiences, "In a sense the central story of my life is about nothing else."[21]

Lewis came to be haunted by a longing awakened through creative depictions of life and places beyond his own: "Such then was the state of my imaginative life; over against it stood the life of my intellect. The two hemispheres of my mind were in the sharpest contrast. On the one side a many-islanded sea of poetry and myth; on the other a glib and shallow 'rationalism.' Nearly all I loved I believed to be imaginary; nearly all I believed to be real I thought grim and meaningless."[22]

Lewis recounts those details that prodded him to faith. He observes that his reading began to close in on him. He found himself gravitating toward those authors who wrote of "roughness and density of life." They did not reduce life to neat formulas and systems. They were imaginative. Their portrayals reinforced this deep-seated longing. Most of these authors Lewis found were Christian. They did not write about neatly packaged approaches to life but of life's complexity. One author who spoke to him most deeply was George MacDonald. The account of MacDonald's influence on Lewis is central to the story Lewis tells in *Surprised by Joy.*

The Baptized Imagination

Lewis was studying for his entrance exams to Oxford University, in Surrey, England, at the home of his father's old college tutor, William T. Kirkpatrick. The Lewis family called Kirkpatrick "The Great Knock." Lewis was living what he considered a rather idyllic life. He would rise each morning and read Greek and Latin literature, relishing the original nuances that elude those who can read only in translation. Lewis would then read the papers he was writing for his tutorials with Kirkpatrick. He found immense enjoyment in the debates that followed. Of course, when he first arrived at Surrey, he lost these debates time after time. Yet, good pupil that he was, Lewis was fine-tuning his skills in logic and dialectic. In time, he would win the debates as often as he would lose. His power as a critical thinker was being strengthened in this rigorous environment.

Kirkpatrick, in his early days, was preparing for ordination in the Church of Ireland. But something happened that remains a mystery to this day, and he abandoned his theological studies and became an atheist, trading a career in ministry for one in the academy. Lewis's atheism was nurtured in this Surrey environment, as much as his sharp mind and keen wit. This is why it is so interesting to discover that an atmosphere almost hostile to any kind of spiritual life would be the very place where Lewis would declare, in his autobiography, that his *imagination was baptized.* How did this come about, and what did Lewis mean when he distinguished this categorical description of the imaginative life?

While at Surrey, it was Lewis's habit to break from the rigors of study by taking walks through the countryside. If occasion permitted, he would pick up reading material for his own enjoyment. He would read these books in the late afternoons and evenings until he went to bed. The schedule repeated itself the next day. On one of these walks, Lewis happened by the train station at Leatherhead. It is a place of no consequence from the looks of it, and yet a place of great consequence by virtue of what occurred there and how it would play out in Lewis's life.

At the station, while perusing the offerings at a bookstall, Lewis happened on a pale blue hardbound Everyman's Library copy of George MacDonald's *Phantastes.* He purchased the book and took it with him to Kirkpatrick's. Here he began his own adventure through Faerie Land, following the pilgrimage of the book's central figure, Anodos.[23] The name *Anodos* comes from a Greek word that means "No way." Anodos is to go on a pilgrimage through Faerie Land but has no way, until a Faerie enchantress supplies it to him.

Of course, throughout the book, Anodos has many adventures. Eventually, he comes upon a large manor house that is both inviting and hospitable, but also without a visible host. Each day a fire is started in the grate, generous meals are served promptly at meal times, and Anodos feels the welcome of the place. Often he steals away to the library and reads stories like no other he has encountered. One so impresses him that he recounts it in the narrative of the book. It is the story of Cosmo, a student in the University at Prague.

While Lewis only refers to this story as important in his own life, the reader should become acquainted with it. The story is set in the late seventeenth or early eighteenth century. Cosmo has all the carriage of one who had been born into means but has fallen on hard times. He tries to make his way as a student. In order to finance his education, he teaches other students fencing. Cosmo is a well-admired student, popular among his peers, but he hides his poverty. He allows no one into his private life. He lives far on the outskirts of the city, where the rents are cheap.

One day, as he is walking home, Cosmo happens upon an old secondhand store. The very odd proprietor rubs Cosmo the wrong way, but he wanders through the store anyway. His eyes light upon a mirror. He is attracted by the ornate carving on its wooden frame. Against his better judgment, since he can ill afford such a purchase, he buys the mirror and takes it home. That evening he attaches the mirror to the wall opposite the door into his single-room flat. The mirror seems to get lost in the clutter of a university student's room. A skeleton, the remains of an anatomy class, hangs from a stand. A taxidermied bird of prey from an ornithology course sits on a desk. Piles of papers, books, and unwashed laundry are strewn about.

That evening, as Cosmo sits down to eat, nearby church bells chime six o'clock. He notices movement in the newly purchased mirror facing him. He looks and sees the most beautiful woman he has ever seen entering his room. Cosmo turns swiftly toward the door to look at her, but no one is there. He looks back at the mirror and sees that the beauty is reserved for the mirror only.

Cosmo rushes to the mirror that he might gaze on the woman's beauty. He notices that sadness colors her face and hangs like a shroud all about her. Cosmo watches as she looks into his room and makes a slow and deliberate pilgrimage through the clutter. She is horrified at the discovery of the skeleton, put off by the grotesque appearance of the stuffed bird. She is also clearly disappointed at the unkempt state of the room. She passes through, stepping over one obstacle after another and, as quickly and mysteriously as she entered, she leaves.

Cosmo is captive to her beauty. He will not leave his post at the mirror. Perhaps the woman will appear again and delight him with her beauty. Morning dawns and still he is there. He refuses to go to school that day. He will sit through no lectures, he will tutor no other students in fencing, for he is preoccupied with one thing; he must see the woman again.

Sure enough, come six o'clock as the church bells chime that evening, the woman reenters into Cosmo's room as it is reflected in the mirror. Again, he is captured by her beauty, but he also wonders why she is so sullen. Cosmo watches again as she makes her way around the room. He notes again her contempt for the skeleton and her utter disregard for the bird of prey. Like before, she has to step carefully through the clutter until she has completed her round, before exiting the room once again. At this, Cosmo guesses that the woman may come at six each evening. Exhausted, having been up all night, he sleeps.

The next day, Cosmo again refuses to go to school, if perchance the lady of the mirror shows up at some unexpected time. But she comes again as the church bells chime at six. Cosmo watchers her every move and notices again the sadness of her face and wonders at the mysteries it hides. He sees again her revulsion at the skeleton and the bird and her seeming disappointment at the messiness of his abode. As the reflected door in the mirror closes behind the woman, Cosmo longs to communicate with her. In that moment it dawns on him that she can respond to the items in the mirror. Perhaps if he rearranges items in his room, he can communicate with her.

Immediately Cosmo starts tidying his room, cleaning here and there and putting away the items strewn about. He gets rid of the skeleton and the bird. He hopes that perhaps the woman will notice the changes and that they will somehow please her. The next evening, as the woman in the mirror enters the room, she goes to where the skeleton had been and sees that it is missing. She looks to the place where the bird of prey had stood. As she surveys the cleaned and tidied room, a very faint smile draws itself across her sullen face; Cosmo is smitten.

The next day, he refuses to go to school again. Instead, he goes to the shops until he finds a picture to hang on the barren walls of his room. When the church bells chime at six, the woman enters the room in the mirror. She immediately notices the painting and goes to admire it. This time the smile is broader, her countenance more beautiful than ever.

Cosmo becomes obsessed, not only in trying to communicate with her but also with attempting to bring some joy to her troubled world. Day after day, despite his poverty, he goes out and buys things to please her; perhaps he is actually trying to please himself because of his obsession with her. Cosmo neglects all of his other duties: no school, no fencing lessons, no friends—only his obsession with the woman remains.

Finally the day arrives when Cosmo feels he must have her. He goes to an occult store and buys a book of spells and with it the necessary ingredients to work an incantation whereby he might force the real woman to show up at his room. That night, as he tries to bring about the incantation, a storm is brewing. The wind begins howling and whistling. Rain is pounding on the roof and against the window. Flashes of lightning interrupt the darkness, followed by cracks of thunder.

As Cosmo throws a last lock of hair into the kettle that is boiling over the fire and reads a few carefully chosen words from the book, the door flies open and the rain and wind come swirling into the room. A flash of lightning reveals the silhouette of the woman, cloaked and drenched with rain. Following a sudden peal of thunder, the woman enters, her face now illumined by the fire on Cosmo's stove, and she speaks. She cries out, "Cosmo, I am under a spell to the mirror; if you love me, break the mirror and set me free!"

Cosmo hesitates. Although the window of opportunity in this moment is so narrow, he takes time to inquire if he shall see her again. She can make him no promises. Cosmo hesitates, and in that second comes a flash of lightning and a crash of thunder. When Cosmo awakens, it is morning. The woman is gone, and so is the mirror. His health is nearly gone as well, due to his days of neglect and his obsession with the woman. Cosmo's shame overwhelms him, but in it, all his new quest is defined.

Cosmo slowly nurses himself back to health. He returns to the antiques store to ask the sinister-looking proprietor if the mirror was returned. He finds that it has been but also that another young man has purchased it. Cosmo sets out to find the mirror. He also returns to the university, not so much to study but to begin teaching fencing once again so he can pay his bills. He follows any and every lead that might even hint of the mirror's whereabouts.

This goes on for several weeks, until the day he inquires after one of his former pupils, who has not returned for his fencing lessons. Cosmo discovers that nobody has seen the student on campus. He also learns that this particular student spends all of his time in his rooms, exiting only to buy decorations and paintings for the walls. Cosmo goes off to find the student. At that moment in the narrative, the scene changes.

The reader is taken to the chambers of the king's daughter. She is tossing, trancelike, on her bed. This woman is the woman of the mirror. As the princess moans on the bed, her chambermaids speak softly to one another. A mighty storm is brewing, such as has not been seen over the town since the day Cosmo encountered the real woman in his room. The chambermaids recount that the last time such a storm occurred, the woman threw on her cloak and rushed out into the night—only to return hours later, soaked through and deathly ill.

As they speak in hushed tones, the princess sits up in her bed and shouts, "Cosmo, then you really do love me!" She puts on her cloak and once again ventures out into the stormy night. She hastens from the palace, near St. Vita's, down the hill to the Charles Bridge, where she crosses the Moldau, and on to the Charles University. She comes to Cosmo and finds him standing with his back against a whitewashed wall. Cosmo's face is as white as the wall itself. His hand is clutching his side. The princess throws her arms around Cosmo and through her tears she cries out, "Cosmo! Cosmo! Then you really did love me!" And with this she notices the blood trickling from between the fingers of the hand at his side. A faint smile draws across his face and his limp body slides down the wall into a heap. Cosmo is dead.

This is the story, with some embellishments, that Lewis read, and after reading proclaimed that his imagination was baptized. What in the story gripped him so? First, it is a great story. Second, if it baptized his imagination, we suspect that the story awakened him to long for something spiritually valuable and life-giving. As George MacDonald would become Lewis's unofficial teacher, perhaps a description can be found in MacDonald's *Diary of an Old Soul*. MacDonald calls this spiritual awakening "Waked enough to feel a woe."[24] Third, perhaps there was something in the content of the story itself, the willingness of one, like Cosmo, to exhibit love for another to such a degree that he would give up his life to save that other.

Whatever it was, it set Lewis on a less ambiguous spiritual quest. Some imaginative content now informed him. His mind at this time was that of an atheist, but his heart was looking for something more meaningful, something that would satisfy the spiritual hunger within. The initiation of this quest is what Lewis had in mind when he said his imagination was baptized.

The Baptized Imagination and Escape from Falsehood

J. R. R. Tolkien wrote that one element that a reader should expect to find in a good fairy story is escape. He did not mean escape as the psychologists happen to use the word—that is, as retreat from the real world into the world of wishful reverie. Tolkien, and also his friend, Lewis, marked the difference between the unhealthy escape of the deserter versus the escape of the prisoner. In a world where materialism seeks to snuff out any form of spiritual passion and interest by denying that feature of our humanity that knows it is more than mere beast, we long to escape into those regions that affirm something fundamental to our humanity, that we are spiritual beings as well as men and women of the flesh.

We long to break free of the cacophony of our culture that inadvertently seeks to deaden the pain of our existence by extinguishing the part of us that longs for the rich and robust life of the spirit. We long to escape the falsehoods and pretenses of being treated as mere commercial targets for industries that want to capitalize on us as simply consumers of products. From age retardants to pornography, from get-rich-quick schemes to staying forever slim diets, from products promising virility to plastic surgery, we long to escape. Sanity is likely only to come by escaping from these artificialities into a more substantive life. It is a life where real love is manifest in heaven's high courtesy of those kinds of sacrifices that continually say to others around us, "I offer my life in love of you," rather than the default that says, "Your life only matters if it is useful for my purposes." The first is heroic and full of love; the latter is swollen in its self-interest and knows nothing of the Cosmo-type sacrifice that loves truly, heroically, and communicates to others that they matter simply by being a person who is living and breathing on this planet. As Lewis's imagination was baptized, he was able to begin discovering that his own life mattered more as he was able to value others, not merely use others for his self-interest.

The Value of the Baptized Imagination

A noteworthy moment in Lewis's fiction demonstrates the idea of a baptized imagination. In *The Last Battle*, the final story of Lewis's Narnian Chronicles, a Calorman knight named Emeth ends up in Narnian heaven. Throughout his life, Emeth had been an ardent follower of the false god Tash. How is it that he should end up in Narnian heaven? Some have accused Lewis of universalism, the complex theological position that says roughly, in some of its configurations, that it makes no difference what you believe: All is relative. At the end of the day, if there is a hell, nobody is going there; if there is a heaven, all will end up there.

Let us remember that no author's theological positions should be judged entirely by his or her fiction, though fiction can convey or contain the author's understanding of reality. And if we were to judge Lewis a universalist by what he put in *The Last Battle*, some significant problems would remain—not least of which is the fact that not all of the inhabitants of old Narnia actually make it into Narnian heaven. As old Narnia dies and darkens, a long procession of Narnian inhabitants march single file up to the door into heaven. Aslan, the Christ figure of these books, stands at the door. Some come to him and hate him and turn into outer darkness rather than enter a world where he reigns supremely. Others see the lion and their hearts flood with adoration. They enter to be near him forever. It is this world the Calorman, Emeth, has chosen to enter. Lewis, even in his fiction, at least in this depiction, does not seem to fit the Universalist label. Still, what does Emeth represent in this book? A close look may help clarify Lewis's concept of the baptized imagination.

The name, *Emeth*, comes from Hebrew and it means "truth." Lewis uses the same word in two other books. This indicates he understood the meaning and was intentional about what he named this soldier. Lewis included a brief footnote in *The Abolition of Man* where he cites the word and defines it.[25]

More significantly, in *Reflections on the Psalms*, written within two years of his writing *The Last Battle*, Lewis also refers to Emeth. In this text, Lewis mentions an Egyptian pharaoh named Akhenaton (the father of Tutankhamen), who was a monotheist. Lewis writes that we do not know if Akhenaton was merely a crackpot going against the grain of the polytheism of his time, or someone illuminated to some degree and following the truth revealed to him. Lewis wonders what we are to make of such historical figures, and what happens to them in the afterlife. Could it be that those who have sought faithfully to follow the light given to them might have opportunity to complete the process until they come to fullness of faith, even if that process occurs after this life is over for them?[26]

The matter centers around what theologians call the *ordo salutis*, or the order of salvation. This doctrine attempts to describe the process and logical sequence of humanity's coming to faith. Every version of the *ordo salutis* is rooted in an awareness that salvation begins in the mind of God and God's work in the created universe. First Peter 1:19-20 says that Jesus was "a flawless, spotless lamb...chosen before the creation of the world." In other words, God was not surprised by the sin of the first couple in the garden of Eden. God's redemptive plan was not in reaction to an unanticipated human event. The *ordo salutis*, as a doctrine, is rooted in the character and nature of God. The doctrine is also connected to the historic incarnation of Christ. His death on the cross somehow sets those who trust in him right with God.

But how much about God and the divine plan must people grasp before they can be saved? Abraham, the "father of faith," believes in God's provision in Christ by looking forward to the Incarnation. We know that Abraham did not have full knowledge of Christ, yet his faith in what he did know, in anticipation of Christ, was sufficient for him to become the model of faith. Perhaps there were others like Abraham, people we've never even heard of. And perhaps Akhenaton was one of these. Lewis wonders, but he makes no absolute claim.

The *ordo salutis* continues as it considers the process of one's own personal faith pilgrimage and its development. The process certainly begins with some kind of regeneration that indicates the initiative has started from God's side of the ledger. It is the wakening enough to feel a woe. This regeneration period may be moments before the actual act of salvation or it may introduce the believer to a process that might take years to complete.

What would happen if a person died after regeneration and before conversion? Would God, who began this work in the individual, allow for the process to be completed after death? Some might object that if God started the process, God could preserve the life of that individual until the conversion process could be completed in this life. This is a valid conjecture. However, let's keep in mind that the Old Testament saints' lives were not preserved until the coming of Christ. When did they get the full picture? So, although God certainly could preserve the life until the fullness of the message was known and responded to, what if that was not the case? It is a matter of theological imagination to begin to consider what this reality might look like.

Lewis is doing this kind of imaginative speculation in *The Last Battle*. Some might object to such speculation in a children's book, and this too might be a fair judgment. On the other hand, one could equally ask at what point we should assist young people in entering imaginative work relative to theology. Certainly nobody in their right mind would believe that a current theological understanding is the last word. We will always need serious students of theology to deepen their grasp of the infinite. Anytime may be a good time to help those who are younger begin to see that God is bigger than our best thoughts about God. So Lewis may be onto something in introducing Emeth, the faithful follower of the truth revealed to him until he could meet Aslan, the fullness of truth in flesh.

The baptized imagination is the beginning of that imaginative process on the road to the discovery of God. For Lewis, as he recalls in *Surprised by Joy*, it all began when he picked up a book from a bookstall at a train station in Surrey.

Chapter 2

Hunting the Woolly Mammoth

Shared Imagination in *Mere Christianity*

At the end of his essay, "On Three Ways of Writing for Children," C. S. Lewis recounts an incident that occurred while he was eating in a hotel dining room. He had been served prunes. Not liking prunes he uttered, "I loathe prunes." At another table near his, the voice of a six-year-old exclaimed, "So do I." The shared experience of disliking prunes bonded these two: the Oxford don and Cambridge professor with a six-year-old.[1]

The shared imagination may be defined as that feature making it possible for the one doing the imaginative work (painting, storytelling, sculpting, composing, writing, public speaking, and the like) to connect with his or her audience. The things the artist and audience share in common are valuable assets aiding communication between the two. Every communicator may long to awaken something new in readers and hearers but he or she will not likely do this as well if he or she doesn't begin with shared experiences. Once the connection is established, then the shared imagination has the opportunity to move the audience from what it already knows into the realm the communicator wants to reveal. Lewis was a master of the shared experience and knew it as an essential asset in communication. Whether writing children's stories, or Christian apologetics, or doing serious academic work, or merely penning a letter to a friend, Lewis was always aware of his audience and sought to connect through shared experiences. In this way, the shared imagination is a rhetorical tool. It operates with an awareness of the rhetorical need of any given moment. It seeks to connect with an audience. It demonstrates empathy for others and therefore gives credit and authority to the communicator.

The Doctrine of the Unchanging Human Heart

In *A Preface to Paradise Lost*, Lewis describes a phenomenon he calls "The Doctrine of the Unchanging Human Heart." Lewis says that he once believed that throughout time all people share common things. One can see many examples that support this impression. G. K. Chesterton, in his book *The Everlasting Man*, asked, "What do we really know about prehistoric man?" Since these persons left no written record, it seems that the best we can do is speculate. Except, Chesterton observes, prehistoric people left paintings on the walls of caves. We do not know why. Were these paintings decorations on cave walls where the stories of communal heroes were recounted (before new heroes were born in the dangers of the next hunt of the woolly mammoth)? Perhaps the paintings were religious iconography, and the caves were places of worship. It may be that the place was a tribal nursery where the children were kept when most of the adults went to hunt and gather their food. Perhaps the paintings kept the children entertained. We simply do not know why the paintings were painted. But we do know that the paintings themselves reveal that these prehistoric ancestors were artists and therefore may not be much different from their modern progeny.

About forty years ago there was a change noted in the performances of Shakespeare. Before that time costuming was most often in Elizabethan garb. When change came, the plays were performed in costuming from any time and any culture. The change allowed artists to show that Shakespeare was always contemporary. His themes spoke of the common struggles that plague humankind. The comedies and the tragedies all seem to begin with misunderstandings of various sorts. In the comedies, the plays conclude with nobody taking himself or herself too seriously, and all get a laugh at their own expense. In the tragedies, all take themselves too seriously, and the stage is often strewn with dead bodies as the curtains close. The dignity and depravity of human beings in Shakespeare's plays reveal something of the unchanging human heart.

A further instance can be found in the performances of pantomime artist Marcel Marceau. Removing the particularity of language, Marceau was able to draw both laughter and tears from his audiences, whether in the Eastern or Western Hemispheres. There is something of shared human experience that transcends time, gender, ethnicity, and language.

Nevertheless, Lewis says he does not believe in "The Doctrine of the Unchanging Human Heart," not because it is false, but because it is incomplete. The great thing about the nature of being human is not merely what we share, but the elasticity of human nature, illustrated by the fact that people can be so different from age to age and place to place. Lewis observed that if someone thinks he or she needs notes while reading Milton, imagine the notes Milton would need if he showed up and started reading a modern novel. He might ask, "What's a toaster?" Or, "What's a DVD?" What is an automobile, or an airplane, or a microwave? Or, what is a video game, or a cell phone, or a can opener? A communicator, effective in the use of the shared imagination, begins with things common to the unchanging human heart and moves to those unique to a given and particular circumstance or point of view.

While Lewis exhibits the shared imagination throughout his work, it is displayed perhaps most prominently in his classic work of apologetics, *Mere Christianity*. Even the title suggests that he is not so interested in peculiar characteristics of the faith that divide Christian denominations from one another. He wants to present mere, or essential, features of the faith held in common among virtually all Christians. Further, as Lewis attempts to connect with his audience he begins by pointing out very common elements embedded in human experience that suggest a hunger for the very things he will then explain. It is important to note that Lewis begins with shared experiences that he then implies give evidence that all share a common nature, having been created in the image of God.

The Shared Imagination and *Mere Christianity*

Assumptions behind the Book

In *Mere Christianity*, Lewis operates with a set of assumptions not only common to all Christians but equally common among those who have carefully observed their world as they sought to make sense of it. He describes a skeletal structure of Christian thought embraced by all Christians. These ideas are based on the scriptures and affirmed by the early creeds of the church. There has been some "fleshing out" of this skeletal structure that is different for the Orthodox, Catholics, and Protestants, but the things in *Mere Christianity* reveal a common DNA and evidence of family resemblances among all branches of the Christian faith. So Lewis uses the shared imagination to appeal to a wide audience of Christians, but it is not merely Christians he hopes to reach. The shared imagination makes it possible for Lewis to reach a wider audience of those outside the faith, as well.

Lewis once wrote, "I am an apologist and a 'rhetor' not a man of affairs nor even (I suspect) of practical prudence."[2] The work of the rhetor is to persuade. This is true if you want to convince others to vote for your candidate in the next election or you merely want them to pass the salt at dinnertime. Again, the rhetor is audience centered and wants to move the audience to *do* something. Of course, persuasion can goad or manipulate others into doing immoral acts as well as moral ones. And this is certainly so with all forms of religious rhetoric. Anthony

Trollope once observed that "only the preacher can compel people to sit still and be tortured."[3] In all persuasive endeavors, we must ask the question, "How does a person who seeks to persuade another do it justly without manipulation?" Because of the risks of abuse peculiar to rhetoric, Socrates reminds his audience in the *Gorgias* that the persuasive person ought to be a just person.[4]

In Lewis, readers see a practice that can inform their own attempts to persuade. He embraces the posture of getting shoulder to shoulder with his readers. His descriptions do not leave the reader dependent on him for more. Building on shared experience, he describes with such clarity and imaginative force that the reader is caught in the wonder of the thing itself. When the Lewis book is closed, the reader remains inclined toward the object, eager to discover more. Even though we have a shared sense of the world around us, no one has a complete grasp of things as they are. Each of us can benefit from what others have seen. Lewis appeals to these shared things in order to encourage his readers to go further. The fact that reality is complex never seems far from his thought. Any present understanding, or image, of the objective world will always have to be revised to give way to something more robust and ever more intriguing. I may be fortunate enough to know a sure word about a given matter, but I will never have a last word about anything. The truth I might know can be plumbed deeper still. This practice of beginning with shared experience and going deeper is never more evident in Lewis than in *Mere Christianity*.

The Argument of the Book

Mere Christianity was originally prepared by Lewis to be broadcast over the BBC during World War II. This medium was new to him, and he had to accommodate himself to this new forum to present his ideas. Nevertheless, the need to be audience centered remained central to his rhetorical goals. So his use of the shared imagination was very important. The broadcast talks were later published as small books. These eventually were brought together under common cover to make up what we now know as *Mere Christianity*. The book has many complex themes. Each chapter, encapsulating a particular broadcast, is focused on a given topic. The book itself is divided into four sections. Due to the limits of this study, we will look at the shared imagination as it occurs in each of these sections.

Right and Wrong as a Clue to the Meaning of the Universe

As Lewis begins his argument, he draws the reader's attention to a common and shared phenomenon evident in every instance of debate or argumentation, whether a formal academic or political debate, a disagreement among friends, or a spat between a husband and wife. In 1939 Lewis wrote in his essay "De Futilitate" that "an accusation always implies a standard."[5] This point is fleshed out in *Mere Christianity*. Disputants may disagree tooth and nail about what is right, but each believes in a standard by which the right or wrong of a matter can be discerned. Further, unless this standard is objective, the entire discussion is an exercise in futility.[6] In other words, the standard is shared, even though the interpretation and application of the standard to the circumstances are not. Lewis illustrates this by appealing to something that virtually all of his readers have experienced. Having established the common bond, Lewis then makes a case for Christianity.

Lewis calls this standard the "Law of Nature." Expositions by Lewis about the Law of Nature are not limited to *Mere Christianity*. His most developed treatment can be found in *The Abolition of Man*, where he refers to the *Tao* and defines it as the "doctrine of objective value."[7] In essence, Lewis believes that one must adjust the tangles of one's intellectual, volitional, and emotional life to the plumb line of reality. Therefore, these arguments, however imperfect, are an appeal to objective reality and for our disputant to return to good sense. Further, each of us, at times, falls short of objective standards. Consequently, bad behavior can be rationalized and justified. We know this is true from our own experience and we have seen others do it as well. While disagreeing as to what is actually right or wrong, the argument grows out of a shared sense that there is some kind of right and wrong that is knowable. Further, Lewis recognizes the shared human practice of trying to live by ideals and yet finding that we fall short of them. Given the fact that these things are relatively common, what can one do about it? How can one improve? Lewis now begins to build on these common observations and imagines for his readers the kinds of possibilities suggested by Christianity.

What Christians Believe

The question Lewis sets before his readers is, "How do we get better once we have violated the inexorable objective standard?" He expects that every honest reader will know exactly what he is talking about; he appeals to the shared imagination. Certainly every worldview that can be taken seriously must account for human existence, meaning, purpose, and human shortcomings. Those who say there is no meaning contradict themselves because, merely in stating this, they try to express themselves meaningfully. Lewis, in *Mere Christianity*, spends only a little time suggesting what competing worldviews offer to solve the problem of human failure. He is interested primarily in setting forth how Christianity tries to resolve this human conundrum. Nevertheless, he recognizes that asking, "What is the source of this objective standard?" is fundamentally a religious question. And, in a very fair-minded judgment, he notes, "If you are a Christian you do not have to believe that all the other religions are simply wrong all through."[8]

Lewis does not develop many of the common items that unite the great world religions in his discussion in *Mere Christianity*. Nevertheless, he does talk about the shared elements found in the world religions in his first work of popular Christian apologetics, *The Problem of Pain*. Borrowing from Rudolph Otto's *The Idea of the Holy*, Lewis enumerates three characteristics true of all the great world religions and then distinguishes the one thing that sets Christianity apart from the others. First, they all believe in some kind of supernatural other, what Otto calls the *numinous*. This supernatural will look different if one is an animist, pantheist, polytheist, dualist, monotheist, or trinitarian monotheist. Even so, a sense of transcendence is present in all of these religions. Second, they all believe in a moral law that people fail to keep. Third, they all believe in a union between the numinous and the moral law. In some way, the divine is the custodian of the law; therefore, failing to keep the moral law is an offense against the divine.

All the great world religions look similarly at these three points. What distinguishes Christianity from the others is found in the question, how does one fix the predicament? How does anyone placate the offended majesty? For Lewis, all the other religions come up with a new set of rituals or practices designed to get one in the good graces of the divine by virtue of the works, or merits, of the religious adherent. Of course, if one could not keep the first set of standards, why should one be very optimistic about fulfilling the requirements of the second set? Lewis employs a kind of shared imagination as he appeals to a common experience of his audience and then seeks to take it further. This notion of the uniqueness of Christianity is developed more fully in *Mere Christianity*, especially as it relates to the importance of the incarnation as God's way to reconcile lost humanity to God's very self.

In *Mere Christianity*, while Lewis admits there is much good and much held in common among all the world religions, nevertheless, he says that "being a Christian *does mean* thinking that where Christianity differs from other religions, Christianity is right and they are wrong."[9] Here Lewis turns the reader's attention to the uniqueness of Christ. He looks at Jesus who enters human history. The incarnation itself is an example of the shared imagination. The God of the universe enters time and space that he might identify with lost humanity and reconcile them to himself. He does this by entering into the common human experience. This ministry is an appeal to human beings to turn to God, but the appeal is made as an insider. Nevertheless, as Lewis recounts the events of Christ's life, he marks that Jesus, God in human flesh, claims to be God. Lewis sees that this claim is either that of a lunatic, or a deceiver, or Jesus is who he claims to be, the God of the universe. Lewis uses an old argument (that is a shared one) to make his case. He borrows his point from Saint Augustine who wrote of Jesus's claims *aut Deus aut malos homo* ("either God, or bad man").[10]

From the shared experience of constantly appealing to objective reality, and the quest to understand human failure as we encounter it in the world, right down to our own lives and shared experience, Lewis moves his readers further along by challenging them to look to the incarnation and recognize that "the central Christian belief is that Christ's death has somehow put us right with God and given us a fresh start."[11] Lewis does not struggle to find the most commendable theory of the atonement. He does not enter into the minute, hair-splitting dogmas that divide (worthy as these may be for consideration). He stays on the simple path because he wants people to discover the simple gospel that "God was reconciling the world to Himself through Christ" (2 Cor 5:19).

Christian Behavior

Building on what he has written, Lewis turns his attention to Christian behavior. He appeals to shared experience while making his case for the moral law and human failure. He looks to the incarnation and to the death and resurrection of Christ as a means to write imaginatively about how humanity is set right with God. Now, he evokes the deep, and common, human desire to want the broken things within us fixed. The appeal is once again to the moral law. "Moral rules are directions for running the human machine. Every moral rule is there to prevent a breakdown, or a strain, or a friction, in the running of that machine."[12] Lewis does not see the keeping of the moral laws as a means of salvation. That work is already finished in Christ. But he does ask his readers to consider in what way the moral law can advance spiritual maturity. Once again shared experience, imaginatively understood, reveals that we cannot neglect our common deep need for restoration.

Somehow this must be reflected in human behavior. Often the hostility of people toward Christianity is rooted in the poor behavior of those who claim to be followers of Christ but who live in a manner that looks nothing like Christ. The experience of seeing such inconsistencies is common. Could we not imagine a way where the resources of heaven might be marshalled for both personal and common good? What would this look like? The need is real, as Lewis observes: "Moral failure is going to cause trouble, probably to others and certainly to yourself."[13] Further, Lewis notes that true moral development requires that we consider a wide range of applications. This too is an imaginative exercise tethered to common shared experience and the deeply rooted desire for a better life. Lewis again interjects, "If we are to think about morality, we must think of all three departments: relations between man and man: things inside each man: relations between man and the power that made him."[14] The Christian faith should, unimpeded, lead to positive developments in one's relationship with God and God's purposes; in one's growth of character; and in cultivating more harmonious relations with other human beings.

The kind of behavior Lewis imagines is not necessarily new. The dream is a *shared* one. And, again, Lewis writes with the assumption that his audience has some inkling of virtue. Therefore, he writes of the cardinal virtues and appeals to some degree of common knowledge. But he is wise not to assume too much of his audience and therefore fills in the blanks as he seeks to push out the perimeters of understanding. The ancients (the Greek philosophers, the biblical writers, and the early church fathers) saw the virtues as necessary to living the good life. As Lewis describes them, the virtues were seen as a means to a greater end. No virtue was expressed by a single act; they were to be habitual behaviors in the lives of those who possessed them or approximated them. Wisdom, or prudence, is the habit of being careful about the decisions one makes. Those who hunger for wisdom recognize their own limits and therefore seek counsel from every available, and reliable, source. As Lewis develops this topic for his audience, he sees that wisdom is not static; it longs to grow by benefiting from others, both in current time and from those who lived in past times. This is essential if one is to gain perspective on any given matter. Therefore, a wise person senses the need for the insights of others in order to gain understanding that transcends his or her own limits. The Christian grasp of wisdom recognizes the need for God and community. This becomes all the more important when the biblical teaching of human brokenness is acknowledged, something Lewis points out frequently in *Mere Christianity*. Lewis again is revealing a dependence on the shared imagination with his audience. As fallen beings it is easy to look at the world through a clouded, self-referential lens. Building on the grace to be found in Christ, Lewis challenges his audience to pursue wisdom.

Writing about temperance, Lewis says this virtue is not to be pursued in order to gain God's graces. Rather, a person who knows God's love and forgiveness will want to cultivate it. Temperance is the habitual ability to resist the enticement of immediate pleasure in order to gain the greater though more remote good. Temperance exercises a kind of satisfaction in the love of God. Temperance is not gnostic, that is to say, it does not deny the pleasures of this life by suppressing desire for these pleasures in pursuit of otherworldly gain. No, the Christian lives his or her life in the flesh as well as in the spirit. Consequently, the Christian, growing in grace, must learn how to live temperately. Temperance is not abstinence; rather, it is the ability to say no to wrong action even in the jaws of pleasure. It cultivates a character that can walk circumspectly. Fulfilled in the love of God, it does not need to find fulfillment artificially. Since struggles in these areas are common, Lewis again utilizes the shared imagination as he portrays struggles he knows his audience has encountered.

Lewis also discusses justice. It is the habit of being law-abiding and concerned for the common good and general welfare of one's society. Consequently justice seeks to secure and protect natural rights for all. It looks out for the welfare of others. It is fair; it renders to others their due. Justice reminds us that moral development cannot be isolated from the responsibilities and obligations we have toward others. Character cannot be developed in a vacuum. The just person will be intrinsically motivated to serve the welfare of another. Pascal wrote in the *Pensees* that Christians had two laws better than all the other laws of statecraft. These are to love God and love your neighbor.[15] When love of God grows cold and love of neighbor is ignored, penal codes thicken and proliferate, filling the shelves of law offices and municipalities. Nevertheless, extrinsic laws cannot do for an individual what the transformation of character can do when justice is cultivated from within. Lewis again seeks to increase his audience's understanding of essential elements of Christianity by beginning with shared experiences and then going further. Each generation, entering into the spirit of Lewis's writing, can take it further still. Understanding in these matters must be dynamic, not static. New applications will always be needed, which means the imagination will always be vital.

Another of the cardinal virtues Lewis writes about is courage. It is the habitual ability to suffer pain and hardship. At the heart of courage are endurance, fortitude, and staying power. As temperance is the ability to say no to wrong action even when it promises immediate pleasure but may have dire long-term consequences, courage is the ability to say yes to right action even in the teeth of pain. Courage, informed by the other virtues, such as justice, will choose to protect against injustice even if it costs one personally. Informed by temperance, courage will know how to deny those personal pleasures and comforts if they are distracting from moral obligation. And, of course, wisdom will be necessary to make wise decisions in these regards.

Lewis addresses much more on a host of other topics essential to the Christian faith. And virtually all that he writes is rooted in his sense of what he believes his audience knows already. This is coupled with his desire to take readers further in their understanding. Thus, Lewis's *Mere Christianity* is an example of what he calls the *shared imagination*. From the original radio broadcast talks, to the actual publications, *Mere Christianity* has connected with millions.

Hope and the Shared Imagination

Having discussed the cardinal virtues of wisdom, temperance, justice, and courage, Lewis focuses his reader's attention on the theological Virtues: faith, hope, and charity. The shared imagination comes through most clearly in the appeal to hope. Here Lewis assumes in his audience a common longing for a future with promise. The reason people endure even in the midst of difficulties is their belief that something better is coming. All ages seem to imagine that the world could be better than it is. Lewis believes at the foundation of this hope is a belief in heaven. Such hope prods believers to work for a better world. Sacrifices are made to correct injustices and improve society for one's own generation and the generations to come. Lewis writes, "The Apostles themselves, who set on foot the conversion of the Roman Empire, the great men who built up the Middle Ages, the English Evangelicals who abolished the Slave Trade, all left their mark on Earth, precisely because their minds were occupied with Heaven."[16] Lewis believed a desire for heaven existed in the heart of his readers no matter how unrecognized or repressed it might be, and he appeals to it. The appeal is an imaginative one since the actual experience of heaven is something future. Nevertheless, Lewis believed the hope of heaven can have positive results now.

On this shared hunger for heaven Lewis writes,

> If I find in myself a desire which no experience in this world can satisfy, the most probable explanation is that I was made for another world. If none of my earthly pleasures satisfy it, that does not mean the universe is a fraud. Probably earthly pleasures were never meant to satisfy it, but only to arouse it, to suggest the real thing. If that is so, I must take care, on the one hand, never to despise, or be unthankful for, these earthly blessings, and on the other, never to mistake them for the something else of which they are only a kind of copy or echo, or mirage. I must keep alive in myself the desire for my true country, which I shall not find till after death; I must never let it get snowed under or turned aside; I must make it the main object of life to press on to that other country and help others to do the same.[17]

Clearly, as Lewis wrote this, he believed his readers shared this sense of hopeful longing for heaven. He also believed that this longing for a better world yet to come gave both the vision for change now as believers worked for justice, and encouraged believers to endure while doing the work yet to be done in this life. Wrongs ought to be righted that the hope of heaven might be most closely approximated now. True Christians should always desire to make this world a better place because their eyes are set on the world to come. Lewis recognized that this shared longing for heaven could have a positive effect on one's behavior.

Beyond Personality; or, First Steps in the Doctrine of the Trinity

Lewis turns his attention in the last section of *Mere Christianity* toward the Trinity, with its wide-ranging applications for human flourishing. Here again Lewis's use of the shared imagination is evident. Certainly he writes for Christians who have, as one of the unique features of their faith, a doctrine rooted in the belief that there is one God eternally existing in three persons, Father, Son, and Holy Spirit. While Lewis will develop this doctrine and apply it in many very practical ways, he begins by recognizing that Christians, however much or little they may grasp it, have some notion of the doctrine of the Trinity. Further, if God created human beings in the divine image, then the relational character of God also must be vital for any kind of rich spiritual development. This fact must be evident whether or not one is a Christian. By acknowledging this, Lewis again is able to connect with his audience through shared experiences, as he imaginatively nudges them to grow and mature.

In an essay called "Membership," Lewis noted that "personality is the road to unity."[18] In essence he was saying that I can only truly understand who I am by understanding myself in relation with others. In unity and harmony with God and with others my real identity is clarified. In serving others, purposes for life are clarified and refined. All of this is predicated on the reality of God and the divine disclosure to us of the Trinity. In *Mere Christianity* Lewis develops this idea further, asserting, "The words 'God is love' have no real meaning unless God contains at least two persons." And, he clarifies, "If God was a single person, then before the world was made, He was not love."[19] How is this to be understood and applied?

Ask any nontrinitarian monotheist, "Do you believe God is a contingent being or a noncontingent being?" You might well be asked what these words mean. *Contingent* implies that something's very existence is dependent on the prior existence of something else. For instance, a wooden table exists because of the tree that existed before the table was made, and because of the carpenter who made the table. Therefore, the table is a contingent thing. Something that is noncontingent is a necessary thing; it is self-existent and utterly independent, needing and having nothing prior to its existence. Once the clarification is made, the response is, "God is clearly noncontingent." Then ask, "Do you believe God is a God of love?" To which the response is generally yes. Then ask, "Who is the object of God's love?" The answer is "We are." Or, "God's creation is the object of His love." But embedded in the nontrinitarian's reasoning and theology is a debilitating contradiction. For if God is noncontingent and yet needs creation (something outside of God) to fulfill the divine nature, then God is both noncontingent and contingent, which is clearly nonsensical. Relational attributes in a noncontingent being presuppose that relationship is necessary in that being. Here again, Lewis, in his treatment of the doctrine of the Trinity, appeals to some common sense he believes he shares with his audience. He then begins to build on some shared common sense, and, using his imagination, takes it further.

The practicality of this is developed throughout the last section of *Mere Christianity*. One can find in the trinitarian God an objective standard for the mending of broken relationships. If we find ourselves estranged from God, and from one another, what is the standard by which the broken pieces might be put back together in a way that makes sense? A puzzle maker is always helped if he or she has the picture of the finished product on the box from which the pieces came. A necessary relationship found in God becomes the model for reconciliation and mending all forms of broken relationships. Further, the grace of God is the glue for cementing the pieces back together. Also, the very trinitarian nature of God reveals a pattern for wholeness and service, for purpose and meaning in relationships. Out of the very longing to have fixed what is broken in us, and that which is broken in our world, Lewis appeals to this shared sense of longing in his audience as he makes his points throughout *Mere Christianity*.

Following the Map: Growth of the Shared Imagination

Lewis's use of the shared imagination enables a writer or artist or anyone who seeks to communicate with others, the means to connect with an audience by building on what they already share with others. Lewis displays with great clarity and dexterity his use of the shared imagination while building his argument in *Mere Christianity*. He rightly observed that "doctrines are not God: they are only a kind of map. But that map is based on the experience of hundreds of people who really were in touch with God—experiences compared with which any thrills or pious feelings you and I are likely to get on our own are very elementary and very confused."[20] The collective experiences are an entry into the shared imagination. Lewis also notes that "if you want to get on further, you must use the map." The shared experience, the map, only prepares us for the next step. Building on the shared imagination we can grow corporately into a greater communal understanding of any given thing. But this is essential for growth in the knowledge of God. Lewis understood this well. Like a craftsman, he is able to connect with his audience and encourage them in faith.

Good communication will always rely on something like the shared imagination. If a speaker or writer hopes to be heard or understood, he or she will think about the audience. There are values and experiences shared by a communicator and his or her audience. These shared values and desires are more than assets or starting points—they are the very condition of good communication. They connect author and audience. *Mere Christianity* has enjoyed rich popular appeal over the decades because Lewis chose to connect with his readers at the point of the shared imagination.

Chapter 3

The Smell of Deity

Satisfied Imagination in *Letters to Malcolm: Chiefly on Prayer*

The satisfied imagination takes delight in the familiar, the simple, the mundane, and the repetitive in a manner that brings our minds back to the eternal source of order and repetition. It works to reenchant the familiar by enabling us to view the commonplaces of life anew and with fresh perspective and insight. It dwells on the things it knows and finds satisfaction there. This is a particularly necessary type of imagination to cultivate in a society that thrives on constant change, and we will examine it through the lens of Lewis's *Letters to Malcolm: Chiefly on Prayer*.

Charged with God's Grandeur: The Satisfied Imagination in the Medieval Cosmology

Lewis first references the satisfied imagination in *The Discarded Image*, a fascinating work that examines the medieval worldview and cosmological model. We are given to understand that artists and poets of the time depicted this worldview again and again. Lewis writes that Marcus Aurelius desired that all people could love the universe as a man can love his own city. He believes this perspective was actually possible in this period. Again, he writes, "Other ages have not had a Model so universally accepted as theirs, so imaginable, and so satisfying to the imagination."[1] This model is central to Lewis's thought and elements of it appear repeatedly in his works. Its cosmology is also central to an understanding of the satisfied imagination because it functions as the framework on which will hang the discussion of *Letters to Malcolm*. Therefore, an overview of its construction will depict its imaginative impact as well as outline various concepts of the satisfied imagination. We will need to suspend disbelief while investigating this

– 31 –

model, as Lewis himself suggests. Approach it as you would a work of art. Don't compare it to twenty-first-century knowledge of the universe.

To begin with, in *Studies in Medieval and Renaissance Literature*, Lewis writes that medieval scholastics were working at a disadvantage. In addition to a pre-Copernican understanding of astronomy, they had lost most of their books; the ones that survived were a miscellaneous collection, often obtained from great distances and at great cost. Therefore, the scholastics were reluctant to say that some books were right and others wrong. Their ingenious solution was to harmonize the texts they possessed, which resulted in a syncretistic masterpiece. Out of this the medieval cosmology was birthed. They took great delight in this work, and with great patience and systematization, they were able, as Lewis writes, to tidy up the universe. Thereby, they created one of the world's greatest and most complex works of syncretism and harmonization.[2] And we ultimately want to examine the ramifications and implications of this model on the mind of medieval people. But first, we must understand the elements of its construction.

Medieval thought held the earth to be the motionless center of the universe around which all the planets revolved. Despite its centricity, the earth's size was comparatively insignificant. The universe surrounding it was inconceivably large, but also finite. You could never get to its frontier, but the frontier existed, nonetheless. Compared to a modern understanding of space, you get the notion of a universe in terms of height rather than distance. Our universe fills us with questions and forebodings because we assume it to be infinite, empty and mysterious beyond reckoning. The medieval understanding of the ultimately finite nature of the universe enabled people to see it as an answer, not a question. It became a final standard by which all else was measured.[3]

The heavens, as we will find, were above all a whole of finely graded parts. Lewis states that this satisfied the medieval idea of unity through plurality, of harmonization and syncretization, which is also a major component of the satisfied imagination. The universe was divided into three regions. The first region was sublunar and constituted the area from the moon down to the earth. This was the region of mutability and contingency in which we on earth dwell. The second region was immutable. It drew its boundary above the region of the moon's orbit and contained the seven "planets": the Moon, Mercury, Venus, the Sun, Mars, Jupiter, and Saturn. Above this existed the third region, the empyrean, the beginning of the true heaven, filled with the divine substance.[4]

This cosmos also possessed unique dynamics. Movement earthward from any part of the universe was considered movement downward. Gravity was explained analogically as the desire of an object to return to its native or proper place. Aristotelian theology stated that the concept of infinity did not exist; therefore, the universe must have contained a compulsive, immovable force that generated all movement by being the end or object of all other things. This force was called the unmoved mover or the *primum mobile*, a force likened to or roughly equivalent with God.[5]

Lewis describes the unmoved mover as the supremely desirable object; thus, the universe is moved by its love for him, not by his love for it, as we might be prone to infer. It does this by approximating (or imitating) his nature as closely as possible at all times. For the ancient Greeks, the circle was the most perfect figure, and therefore movement in a circle was the closest approximation to perfection. Every sphere moved because at all times it had an unceasing desire to mimic God's perfect nature in its love for him. Each sphere passed its knowledge of God to the sphere below it. Thus, through each successive sphere down toward earth, movement became slower, impulse weaker, and knowledge of God less, because the *primum mobile* was at many removes.[6]

In order for these spheres to be capable of such movement (the incessant desire for God), each was inhabited by a rational creature called an *intelligence*. Also present in the spheres between the moon and the empyrean were the angels, of which existed nine classes containing triads of three groups of three classes. At the top hierarchy were the seraphim, cherubim, and thrones, exclusively absorbed in contemplation of God and unconcerned with the universe. Beneath these were the dominations, virtues, and powers, who exerted some influence on the created universe. The lowest hierarchy was responsible for human affairs; these were called principalities, archangels, and angels.[7]

Lewis writes that one of the main features of the medieval model was its orderly and varied reiteration of the same subject, an important function of the satisfied imagination. As stated earlier, the medieval mind desired to harmonize all knowledge. This resulted in massive and ordered amounts of reiteration. For example, Lewis describes the angelic triads that existed in the model. Each triad contained an agent, medium, and patient. In this way knowledge of God was passed down from the highest spheres of the heavens to the lowest. At the top level, God existed as agent, the seraphim as medium, and the cherubim as patient. In simpler terms, God functioned as the object of love, and the seraphim below God were the recipients of that love, who in turn passed knowledge of God's love down to the cherubim beneath them. This triad was repeated all the way to the lowest spheres. There were triads of faculties within the angels themselves, triads within the universe, triads within human beings, and triads connecting each. It was a dizzying amount of reiteration.[8]

Not only were the skies peopled, as it were, but the planets also exerted influence on humans and on the earth. The beam of each planet penetrated to the earth and produced the various metals associated with each: the moon produced silver, the sun gold, and so forth. But the planets also influenced human psychology and events. Because of this, Lewis argues, theologians of the time had to fight against a strong astrological determinism that negated the idea of free will. But it was generally accepted that a person, acting in wisdom, could get over a bad horoscope. Even if a person didn't live out of this determinism, the freedoms of humans to live randomly marked them as inferior, says Lewis. It was the regular and monotonous activities of the heavens that were seen as superior. This is again the influence of Aristotelian thinking; true freedom is an existence that is mapped out and follows a certain course, not an ability to do whatever one wants.[9]

One begins to understand the complexity of the heavenly model, and how the medieval mind reveled in this important facet of the satisfied imagination. But there is more. In addition to planetary influence, these heavens were filled with light and sound. We know today that the heavens are largely empty and completely dark. Medieval thinkers did not believe this. The heavens were neither dark nor silent. The darkness of night was explained as the cone of the earth's shadow when the sun was below it. Otherwise the heavens were perpetually filled with sunshine. And sound. This was the music that upheld the universe. One couldn't hear it because, paradoxically, one had always heard it. One would notice its absence only if it suddenly ceased. We might liken this to the unusual quality of quiet that descends when a storm causes the power to go out. While it is on, we don't realize that electricity produces a sound because we always hear it, and thus are auditorially immune to it. Only when it is gone do we sense a deeper silence.[10]

Lewis gives life to this idea of lighted, animated heavens in *Out of the Silent Planet.* The protagonist Elwin Ransom has been forced by villains Weston and Devine to journey in a spaceship to the planet Malacandra. He experiences the life-giving and energizing effect of the heavenly light as he travels through space: "There, totally immersed in a bath of pure ethereal colour and of unrelenting though un-wounding brightness, stretched his full length and with eyes half closed in the strange chariot that bore them, faintly quivering, through depth after depth of tranquility far above the reach of night, he felt his body and mind daily rubbed and scoured and filled with new vitality."[11]

Ransom even acknowledged the spiritual influence of the heavens as he felt the old paradigm of space as cold, black emptiness sloughing off of him like an old skin: "He had not known how much it affected him till now—now that the very name 'Space' seemed a blasphemous libel for this empyrean ocean of radiance in which they swam. He could not call it 'dead'; he felt life pouring into him from it every moment. How indeed should it be otherwise, since out of this ocean the worlds and all their life had come?"[12]

Today, we understand space such that we always think of looking *out* on it. But medieval people viewed this vast panorama of music, light, and movement as looking *into* the universe. One of the triads alluded to earlier, propounded by the thirteenth-century monk Alanus, is that of the divisions of the heaven from the earth. Alanus defined the heavens in terms of castle, city, and lands. The castle of God the king was associated with the empyrean, the highest region beyond the highest sphere. In the city outside the castle lived the nobility, the nine orders of angels or intelligences associated with the planets. The lands outside the city wall constituted the third division, the region beneath the moon's orbit where those on earth dwelt.[13]

The ordered and monotonous movements of the heavens were viewed as a delightful dance, festival, or carnival. To dwell outside the city wall was to be excluded from what Lewis calls "the high pomps" occurring within the city and to experience longing to take part in it. Lewis likens this longing to animals staring at the fires of an encampment they cannot enter, or as rustics staring at a city.[14] It is those in the region of mutability staring into the regions of immutability or those caught up in living randomly staring into the kingdom of perfect order. And again, order and monotony are outworkings of the satisfied imagination.

The idea of yearning is appropriate here, but a yearning for repetition, a creaturely yearning to be part of that repetitive cycle in the heavens that is every moment imitating the nature of God to its fullest extent possible. It can now be seen why medieval people had a passion for repetition and for asserting the nature of things as they were. They wanted to participate in some small way in what was happening inside the city walls. They accomplished this through the pageantry and ceremony of ecclesiastical and social hierarchies, because these functioned as dim reproductions of the heavenly hierarchies.[15] And pageant, according to Lewis, was a "group of symbolical figures in symbolical costume, often in symbolical surroundings." It was simply a way that meaning could be conveyed iconographically.[16]

This somewhat lengthy overview of the medieval cosmology outlines how the medieval imagination utilized the satisfied imagination. It could be satisfied only by creating in this specific way, within these specific parameters. Both the creation and byproducts of this model represent a picture of the satisfied imagination at work. We have attempted to show how minds that loved order, repetition, balance, and harmony found delight and satisfaction not only in the model they created, but, more importantly, in what that model ultimately pointed to. Remember that each piece of the heavenly model was orderly, influenced, every sphere achieving its own perfection. One can trace this spiral of complex perfection right up through the heavens to the Prime Mover, the one that prompts all this order and striving toward perfection, this lovely glory and movement and complexity of the heavens. Without the Prime Mover, the heavens would fall into chaos and disarray. Thus, by extension, the beauty of and delight in the model are really the beauty of and delight in God.

Ultimately, this is what the satisfied imagination attempts to achieve: a delight in the familiar, the simple, the mundane, and the repetitive, such that it carries our minds back to the eternal source of order and repetition. How we do this will be the primary focus of *Letters to Malcolm*, where Lewis embodies examples of the satisfied imagination. In experiencing such delight, we are participating in the nature of God at some far distant remove. We ourselves are outside the city wall, which we cannot enter in our lifetime. But we sense the glory, order, structure, and influence of the divine nature in our lives. The satisfied imagination helps us to enact in a small way the "high pomps" of God's heavenly kingdom right here on earth.

One final example will help to both solidify and further inform the nature of the satisfied imagination. In his essay *Tremendous Trifles*, G. K. Chesterton tells the tale of two young brothers playing in the front garden of their home. This garden is no larger than the size of a dinner table and consists of some strips of gravel and a tiny patch of grass. The milkman, who is really a fairy in disguise, stops by and grants each of the brothers a wish. One brother, Paul, decides to be a giant because he has long desired to view the great wonders of the world and as a giant he could travel wherever he wished quite easily. He is granted his wish. He strides to the Himalayas and finds them as insignificant as the rockery in his front yard. He wades across the ocean to see Niagara Falls, and it reminds him of the tap turned on in the bathroom. He walks around the world for a few minutes trying to find something large. He is unsuccessful and so lies down on a couple of prairies and falls asleep of boredom. Unfortunately, while asleep, he has his head cut off by a backwoods philosopher who believes that the evil of pride means being out of proportion with the universe.

Paul's brother Peter chooses to become a pygmy. At half an inch tall, he suddenly finds himself in a dense jungle with strange, tall trees and an impossibly shaped mountain that is, of course, the house. In this world, Peter has yet to come to an end of his adventures. Says Chesterton, "In other words, we may, by fixing our attention almost fiercely on the facts actually before us, force them to turn into adventures; force them to give up their meaning and fulfill their mysterious purpose."[17]

Like the medieval scholastics, Chesterton is reenchanting the familiar by attempting to make a point about how we overlook the commonplace. These commonplaces of life are where the satisfied imagination begins to flicker in our minds. It is the mind dwelling on the things it knows, and finding satisfaction there, just like the medieval poets and scholastics did with their cosmology. In a society that is becoming increasingly enamored of change, a delight in sameness can seem positively regressive in terms of cultural "progress." Nonetheless, this delight is a necessary tonic in an age of distraction. Call it the byproduct of the "grass is greener syndrome," but most people will have extreme difficulty in finding the common, daily, and routine details of life enchanting. Yet demanding as it may be, this is the task of the satisfied imagination: participating in the glory of heaven that we only perceive, when we perceive it at all, through a glass darkly.

Participating in the High Pageantry of Heaven: *Letters to Malcolm*

Letters to Malcolm: Chiefly on Prayer is a collection of letters written by Lewis to an imaginary friend named Malcolm. As the title states, these letters focus primarily on various facets of prayer, including prayer as worship, petitionary prayer, the problems of prayer, making desires known to God, the idea of divine impassibility, and the fear that no one is listening. All are relevant to a robust understanding of prayer. The work includes several letters on the nature of our relation to God and material reality, as well as how our pleasures function as prayer.

Without taking the obvious defects and errors of the medieval model literally, it can still help foster an analogical understanding of our relation as earthbound beings to the God of the universe. As previously outlined, the satisfied imagination enables us to participate in a small way in the high pageantry of heaven. It does this through instilling a delight and even an increased insight into the familiar, the simple, the mundane, and the repetitive so our minds will be carried back to God, the ultimate source of order and repetition. In experiencing delight, we participate in the nature of God. But we are ultimately outside the city wall, looking with longing at the distant city where revelry, feasting, pageantry, and festival are occurring. We yearn to be part of the perfection that makes this possible, but are removed from participating in it fully. However, there are times when we sense its glory, order, structure, and influence in our lives. Our efforts to replicate it in worship, prayer, and liturgy become attempts to participate and to remember. But before we can participate and remember, we must gain a deeper knowledge of that repetitive reality that we experience every day and in which we are trying to find satisfaction.

In *Letters to Malcolm*, Lewis speaks of God as the ground and supplier of both our personal reality and the reality of the material world. Thus, we must begin to see God in the world around us, realizing that God is present in each thing and person differently. And because this reality is so familiar, we must be constantly reminded of it through holy places, things, and days. For without them, our belief in the holiness of the world around us will shrink and fade. It is why medieval minds created a cosmology that had this concept built into it. It constantly reminded them of the ultimate reality being enacted in the high heavens, and by extension, but with weaker impulse, on earth.

One problem though, writes Lewis, is that the holy days and places themselves can become commonplace and cease to fulfill their function of keeping us aware of the reality that we cannot see. The world is crowded with God, says Lewis, and God walks abroad incognito. The incognito is often not difficult to observe; the real task is in remembering, in waking up and staying awake. If the material world has its ultimate being and reality through the upholding action of God, then everything can be seen rightly as the products of divine activities.[18] This notion is extremely significant for the satisfied imagination. It enables us to find satisfaction in the familiar, in the material world around us.

Bearings on the Bright Blur: The Self and the Material World as End Products of the Divine

But how do we actually find satisfaction in the world around us? Let's examine Lewis's understanding of the reality of self and the material world a bit more closely. Lewis states that in attempting to place oneself in the presence of God in prayer, two ideas get in the way. One is the "bright blur," a place in a person's mind associated with God. The second is the idea of the self. The problem is that neither of these is real. Both of them are constructs created by the real "I." Material reality, my notion of God, and what I call "myself" are realities of such depth that I can never know or understand them. The real "I" has created them out of miscellaneous psychological bits and pieces to suit my needs.

But this creation is not the actual reality. Unless I could watch creation as it bursts directly from the hand of God, I can never go deep enough to find the ultimate reality of anything. This doesn't mean I cannot know anything; truth can always be more deeply understood. However, we cannot ever get to the bottom of it. Thus, the one reality we can know for certain, writes Lewis, is a relationship between subject and object: myself as the subject and the material world as the object. Except when I am asleep, this relation always exists. And because God creates, sustains, and empowers all material reality, including myself, at every moment, this subject/object interaction is essentially the meeting of God and myself. God is the ground of my being and the ground of the material world.[19]

Lewis writes that if we can see our two ideas of self and material world as facades rather than ultimate realities, then we can also begin to see them as the end products of divine activities. But to do so, we must continually break the ideas or constructs we make of these things. Lewis suggests that we start by breaking the idol we make of the "bright blur," our hazy notion of God. This is important for several reasons. Remember, we are attempting to understand how to activate the satisfied imagination through the repetition and seeming monotony of our lives. In prayer and in life, we can cultivate awareness that the "real world" and "real self" are not really ultimate realities. Within and beyond them exist realities that we cannot fathom because we cannot see them being created from the hand of God. God is the ground of all reality; therefore we can never have an ultimate understanding of it, because we can never fully understand God. All our understanding must be, in some respect, false. Hence the need to constantly break the idols we make of reality. Not that our understanding is untrue; it is simply incomplete. A tree does not have to give up its existing rings when it adds new ones.

And so in prayer it is the real "I" beneath my pseudoself that attempts to speak with God or to see the material world as the outcome of divine workings. Fostering this awareness can create a possible theophany, or experience of God, at any given moment. When my perspective is so adjusted, all manifest reality becomes a conduit for seeing the divine.[20] Remember Chesterton's advice to fix our attention fiercely on the facts and force them to turn into adventures, give up their meaning, and fulfill their mysterious purpose? The fierce attention is essentially a way to remember that the facts aren't the actual reality, but the thin scrim of some unbelievably alien manifestation of God's power. Again, ultimately, this understanding turns the mind Godward, and, as Lewis writes, enables it to "run back up the sunbeam to the sun."[21] A stanza from Gerard Manley Hopkins's poem "God's Grandeur" is appropriate here:

The world is charged with the grandeur of God.
It will flame out, like shining from shook foil;
It gathers to a greatness, like the ooze of oil
Crushed. Why do men then now not reck his rod?
Generations have trod, have trod, have trod. (1–5)[22]

This is one of the primary ideas of *Letters to Malcolm*. We only begin to see the grandeur when we recognize that reality is ultimately iconoclastic in Lewis's view. God works in us to constantly break the idols and images we make of the deity. We cannot ultimately understand the reality that is God, any more than we can understand the material world or ourselves. Thus, it is vitally important to position our understanding of these as the products of divine activities. We must see through the scrim. This will allow us to understand differently, to take Chesterton's fierce look at the world around us, and create a space where the theophanies that Lewis writes about can lead us to adoration and worship, to participate at a distance in those beautiful and pure movements of heaven.

In a letter to his friend Malcolm on this subject of prayer as worship or adoration, Lewis recalls a walk they took together through the Forest of Dean in the Wye Valley of England. On this walk, Lewis had thought that to pray in this way, one had to begin by thinking about God's goodness and greatness, creation, redemption, and the blessings of life. Malcolm stooped to a cold running brook, splashed his hot face and hands in a small waterfall and said, "Why not begin with this?"[23] This echoes Marcus Aurelius's pleasure rooted in place. Thus, like Malcolm and Aurelius, we must begin where we are.

Lewis reminds Malcolm how well this simple method worked: "That cushiony moss, that coldness and sound and dancing light were no doubt very minor blessings, compared with 'the means of grace and the hope of glory.' But then they were manifest. So far as they were concerned, sight had replaced faith. They were not the hope of glory, they were an exposition of the glory itself." A bit later he writes, "I was learning the far more secret doctrine that *pleasures* are shafts of the glory as it strikes our sensibility. As it impinges on our will or our understanding, we give it different names—goodness or truth or the like. But its flash upon our sense and mood is pleasure."[24]

The fact that Lewis is equating the pleasures or satisfactions we experience as worship and as shafts of the divine striking our sensibilities aids our understanding of the satisfied imagination. The small and even momentary pleasures we experience daily, such as the flash of birdshadow across a sunlit lawn, the first tips of daffodils jutting up through the winter-weary ground, a compliment about something we've done, can, as Lewis writes, be a channel for adoration.

Again, let us focus on our relationship to the material world and the knowledge of that world as an outworking of divine activity. Remember that the satisfied imagination seeks, through the repetitive trivialities of our daily lives seen in an eternal light, to participate in a small way in the high pomps of heaven. Our pleasures and an attendant recognition of them are one way to achieve this. And Lewis suggests that the mere experience of these tiny theophanies is itself adoration. We are drawn into gratitude for these glimpses and thus our mind runs back up the sunbeam to the sun.

In this scenario, we might liken our experience to that of the planets in the medieval cosmology that are always approximating God's love to the best of their ability. In this understanding of the satisfied imagination, Lewis believes that there would be no pleasure too small or ordinary to be receptive to God in this way. The feel of the morning air on our skin or our slippers could elicit such a response.[25] But of course our minds will often *not* run back up the sunbeam because of certain obstacles in our way.

The Material World Is on Fire: Overcoming the Four Obstacles to the Satisfied Imagination

Lewis outlines four obstacles in *Letters to Malcolm* that prevent us from perceiving these pleasures. One is simple inattention; another is the wrong kind of attention. We could imagine that the pleasure is simply taking place within us and ignore "the smell of Deity that hangs about it."[26] Or we might hear just a roar, rather than the roaring of the wind. A third is greed, desiring the pleasure again and again. The fourth is the conceit that not everyone is privileged to have the understanding I have been vouchsafed. The ability to recognize God in our pleasures is a discipline, but for Lewis, as it succeeds, it gives him bearings on the bright blur. As we learn to avoid these obstacles to identifying pleasures and develop an awareness toward them, the blur becomes brighter and clearer.[27]

Lewis writes that these small pleasures are important in learning adoration of God. How will we be able to adore God on large occasions if we have not first learned on the small occasions? "Any patch of sunlight in a wood will show you something about the sun which you could never get from reading books on astronomy. These pure and spontaneous pleasures are 'patches of Godlight' in the woods of our experience."[28] Of course, these small adorations are not the whole story in our striving to participate in God's nature, and Lewis cautions against our seeing them as such. But overcoming the obstacles to sensing these small pleasures is an important beginning for the satisfied imagination. And it is to implementing the satisfied nature that we now turn.

What better way to begin than by utilizing the medieval tactic of harmonization to outline a strategy for exercising the satisfied imagination, as understood in *Letters to Malcolm* and informed by the medieval cosmology? Proper use of the satisfied imagination necessitates recognition of and movement through four phases: problem, need, means, and end.

First the problem, as identified in *Letters to Malcolm*. There is a sense in which we are asleep and must wake up in order to recognize when something is giving us pleasure. Often something may rivet our attention momentarily, but we might not associate it with pleasure. These are striking at us all day long, but until we wake up enough to identify them as such, they will remain peripheral to our experience. We may identify them as pleasures, but not as shafts of the divine striking our sensibilities. It is this deeper reality to which we must awaken. But, as Lewis writes, obstacles such as inattention, wrong attention, pride, and a desire for repetition inhibit our waking to cognizance of the true nature of these pleasures.

According to medieval cosmology, this problem of waking up is due to the fact that we are the rustics outside the city wall, barred from the glory of the city.

Our ability to live randomly, to have choice and free will, further adds to our problem by preventing us from acting in a way commensurate with the movements of the heavens in relation to God. And just as astrological determinism plagued medieval thinkers, a form of determinism plagues us today. It might best be summed up in the words *It is what it is*. This platitude covers a multitude of reasons to rationalize behavior that would prevent us from living intentionally.

The second phase in this strategy of the satisfied imagination is, as Lewis writes in *Letters to Malcolm*, the need to wake up and stay awake. Coming awake encompasses a need for awareness, recognition, revelation, and victory over the four obstacles. To use Lewis's term, we need clarity on the bright blur. Similarly, the need for medieval thinkers was to gain an ability to live not randomly but according to nature: to live in a manner consistent with the perfect movements of the heavens, which approximated God's nature at all times.

The means to enact the need of phase two is what we begin to implement in phase three. The first requirement is to position ourselves in relation to the material world. As Lewis shows us, God is the ground of both material reality and our own reality as humans. The life or being of both is sustained and directed by God. Thus, our understanding of self and material reality must be altered to see both as the end products of divine activities. This will require the fierce look that Chesterton writes about, a dogged determination to see through facts to adventures. It is what Lewis wrote elsewhere about the quality of George MacDonald's imaginative works that "turned out to be the quality of the real universe, the divine, magical, terrifying and ecstatic reality in which we all live."[29]

Even when the obstacles to recognizing pleasures are overcome and we have positioned ourselves correctly toward reality, we have yet another hurdle to overcome. We must force ourselves to remember. I (Mark) used to read the two books of Kings in the Bible from start to finish with ever-increasing disbelief. These books chronicled a long litany of kings who failed to follow God and the resulting disasters of poor kingship. Lightly sprinkled throughout were a few kings who faithfully followed God, thus allowing the nation to prosper. But ever and anon, another king ascended to the throne, abused his power, and destroyed all the good for which the previous king had toiled. My disbelief always took the form of the same question: How could they possibly forget the blessings of a faithful rule? I realize now precisely how they could forget, because I do it all the time. My life lulls me into a sleep that dulls my apprehension of the world around me. I must constantly be reminded of God or else I *will* forget him. This is the purpose of our holy days, places, and things. These times are set apart specifically for remembering.

For the medievals, the model itself helped them to remember. Their poets and artists created art that drew the mind back to the model through endless repetition and reiteration. They created pageantry and ceremonies as a result of the desire to participate in the glory of the city from outside the city wall, because doing so was living as closely as possible according to nature rather than randomness.

Finally the end, the fourth phase, for which all this striving is the means, is our ability to worship and participate in God's nature through theophanies or revelations experienced chiefly through our pleasures—in short, to experience the satisfied imagination. Just as medieval people sought participation in the pomps happening within the city walls, we seek to experience an imagination satisfied with dwelling on the familiar through understanding that we, others, and the material world are on fire with God "at whose right hand are pleasures forevermore."[30]

Waking Up to Ecstatic Reality: The Satisfied Imagination as Corrective

The satisfied imagination does not encourage narrow-mindedness, as one might be inclined to think. We might assume that what exists before our eyes needs no closer look, thus leading to a lack of desire to delve into fresh ways of seeing and experiencing life. But we would not think this if we could perceive reality at the level to which the satisfied imagination attempts to point us. As we use this imagination, our understanding of the bright blur gains clarity. This is expansion rather than contraction. The satisfied imagination exists to tether us to what is orderly and beautiful and worthy of notice in the familiar as we wake up to it and its charged grandeur.

Perhaps its most vital and important corrective is to counteract a worldview without meaning. Contrast the satisfied imagination of the medieval scholastics and their love of and delight in the model with the prevailing philosophy of meaninglessness touted in culture today. Lewis writes about the difference of a man of genius in the medieval period versus his modern equivalent: "Such a man today often, perhaps usually, feels himself confronted with a reality whose significance he cannot know, or a reality that has no significance; or a reality such that the very question whether it has a meaning is itself a meaningless question. It is for him, by his own sensibility, to discover a meaning, or, out of his own subjectivity, to give a meaning—or at least a shape—to what in itself had neither."[31] In a world that doesn't encourage us to form beliefs around ultimate meaning, the very nature of the satisfied imagination demands the realization that manifest reality is bursting with meaning; it is the meeting point of God with the self and material reality. It is Hopkins's world charged with the grandeur of God. It is Lewis's terrifying and ecstatic reality.

An extension of meaninglessness is the insidious trap that joy, pleasure, and truth are to be found somewhere "out there" rather than right here. Or they are to be found in some imagined brighter future when a host of things will finally be true about us or for us. This "grass is greener" mentality leads us to believe that whatever is new, different, or sexy, and will divert us from our prosaic and monotonous lives, must be pursued at all costs. It is a frenetic notion of cultural progress that creates a fear of abandonment. It is a virulent form of chasing after the wind that does not encourage a return to the familiar, to the self, or to the material world, which redefines my position in relation to both and to God. Rather, it is avoidance. In this mindset, we are trapped in a blind reliance on externals to produce fulfillment. Thus, we experience a decreasing power and desire to find or enact this fulfillment in everything for which the satisfied imagination stands.

We often believe our lives are dull, whether at home, at work, or anywhere else. We look to the next big thing, the next change, the new job, or the new relationship to find real satisfaction, not understanding that it is offered to us already in the unvarying existence of our lives. Our real problem is that we cannot see it or don't know to look for it, or don't believe that such an experience is possible. We have been lulled to sleep. We are all guilty of this, especially in an age where constant change has become the constant and we are offered ever more diverting diversions. Our lives are scheduled, maximized, and digitized to the hilt. Again, the satisfied imagination demands that we first wake up to its realities and then, through discipline, force ourselves to slow down enough to remain awake. Constant movement is the enemy of the satisfied imagination.

Thus, a final corrective works as a much-needed way to counteract a world in which everything is increasingly fast-paced, where there is no time for reflection, or quiet, or contemplation; where the pace of life and the use of technologies erode real relationship while promising connectivity; where there is no time or, worse yet, no inclination, for recognizing how simple pleasures can bring clarity to our understanding of God. This recognition naturally leads to creating space and time in a hyperlinked world to slow down enough, begin to wake up, and even begin to realize our need to wake up. Ultimately, it is in waking that we begin to get glimpses of God's glory through our pleasures and to realize with Lewis that "joy is the serious business of heaven."[32]

Chapter 4

Breaking Out of
the Dungeon

Awakened Imagination in *An Experiment in Criticism*

C. S. Lewis writes of the baptized imagination as described previously, and he distinguishes another type of imagination similar to it but of significant difference. It must be given its own category and treated differently in regard to form and use. Lewis calls it the awakened (or awakening) imagination. While the baptized imagination speaks of the awakening of imaginative hunger and thirst for the transcendent (and therefore a spiritual awakening, a first step in what theologians call *regeneration*), the awakened imagination is a more generalized category. It may speak of theological or spiritual awakening, but it is not limited to spirituality per se. It may refer to the imaginative awakening of an idea in philosophy or economics or an author's first glimpse of an idea for a story; a development along the lines of the first imaginative grasp or picture.

Making Sense of Continuity and Change

Lewis writes of the awakened/awakening imagination in his essay, "Dogma and the Universe." While here Lewis's concept is spoken of in the context of theological dogma, the applications are certainly not limited to theology. In the essay, Lewis questions the assumption some hold "against Christianity that its dogmas are unchanging, while human knowledge is in continual growth. Hence, to unbelievers, we seem to be always engaged in the hopeless task of trying to force new knowledge into moulds which it has outgrown."[1] He later refines the question he seeks to answer in the essay: "How can an unchanging system [such as Christianity] survive the continual increase of knowledge?"[2] The question is one concerned with the manner of continuity and change.

Growth requires a change, not of kind but of degree. Without continuity there is no growth. As Lewis notes, "Humanity does not pass through phases as a train passes through stations: being alive, it has the privilege of always moving yet never leaving anything behind. Whatever we have been, in some sort we are still."[3] He also observes, "Wherever there is real progress in knowledge, there is some knowledge that is not superseded. Indeed, the very possibility of progress demands that there should be an unchanging element."[4] This is necessary to the idea of continuity. Mortimer Adler called the development of Western thought "the Great Conversation."[5] He discovered, in those books he called "the Great Books," 102 ideas most discussed in the Western world. For each of these ideas he wrote an essay that begins with the earliest occurrence of the idea and then traces how the idea developed in response to some fresh challenge or new feature related to the original idea. In this Adler followed the development of the idea throughout Western civilization. As generations sought to think more deeply about concepts held by their progenitors, they honed and refined the great ideas. To some degree this development was an imagined one. Continuity was maintained as the idea developed along a particular trajectory. And the awakened imagination provided passage over the threshold that others could surmount if they were to take understanding to new heights.

The awakened/awakening imagination is sensitive to the progressive development of an imaginative grasp. If true meaning is to be understood about anything in a world where meaning is dynamic, then any kind of imaginative grasp must be a process. Lewis writes, "I claim that the positive historical statements made by Christianity have the power, elsewhere found chiefly in formal principles, of receiving, without intrinsic change, the increasing complexity of meaning which increasing knowledge puts into them."[6] Thus, the awakened imagination seeks to make sense of continuity and change.

Theological Trajectories

When the awakening imagination is understood in connection with Christian thought it is legitimate to think of its application in terms of what might be called "theological trajectories." Some explanation is necessary. When Moses was inspired to pen the book of Exodus as Israel stood at the threshold of its national life, he gave the people a legal structure on which they were able to flesh out their developing cultural and national life. This was to be instruction that allowed Israel to face its new life in Canaan with confidence. Unfortunately, the people's disobedience led to a longer stay in the wilderness than they first expected.

At the end of forty years God inspires Moses to give a second draft of the law. It was appropriately called Deuteronomy (literally: *the second law*). One cannot help but wonder why God nuanced this second revelation of divine law. Was he sitting in heaven for forty years regretting things he left out, and therefore chose to add bits and pieces that came to him over time? Of course not! If he is omniscient then he does not think like mere mortals think. He does not have new thoughts—he does not have to begin with a presupposition and through a series of inferences arrive at a coherent conclusion as the fruit of some logical process. The ancients said that knowledge was immediate for God. He always knows. When 1 Peter describes Jesus's work on the cross, the author says of Christ, "[he was] a flawless, spotless lamb....chosen before the creation of the world" (1 Pet 1:19-20). C. S. Lewis said, "God saw the cross in the creation of the first nebulae."[7] There are no surprises for God.

So why did God give a first installment of the law in Exodus and later give another installment in Deuteronomy? Perhaps God gave the law to Israel in an incomplete form and let them wrestle with it as they saw circumstances not described in the law but that could be resolved through imaginative applications of it to those circumstances. When God gave the book of Deuteronomy, God refined the Jewish understandings of the moment, correcting their misapplications, and also confirming their wise applications, of the earlier law, giving a second coordinate from which to develop the trajectory of their thought. Coordinate one: Exodus; coordinate two: Deuteronomy.

Further, in the midst of giving the law, God gave orders for the distribution of property once the children of Israel reached the promised land. Moses announced God's revelation that the property was to be distributed through the male heirs. As soon as the word of God was given, the five daughters of Zelophehad objected. During an age when the ground was known to swallow up dissenters, one can imagine people stepping away from these women for safety's sake. To Moses's credit, he asked why the daughters were struggling with the law as it was just given. The women responded that their father had five daughters and their father's legacy would not fall to his progeny but would go to his brother's sons, that is, the cousins of the daughters of Zelophehad. Moses did not dismiss the women or their objection. He went to God in prayer, and God responded that the daughters of Zelophehad were right! The revelation just given did not come with a full range of possible applications. When the demand for a more robust equity to the descendants of Zelophehad was made, God affirmed the request. God also validated the use of theological trajectories. While tethered to scripture, and following the lines of clearly granted coordinates, the imagination awakened into richer applications.

The next coordinate after the law was the record of the history of Israel. Here the children of Israel could learn from the successes of past generations to properly apply the law in the matter of fresh challenges. They could also learn from the consequences of the failure to properly apply the law. There was room in their national life to cultivate something like the awakened/awakening imagination. More coordinates would follow, the most outstanding of which was the incarnate life of Christ. Here was a living example of what God's revelation would look like when lived out authentically in flesh and blood. The prophetic books and the epistles to the churches were further coordinates providing correctives when the culture stepped outside its proper bounds.

In all, we see that biblical revelation did not come with an exhaustive set of applications. Its word was trustworthy and true and perpetually relevant. The Bible was not merely a book with application for the agrarian culture in which it was given. It had relevance for an industrial age never conceived by Moses or Paul. And it has relevance for the technological age and whatever age may come next. The scriptures themselves affirm this kind of thinking along a theological trajectory, tethered to the text and following along clearly prescribed coordinates. This process of application is, in part, an imaginative one. Lewis was right to see one application of the imaginative life flow along these lines. But there is more to grasp when considering the awakened/awakening use of the imagination.

Sometimes the imagination can awaken through creative pictures or visuals that seem simply to pop into one's head. Of this kind of inspiration Lewis observes, "It came. I doubt if we shall ever know more of the process called 'inspiration' than those two monosyllables tell us."[8] Lewis says his own imagination was awakened by such pictures. He said that the Narnian Chronicles grew from a picture of a faun with an umbrella carrying Christmas parcels in the snow. It was a single frame, one image; Lewis's attempt to discover what this picture meant became the inspiration unfolding the Narnian books.

Not all are, or will be, inspired the way Lewis was. His was clearly a very visual imagination. He said he did his prayers by picturing those he was praying for; it was a prayer by means of images. So this example of what Lewis called the awakened/awakening imagination, or what he elsewhere calls the pictorial imagination, is highly effective.

However, visual imagination should not be codified as the only way one's imagination might work.[9] Those who find inspiration coming along these lines must realize, as Lewis did, that the picture must go someplace if it is to become a story. Here Lewis uses another term synonymous with the awakening imagination: the cinematographic imagination. This is not so much an imagination of pictures but moving images (the dance compared with the sculpture). It creates a visual, moving narrative. Lewis praises John Gower for this approach and notes of his *Confessio Amantis*, "Excellence in Gower's sea-pieces [that] has led some to suppose that he was familiar with sea travel—as he may well have been; but it is in fact, only one manifestation of his devotion to movement and progression, his preoccupation with things that change as you watch them."[10]

The Awakened Imagination and *An Experiment in Criticism*

Lewis was constantly growing and developing in his imaginative grasp of many topics and subjects. One can see displays of the awakening imagination throughout his books. It has one of its finest embodiments in Lewis's *An Experiment in Criticism.*[11] Lewis observes that "the process of growing up is to be valued for what we gain, not what we lose."[12] In the experiment Lewis wants to know if a book might be judged good or bad by how it is read. This may sound subjective, but if a good book is one read often by many in a particular way, his judgment has merit, because Lewis gives definition to many types of readers as well as many types of literature.

Among readers, he makes a distinction between the few and the many. The few read a book only once; the many are likely to return to a book they like and read it over many times during their lives. The many use books; the few receive from books, and their lives are in some ways enlarged by what they receive. Lewis also notes that the many and the few can be distinguished by how they approach art and music as well. He writes that "the first demand any work of art makes upon us is surrender. Look. Listen. Receive. Get yourself out of the way."[13] Lewis remarks that this is not merely a passive act, though it may seem so at first. The fact is, before an observer can make any artistic judgment he or she must properly understand the thing as it is. Any true judgment will be found in statements that can be supported by the object itself. "As the first demand of the picture is 'Look,' the first demand of the music is 'Listen.'"[14] In this regard, reading literature, viewing art, and listening to music are acts of justice. If justice is to be understood as rendering to something its due esteem, then the awakening imagination is movement toward a kind of justice.

To further justly render to books their due, what some might call a close reading of the text, Lewis classifies different types of literature and defines these types according to category. He describes myth as "a particular kind of story which has value in itself—a value independent of its embodiment in any literary work."[15] No matter what kind of embodiment, poetry, novel, satire, or even ballad or film, the story works. The elements have a kind of power in and of themselves. They tend to hold the reader breathless in wonder and delight. The myth, Lewis observes, "works upon us by its peculiar flavor or quality, rather as a smell or a chord does."[16] The experience of reading the myth Lewis suggests is both grave and awe inspiring. "We feel it to be numinous. It is as if something of great moment has been communicated to us."[17] It is held up to "the fully waking imagination."[18] The myth has a kind of permanent staying power; one cannot escape it.

Lewis also defines fantasy and by it means "any narrative that deals with impossibles and preternaturals."[19] He sees the need to define more precisely and describes the fantasy of the egoistic as the fantasy of the disinterested. The egoistic fantasy demands the reader be present as the hero, whereas the disinterested reads the fantasy as a spectator. Those who would be the hero as they read "project themselves into the most enviable or most admirable character."[20] Lewis wonders whether or not "all the reading of the unliterary is of this sort and involves this projection."[21] The imagination is not awakened to the wider world. It is, rather, shut down to a narrow focus on oneself. It is flattery to the ego. It leads to a superficial realism and deception. As Lewis observes, "Nothing can deceive unless it bears a plausible resemblance to reality."[22]

Realisms in Literature

Lewis cautions his readers about realisms in literature. As is typical of Lewis, he defines things precisely. He writes of "realism of presentation," where the author presents to the reader "sharply imagined detail."[23] This he contrasts with "realism of content," where "a fiction is realistic in content when it is probable or 'true to life.'"[24] The realism of presentation can be found in works such as *Beowulf*, or Tolkien's *The Lord of the Rings*: the reader does not suspect that the world is real, but the descriptions are detailed and coherent, making that imagined world come alive. Things are true in that world. The laws of that world are coherent rather than capricious. Of course it is necessary to "suspend belief" and enter the author's imagined world in order to have the story affect us. It does no good to be constantly saying, "Oh, that could never happen!"

The point of the story is to entertain. It is written to be enjoyed, and significant to the enjoyment is the realistic presentation of that world. On the other hand, those books that provide realism of content may seem true to life but are the most likely to deceive the reader by building up false expectations. Nobody expects orcs and dragons in the "real world," but someone may expect to be the popular student at school, or the successful businessman, or the winner of the beauty pageant. When the content of the story seems real but improbable, it raises expectations that are unlikely to be satisfied. These, in turn, lead to growing disappointments with oneself and the world. The stories, on the other hand, that come from the mythical worlds born out of realism of presentation, imaginatively conceived, are less likely to raise such false expectations and disappointments. But they are very likely to entertain and give pleasure without self-aggrandizement.

Considered Objections as a Quest for Truth

One characteristic of Lewis's writing, observed throughout the corpus of his work, is the tendency to consider objections that might count against his point. This too is characteristic of the awakening imagination. He is unafraid to consider these objections. This suggests in him a real interest in discovering truth. He is questing for answers in his intellectual inquiries. He is not trying to manipulate the answer. Consequently there is something very satisfying for the reader who joins him in any given quest. When Lewis speaks of "realism of presentation" versus "realism of content" as discussed above, it raises the curious notion that literature should be true to life.

As Lewis explores this option, he begins to call it into question. He observes that all but bores say the obvious when recounting a story.[25] It tends to be the exceptional that gets retold—something noteworthy and, perhaps, uncommon. This is why a story is told in the first place and holds the attention of the hearers. Curiosity is awakened and attention is focused. People want to know the unexpected outcome of the story. They wait for the surprise that is coming. The story may finally raise the hopes of the reader that perhaps he or she might one day develop such endurance and courage. Perhaps there might be developments beyond the tendency towards jealousy or envy, those things that lead to inordinate suspicion and eventual tragedy. The literature can awaken in the hearts of the readers the desire to be better men or women. This may occur instead of reading into the plot, or the characters, the false notion that the reader already possesses such qualities and is therefore better than most.

Lewis also sees good literature as inspiring a love in the reader that is not abandoned as he or she gets older. Lewis rightly observes, "The process of growing up is to be valued for what we gain, not for what we lose."[26] The loves of childhood do not have to be abandoned in order to acquire new ones. A tree does not have to give up its interior rings just because it adds new ones. Real growth requires both keeping the old and adding the new. Remember, this is what allows for continuity of development. To dismiss literature as childish or adolescent is as if an ad hominem argument has been used against a book. Rather than describe by means of a failed plot, or deficient character development, or poorly stylized writing, one simply calls the book a name: adolescent. It is not argument and sets forth no proof. Lewis reminds his readers often enough that we must explain why a thing is bad before we dismiss it as bad. If not, we run the risk of manipulation.

Further, to dismiss books that we loved when we were young for the sole reason that we have now aged is to engage in what Lewis calls "chronological snobbery."[27] This can occur not only in the life of the individual but also within any given culture or age. We can be dismissive of others older and representative of some bygone era. There is a chronological arrogance that could be suggested by such flimsy grounds of judgment. Certainly the reader's interests and tastes may develop over time. But this does not require abandoning those things that brought delight in the past. "The real way of mending a man's taste is not to denigrate his present favorites, but to teach him how to enjoy something better."[28]

In keeping with his willingness to look at objections to his own point of view before either dismissing them or capitulating to them, Lewis admits the risk of using literature. Before trying to figure out what a poem might mean, a reader should remember that it is first an object. Attention to the object, as it is, must precede any judgments about it.[29] For example, the literary critic might fall into the temptation of using "To value them chiefly for reflections which they may suggest to us or morals we may draw from them, is a flagrant instance of 'using' instead of 'receiving.'"[30] The book is pursued only for its use. As Lewis notes, "Since everything can be a symbol, or an irony, or an ambiguity—we shall easily find what we want." And he suggests further, "We are so busy doing things with the work that we give it too little chance to work on us. Thus increasingly we meet only ourselves."[31] The old adage rings true again—we reap what we sow. If we sow barley, we reap barley. Sow wheat, reap wheat. Sow self, reap solitude. In a passage that hints of his coming conclusion, Lewis writes, "In reading imaginative work, I suggest, we should be much less concerned with altering our own opinions—though this of course is sometimes their effect—than with entering fully into the opinions, and therefore also the attitudes, feelings and total experience, of other men."[32]

The awakening imagination is necessary to any genuine quest for truth. In this regard, Lewis says a true lover of literature will always appreciate a well-told story, an elegantly written essay, or a poem that is a delight to the ears even if he or she adamantly disagrees with the values or sentiments of the writing. The reader is not merely looking for agreement. There is a desire to know, to see, to hear and understand. The longing is to break out of the dungeon of self into the wider world and be able to recognize that which is different from oneself.

The Point of *An Experiment in Criticism*

As mentioned, the point of *An Experiment in Criticism* is to discover a way to judge a good book from a bad one. Someone might ask why such an experiment is necessary. As long as critics write about books, judgments are being made at some level or another. As previously mentioned, Lewis wrote that "an accusation always implies a standard."[33] What is the basis for any critical judgment of a book? If the standard is self-referential then judgments are nearly anarchistic; it is one individual's taste over against another. There is nothing objective to validate any judgments and all such literary discussions amount to meaninglessness. It is as if everyone ought to like pistachio ice cream over all other flavors simply because I like it best. Further, it is possible that one may assert that his or her literary subculture is the determining source of all literary judgments. It is the will of one party over another whereby judgments may be affirmed. Unfortunately, this too lacks substance. Literary tastes can change over time, and those of various parties can be fickle and thereby prove to be unreliable and subjective. This is duly noted by Benjamin Jowett, the great English translator of Plato's *Dialogues*. He observed in his discussion of Plato's *Meno*,

> Few students of theology or philosophy have sufficiently reflected how quickly the bloom of a philosophy passes away; or how hard it is for one age to understand the writings of another; or how nice a judgment is required of those who are seeking to express the philosophy of one age in the terms of another. The "eternal truths" of which metaphysicians speak have hardly ever lasted more than a generation. In our own day schools or systems of philosophy which have once been famous have died before the founders of them.[34]

In his discussion of Jeremy Bentham, Jowett writes that "the systems of all philosophers require the criticism of 'the morrow,' when the heat of the imagination which forged them has cooled, and they are seen in the temperate light of the day. All of them have contributed to enrich the mind of the civilized world; none of them occupy that supreme or exclusive place which their authors would have assigned to them."[35] The warning is a fair one, reminding that any age, as well as any individual, can become so self-referential that it can inflate the understanding of the person or party as well as the time and place and miss out on the greater reality. This kills the awakening imagination and imprisons one in the dungeon of self-reference.

An illustration of this kind of self-reference can be seen in Lewis's *The Pilgrim's Regress*. This book was written a year after his conversion to Christianity. It is remarkably perceptive and somewhat theologically sophisticated given how early it comes after this change in his life. In the story a boy named John has a vision of an island. He sets out on a quest to find this island and has many adventures along the way. In his travels he meets a group of people called "Stay at Homes." The citizens of this village have no clue how provincial they are. They are convinced that their understanding of things is the dominant grasp of matters worldwide. And they also believe that things they have never heard of cannot be important to others. Of these people, Lewis observes, "That is always the way it is with stay-at-homes. If they like something in their own village they take it for a thing universal and eternal, though perhaps it was never heard of five miles away; if they dislike something, they say it is a local, backward, provincial convention, though in fact, it may be the law of nations."[36]

A similar sentiment is expressed by Rudyard Kipling in the opening line of his poem, "The English Flag." He writes, "And what should they know of England who only England know?" Not until you have traveled beyond the present grasp of a thing, and looked back, can you properly evaluate it. The strength of one's own position can only be properly tested as it runs up against another. Lewis's friend Owen Barfield said it this way: "The Experience of oneself over against that which is not oneself is a *sine qua non* of human consciousness."[37] One further observation by Jowett is equally instructive. In a discussion about utopian literature, he wrote, "No philosophy has ever stood this criticism of the next generation, though the founders of all of them have imagined they were built upon a rock."[38]

The Experiment

Lewis is very aware that if literary criticism is to be considered a valid discipline, then there must be some way to make literary judgments that give credence to the practices of the critic. Lewis is not suggesting that the approach he is setting forth in *An Experiment in Criticism* is *the* way to see these things, but he *is* setting it forth as a matter to be considered and discussed. How can literary judgments be made that have merit? And, for consideration of this present study, in what way might this be considered an imaginative exercise? As in all rhetorical work, the proof in the pudding is whether or not an audience is persuaded. A communicator has achieved desired outcomes if the audience responds in a manner he or she hoped to produce. When it comes to writing books, Lewis believes that a good book is one that elicits from readers a particular response and a bad book is one that receives a different kind of response.

It all sounds pretty controversial. And certainly, both good and bad books may have a variety of audience responses. Nevertheless, Lewis does believe there can be a similar response to a good book by a particular audience. If this is the case, then what qualities does this particular audience tend to possess? Remember,

Lewis identifies two kinds of readers: those who use books and those who receive books. The user sees the value of a given book only if it serves some purpose brought to the reading. He or she is a utilitarian when it comes to what he or she chooses to read. Among this class of readers Lewis identifies the person who reads professionally. The academic may have once been a lover of literature but now sees books only as tools. Having lost the love of books, he or she reads only those things that are necessary for his or her work. Another user of books may be the self-help fanatic who only reads books for their medicinal help. It is unlikely this person will read a book for the sheer pleasure of the story. This person discards the book like one discards bones after having eaten the meat. The idea of a second or third read of a book is foreign to this type of a reader. Others read to stay in the know. They treat reading the way some treat fashion. They want to be current, to read the books those in the know happen to be talking about. Lewis imagines a cocktail party occurring at a house; the guests are all of this fashionable type discussing books to show they are on top of things. Their interest in particular books will last briefly and will be discarded as they rush on to the next book on the top of the best seller list. At this party, as Lewis imagines it, the only truly literary person is the little boy who was put to bed early and is reading *Treasure Island* by flashlight under his covers because he can't put the book down.[39]

By contrast to the user, Lewis imagines another type of reader: the receiver of literature. He or she reads, initially, with a degree of passivity. Receivers enjoy entering the world created by the author. There is a suspension of disbelief in the hopes of actually receiving what the author intended to give. Their hearts rise and fall with the emotion of the book. They are angered at injustices and refreshed by the romantic connections. They are given incidents in the story and respond with ordinate or just sentiments. They receive what has been given and relish it. They also ponder what they have gained from such books and tend to return to the books for more.

Lewis says the mark of a good book is that a reader will want to read it over and over again. Even though the twists and turns of plot are now well-known and the paths have been often trod, the reader goes back to the book for the sheer love of the world created by the book itself. The phenomenon may be observed readily in the response of a child to a particularly appealing bedtime story. Delighted by the world created, the child shouts out at the completion of the story, "Read it again!" or, "Tell it again!" Lewis suggests that though the child knows what is coming before it comes and is already familiar with how it ends, he or she longs most of all for the world created by the author. Lewis believes that it touches the reader or hearer of the story at that place where all tend to long for the only other world we can ever really know, which is heaven.

Lewis believes that this longing for heaven is something common in each of us. Often, however, the longing is truncated by pursuit of some artificiality, what he calls "the sweet poison of the false infinite" in his novel *Perelandra*.[40] Where the longing may be present, the quest for the proper object of the longing may be sidetracked. It is here that a good book may reawaken the longing and set the heart questing for its true north. Lewis writes in *An Experiment in Criticism*, "In coming to understand anything we must reject the facts as they are for us in favor of the facts as they are."[41] In other words, we must break out of the dungeon of self and discover the wider world as it is, not as we would have it be. The capacity to receive literature is either truncated in self-reference and utility, or is yet to be awakened and encouraged in an ongoing awakening to the wider world of the real.

In the epilogue of the book Lewis powerfully reveals that he wants to break out of his own subjectivism. He observes that his own eyes are not enough for him. He wants to read what others have written. He longs to see what others have seen. It is necessary if he is to grow and gain a wider understanding of this wide, wide world and discover his true place in it. The awakening imagination demands it. He writes that even what others have written is not enough for him; he would read what they have imagined. Even this is not enough; Lewis says that he regrets that the brutes cannot write books. Gladly would he see and discover how the world presents itself to the eye of a mouse or a bee, or how it comes charged to the olfactory sense of a dog. Lewis acknowledges that this is a spiritual exercise and concludes with this observation: "Literary experience heals the wound, without undermining the privilege, of individuality.... In reading great literature I become a thousand men and yet remain myself. Like the night sky in the Greek poem, I see with a myriad of eyes, but it is still I who see. Here as in worship, in love, in moral action, and in knowing, I transcend myself; and am never more myself than when I do."[42]

The Fruit of the Awakened Imagination: Awareness

The experiment of judging a good book from a bad concludes with the suggestion that good books are read in such a way that the reader begins to see the world as something separated from the self. Paradoxically, the individual gains, in the process, a clearer sense of self as one individuated from the objective world. Here, both the knower and the thing known have intrinsic value. In this regard the awakening imagination is a sort of threshold to justice, for it allows one to enter into a process of rendering to things their due. As Lewis observes, "In the moral sphere, every act of justice or charity involves putting ourselves in the other person's place and thus transcending our own competitive particularity."[43] For this to happen, one must have a place for the other without regard to utility. As a result, not only is a progressive clarity of the real world discovered, but greater empathy for others is also approximated.

The activity of good reading, of entering the world of good books, is an invitation to break out of the dungeon of self. Here is the opportunity to see the wider world in a somewhat disinterested way; not in a way uninterested, but in a way whereby one can enjoy without having to possess or control. This is the fruit of the awakened imagination. Rather than the transforming imagination that must project onto things what it wants them to be, the awakened imagination becomes aware and in awe of things as they are. One's place in the world can be assumed without fear or pretense.

Chapter 5

On the Shoulders of Giants

Realizing Imagination in *The Discarded Image*

Without a use of the imagination that can help us increase our understanding of the complex world in which we live, human flourishing will be truncated. The realizing imagination helps us understand this complex world. It is like the opening of a rose in bud as it matures to full flower. Lewis thought the realizing imagination one of the most important uses of the imagination and saw it as characteristic of the Middle Ages. The medieval imagination highlighted a developing understanding of the complexities of the real world. It is this sort of understanding that allowed Lewis to write, "I believe in Christianity as I believe the sun is risen, not only because I see it but because by it I see everything else."[1] This dynamic process is capable of accounting for newly acquired data. But the process is only likely to work based on the character of the observer.

To function in a universe more complex than our capacity to understand, we must begin with a sense of humility, or honesty; to do less is to cultivate pretense and pride. Growth in character then is also necessary to the flourishing of a realizing imagination. Philosopher Basil Mitchell writes,

> The sort of person one is, is itself profoundly affected by the character of one's basic convictions. It is evident, therefore, that if these convictions are to change radically, it will not, as a rule, be due to this or that particular piece of evidence, or this or that fresh experience but as a result of a steady accumulation of considerations which together persuade the individual that his or her existing mind-set is no longer adequate and requires either to be drastically revised or abandoned altogether. And this process of change cannot be purely intellectual, because strong emotions and entrenched habits are involved.[2]

The need to define the realizing imagination as we do has its own implications. Lewis writes, "Reality is Iconoclastic."[3] This is Lewis's biggest idea. It is alluded to in every book he wrote (even his pre-Christian writing), but it has its most robust exposition in *The Discarded Image*. What did Lewis mean by the concept "reality is iconoclastic"? Again, the world presented to our senses is always far more complex than our best understanding of it. To accommodate ourselves to complexity and to correct misunderstanding, we must constantly develop.

An iconoclast is somebody who breaks idols. You may have an image of God. Nevertheless, this image may be modified by new insights provided by a recent discussion, a book just read, or a convincing lecture or sermon just heard. In these cases, pieces of the puzzle of understanding have been linked in such a way that a fuller vision of God has now come into view. Yet if you hold onto that present understanding too tightly, however helpful it might have been in the past, it will begin to compete against the possibility of your gaining a better, more accurate knowledge of God. In cases like these, the image once helpful calcifies into an idol.

But *reality is iconoclastic*. Lewis reminds us that God, in divine mercy, kicks out the walls of any temples we may build because God wants to give us more of himself. As Lewis says, God cares nothing about temples built, only about temples building.[4] "He must constantly work as the iconoclast. Every idea of Him we form, He must in mercy shatter. The most blessed result of prayer would be to rise thinking, 'But I never knew before. I never dreamed...' I suppose it was at such a moment that Thomas Aquinas said of all his own theology: 'It reminds me of straw.'"[5]

This idea is imaginatively embodied in a conversation between Aslan the lion, the Christ figure of Narnia, and Lucy, the most spiritually sensitive child to enter Narnia. On her second adventure in Narnia, *Prince Caspian*, Lucy sees her beloved Aslan for the first time. She exclaims, "Aslan! You're bigger!" The lion responds, "I am not. But every year you grow, you will find me bigger."[6] The cultivation of the realizing imagination is vital for cognitive development. In other words, we finite beings should cultivate a dynamic, ever-growing understanding of everything, and most certainly of the infinite God.

The very councils of Christendom remind us that no theology is ever finished but is always developing. All theology is approximation. We get no last word about God, but we can have a sure word about God (because God reveals himself to us). But even in God's revelation of himself, our understanding must be a developing one. No one has ever plumbed the depths. As Habakkuk the prophet noted, in the display of God's glory there is "the hiding place of his power."[7]

Every revelation of God is both a disclosing and a reveiling. If God displays power by creating Mount Everest, we are in awe . . . but have yet to see the full extent of God's power. If God creates the entire Himalayas, we are overwhelmed by the majesty, but even then have not seen the full capacity of the divine omniscience. If God speaks and brings the universes into being, we are speechless before the grandeur of God, but still we are blinded to the infinite reaches of what God can, and might, do. Lewis's God is big and his assessment of human capacities is realistic. Reality is iconoclastic. Reality always acts as its own corrective when we misunderstand it.

This idea is not new with Lewis. He recounts an idea often expressed throughout history. Baron von Hügel wrote, "Beware of the first clearness."[8] We must always move beyond a first grasp into the wider horizons. That is, we must seek the second clarity, and the third, and so on. Robert Browning said in his poem "Rabbi ben Ezra," "Then welcome each rebuff / that turns earth's smoothness rough."[9] We can think we've understood the earth. We can deceive ourselves into imagining that it is nice and smooth and round, "a place for everything and everything in its place." But this is a self-deception, for the world is not smooth and round. It has texture, peaks and valleys, complexities to awaken us and excite us. This is visible on every landscape and at every turning of the road. Welcome those realities that help you to see the world the way it is rather than some way you think it must be.

If we fail to see that there is always more to be known, our developing grasp of the universe will come up short. We must realize the need for and be receptive to growth. The realizing imagination is the means whereby that receptivity can flourish. This relates precisely to Lewis's understanding of the realizing imagination, and to *The Discarded Image* as Lewis's best exposition of it. On December 30, 1952, Lewis inscribed in Joy Davidman's copy of *The Great Divorce*, "There are three images in my mind which I must continually forsake and replace by better ones: the false image of God, the false image of my neighbours, and the false image of myself." Lewis then adds, "(from an unwritten chapter on Iconoclasm)."[10] Perhaps *The Discarded Image* was that chapter, finally written and expanded into a book.

The Discarded Image: An Embodiment of the Realizing Imagination

The Discarded Image is one of Lewis's most important works. This book and *Letters to Malcolm: Chiefly on Prayer* were the final two books he wrote before he died on November 22, 1963. It was the summation of Lewis's Prolegomena

Lectures on Medieval Literature, which he gave many times at Oxford University. Lewis taught medieval literature at Oxford and later at Cambridge. It was the focus of his academic attention. His entire adult life plumbed the depths of this body of work. And since he gave these lectures over and over, one can imagine that the deeper he read and the more widely he studied the authors and influences of this period, the more refined his thinking became, filtered through the grid of a lifetime of thoughtful reflection. We suggest that *The Discarded Image* is to Lewis what the *David* and the *Pieta* were to Michelangelo, or the *Las Mininas* was to Velasquez, or the *Mona Lisa* to Da Vinci.

Since the book represents Lewis's own developing thinking about the medieval worldview, it provides an example of what Lewis thought about the nature of the realizing imagination. Also, since Lewis gave the book the title *The Discarded Image*, it represents Lewis's acknowledgement that all worldviews must, in time, give way to more robust ones. That is, sound thought on any topic must be dynamic, not static.

Something else testifies to the significance of this book. Not only was Lewis forging its content over his lifetime. This book was also his swan song, his last literary statement and final testament to his reading public. In this regard, *The Discarded Image* may even have a slight prophetic feel about it. Often enough Lewis warned against the contemporary idolatries of his own day, idolatries that still reverberate into our own. Lewis sees the future as he examines the past. Just as the medieval worldview had to become a discarded image, so too our worldviews must give way to new pictures of the world. If Lewis is right, then certainly our own worldview must give way to something more responsive to the universe as it actually is.

If this is so, then *The Discarded Image* could become recognized as one of Lewis's greatest works in Christian apologetics. It testifies to the fact that the universe is big and we are small. And if the universe has meaning at all, then we must always account for the coherence that continues to point us to God. Whether or not this book does prove to be one of Lewis's greatest apologetics is a judgment that will have to be made by some future generation. Nevertheless, this book is worthy of serious reflection, and it is a book that embodies the realizing imagination.

The Beginnings

Lewis begins *The Discarded Image* by stating that primary sources should be consulted whenever studying any period in literature. An opinion of a period in literature can best be formed by a collective or composite picture pieced together from a wide range of sources from that period. We must turn to commentaries only when the hard, misunderstood passages in a given text are too difficult for us to decipher. The topography of an area can be studied by looking at a map or by exploring countryside: each has its assets and its liabilities. Certainly the big picture provided by the map keeps one from getting lost. But it never reveals to the eyes or the touch the texture of the land or its flora and fauna. Similarly, commentaries on an age never give the close-up perspective one gets from immersing oneself in the actual literature. Given time, the particular books begin to appear on the canvas of our mind like dots of color on a Surratt canvas. In time a picture begins to emerge. Generalizations of the period, drawn from the books, take on an air of authority.

Lewis has drawn, from his wide range of reading, a picture of medieval literary background helpful to the person just beginning his or her own exploration of the period. Lewis would warn that his book is available for the person who has not yet had the time or opportunity for fuller exposure to the material. But Lewis writes to nudge the student to go from *The Discarded Image* to a firsthand experience with medieval literature. Lewis opens up more than wardrobe doors. Those who read him will discover many other worlds. Yet Lewis's own experience with this particular material gives him authority to say that the characteristic of the age was the realizing imagination.

The Medieval Situation

Lewis observes many things as he writes of the medieval model of the universe. As it comes to the reader through the books of the period, the medieval world picture was no spontaneous, imaginative response to environmental circumstances.[11] It was far more deliberate. The medieval mind "depended predominately on books" to piece together its view of the world.[12]

That means this world was the ripe fruit of reflection and contemplation. Medieval readers and scholars tended to trust the authors they read. Of course, the sources could contradict each other. These tensions had to be reconciled and harmonized.[13] And since "he was an organizer, a codifier, a builder of systems," the medieval scholar developed systems that were both works of art but also dynamic and growing.[14] There was nothing static about his understanding. The universe was freighted with wonder and awe. It was the product of a "realizing imagination."[15] While reading about these things in Lewis, one cannot help but wonder if Lewis's own sense of awe and wonder was drawn from these texts.

Lewis notes that the medieval imagination developed because the artists gave attention to their matter. In this regard, they were objectivists. Their curiosities about the real world came to them through their observations and the books they read. And this led to a sense of unquenchable wonder. They had great confidence in their matter, discovered in both the world they inhabited and the manuscripts they received from the preceding generations. Lewis points out that medieval culture was bookish, yet it operated with a limited number of antiquarian sources. Lewis asks his readers to consider the image of a group of people shipwrecked on an island trying to build a culture on the books that happened to survive the shipwreck.[16] This was the situation of the Middle Ages. The science of textual criticism was not yet established. Source archaeology was not as developed. The medieval scholar was limited to the works of local monasteries. This was not insignificant material but, like Swiss cheese, there were plenty of holes in the content. Nevertheless, the scholastic mind received with gratitude the manuscripts available to it and studied them thoroughly, perhaps more thoroughly than we study our texts today.

Lewis reminds his readers, "Characteristically, the medieval man was not a dreamer nor a spiritual adventurer; he was an organizer, a codifier, a man of system."[17] He sought to make sense of his material and even, where conflicts existed between his sources, he sought ways these might be reconciled. Lewis holds up Thomas Aquinas's *Summa* and Dante's *Divine Comedy* as well as the Salisbury Cathedral as models or archetypes of medieval productivity and synthesis.[18] The scholastics desired unity and proportion with such earnestness that, when seeing contradictions in the ancient, surviving sources, they thought that "there must be some explanation which would harmonize them."[19] Lewis summarizes,

> It is out of this that the Medieval picture of the universe is evolved: a chance collection of materials, an inability to say "Bosh," a temper systematic to the point of morbidity, great mental powers, unwearied patience, and a robust delight in their work. All these factors led them to produce the greatest, most complex, specimen of syncretism or harmonization which, perhaps, the world has ever known. They tidied up the universe.[20]

This "tidying up" was an exercise of the realizing imagination. It was also an exercise in justice and humility. Justice was understood as rendering to a thing its due. It must be understood not merely as the punishment of the evildoer but also the praise of the well doer. It sought emotional harmony with ideas that seemed right. Again, their confidence was in their matter. They did maintain a healthy hermeneutical suspicion of their grasp of that matter. Therefore, they kept at a thing until they believed they had grasped it accurately. The thing itself, whatever it might be, merited such effort just by being the thing it was.

And since their world was one of complexity, they avoided the oversimplifications that can sometimes characterize our own age. Often they were unwilling to quickly pigeonhole a dissenting point of view. By contrast, present practices often tend simply to name a perceived assumption in an opposing view and, by that act, consider it refuted. The substance of the opponent's point of view often is not considered. It is not uncommon today to suspect the integrity of the person who holds a dissenting view simply because it is contrary to our own.

By contrast, the medieval mind would begin with confidence in the matter at hand. This world, its manuscripts, even opposing points of view, merited an attempt at understanding and an ever more robust attempt at "tidying up." This was an act of justice, for their material demanded such a response. Of course it wasn't done perfectly; there were exceptions. But the effect, by and large, was significant, and deliberately achieved. Furthermore, humility was necessary. Chesterton once observed, "One sees small things from the mountain top but large things from the valley." Chesterton also rightly observed, "The world will never starve for want of wonders only for want of wonder."[21] One could say this use of the realizing imagination was an exercise in justice and humility.

A further characteristic of the realizing imagination led Lewis to note that the medieval mind tended toward embellishment. An author unashamedly worked with an old story. His source had merit and the story was worthy of retelling. Nevertheless, he retold the story with his own embellishments. Lewis notes this habit of the medieval imagination in numerous places.[22]

Some of this has lived on in our day, especially in film. So many movies retell old material, worthy stories that merit the retelling, especially in an age where people, less informed than they realize, need to have the old tried and true stories brought into the imaginative enjoyment of a new day and new culture. *West Side Story* is the retelling of Shakespeare's *Romeo and Juliet*. *O Brother, Where Art Thou?* is the retelling of Homer's *The Odyssey*. *Bridget Jones's Diary* is the retelling of Jane Austen's *Pride and Prejudice*. *The Lion King* is the retelling of *Hamlet* (as is *Prince Caspian*). *August Rush* is the retelling of Charles Dickens's *Oliver Twist*.

And there are hundreds of examples in our culture's films that echo something like the gospel story, that is, of one giving up his life to save another: *The Titanic* (Jack gives up his life to save Rose), *Avatar* (which means incarnation in Sanskrit), Disney's *The Jungle Book* (which quotes John 15 in the Bible, near the end of the film, "Greater love hath no man than this, that a man lay down his life for his friends" [v. 13 KJV]), *Beauty and the Beast*, *Tangled*, and *The Little Mermaid*. This medieval characteristic of embellishing old stories has not died. The realizing imagination is an embellishing imagination, with powerful imaginative value.

Reservations: Then and Now

Lewis observes that the scholar in the Middle Ages entertained the possibility that all of his sources carried a certain weight or authority, even the conflicting ones. As noted, he sought synthesis because he lacked the capacity to say, "Bosh!" Was this simply a tending toward naivety? While this could be the case, Lewis said the era's scholars were less likely to be taken in. They worked with provisional models, and they knew it. While their worldview was developing, it was never static. As Lewis observed, "Great masters do not take any model quite so seriously.... They know it is, after all, only a model, possibly replaceable."[23] He noted the medieval man was less likely to take his metaphors as seriously as people do today.

He gives an example. Gravity was not discovered by Galileo. The phenomenon we call gravity was known and experienced in the Middle Ages as well as in all earlier ages. The issue was not in discovery or invention, but in description. How is the phenomenon of gravity explained? The medieval metaphor said that everything has a kind of homesickness, a *kindly enclyning*, a desire to go home, and therefore everything longs to return to its proper place. Let go of the rock in your hand and it falls to the earth out of a desire to return. Certainly scholastics knew that stones have no literal aspirations to return home. Nevertheless, Lewis says if we could ask the medieval scientist why he spoke as if stones did have such aspirations, he would likely "retort with a counter question, 'But do you intend your language about *laws* and *obedience* any more literally than I intend mine about *kindly enclyning*? Do you really believe that a falling stone is aware of a directive issued to it by some legislator and feels either a moral or prudential obligation to conform?'"[24]

Here Lewis awakens his own readers to an opportunity for engaging the realizing imagination. The familiar way of talking about the laws of gravity, in our own day, has blinded us to the fact that "laws of gravity" is itself a metaphor. Furthermore, due to our own common uses, when we consider how the ancients described gravity, we think they were backward or ill-informed as they employed their metaphors. Of course this exhibits the tendency toward cultural insensitivity. But it also reveals how little we are aware of our own metaphors. Even less do we see this unfortunate cultural arrogance and superiority as we look to the past.

It is we who have believed that our descriptions are the preferred or permanent ones. We fail to realize that our own worldview will also become a discarded image. While medieval depictions had to give ground to new descriptions, an honest look at the past may remind us that our own models and metaphors are not permanent. Even the truths we know must give way to a deeper understanding of those truths and a wider application than presently conceived. Lewis notes that "Scientific theories . . . are never statements of fact."[25] Further, Lewis observes that "the ignorant were more aware of their ignorance then than now."[26]

The realizing imagination surrendered to the material before it, that is, it surrendered to objective reality. Therefore, it was less likely to fall into the temptation to be self-referential, which is a significant problem in our day. For example, one might hear someone say, "Prague is the most beautiful city in the world." To be accurate, the one making the statement would actually have to have seen every city in the world. The statement could be more measured by the person saying, "Prague is the most beautiful city I've ever seen." Still, one could ask, "What other cities have you seen?" To substantiate this claim, it is legitimate to ask, "What is your standard for beauty and how would you apply it to a city?" Without substantive support and intellectual rigor, we are reduced to merely saying, "I like Prague."

The realizing imagination is necessary if we would make substantive statements about our experience in the world. This use of the imagination, surrendered to the thing itself, seeks to know, understand, and describe the world as it is. Lewis engages the realizing imagination in this book, describing the medieval world with its models and practices so his readers can benefit. Lewis's model can benefit his readers as they attempt to describe their own world and experience without being merely self-referential.

Lewis wrote with precision at this point when he noted,

> Historically as well as cosmically, medieval man stood at the foot of a stairway; looking up, he felt delight. The backward, like the upward, glance exhilarated him with a majestic spectacle, and humility was rewarded with the pleasures of admiration. And, thanks to his deficiency in the sense of period, that packed and gorgeous past was far more immediate to him than the dark and bestial past could ever be to a Lecky or a Wells. It differed from the present only by being better. Hector was like any other knight, only braver. The saints looked down on one's spiritual life, the kings, sages, and warriors on one's secular life, the great lovers of old on one's own amours, to foster, encourage, and instruct. There were friends, ancestors, patrons in every age. One had one's place, however modest, in a great succession; one need be neither proud nor lonely.[27]

Note well Lewis's statement that medieval humans had a "humility [which] was rewarded with the pleasures of admiration." It is reported that Isaac Newton said with true gratitude and humility, "If I've seen farther than others it has been while seated on the shoulders of giants." Today, the attitude of many might be embodied in the comment, "It's amazing that we've accomplished so much in our day given the pygmies that preceded us." While this description may be overstated, the sentiment is there nonetheless. The interpreter lacks suspicion of his or her own arrogance. Humility and its complementary characteristic of honesty vaporize in some forms of dismissive critique. Couched in the dismissal is the attitude that somehow our party has reached the zenith of understanding, and it is unlikely that anything worthy of consideration will emerge in the point of view of our detractors or those we are dismantling.

How far we've moved from the Newtonian humility; even medieval realizing imagination escapes us. If our position has merit, we should be able to hold up its excellences, in a reasonable way, before our detractors. If we cannot, then we must go slow and be less quick to judge. Most judgments, growing out of self-referential blindness, betray an arrogance and may even mask insecurities. Lewis's friend and fellow Inkling Charles Williams observes, "Not one mind in a thousand can be trusted to state accurately what its opponent says, much less what he thinks."[28]

This is not an overidealization of the medieval thinkers. They were as liable, due to their fallenness and finitude, to get something wrong as we are in our current age. But because they were more curious about their sources and more meticulous to understand what others had said or written, they were less likely to go awry in the same way as we moderns. And because they were very attentive to their matter, they were less likely to dismiss before they understood as fully as they might. Again, there were exceptions, but the practice of the realizing imagination was far more common. As Lewis describes the medieval world, he allows his readers to apply some of these practices to their own time and place.

Selected Materials

Lewis says that the medieval worldview was founded on certain literary sources. The realizing imagination is therefore grounded and informed by what has come before while seeking to craft a fresh understanding of what is ahead. Lewis writes, "There are perhaps no sources so necessary for a student of Medieval Literature to know as the Bible, Virgil, and Ovid, but I shall say nothing about these three."[29] He assumes a well-rounded and liberally educated student will already be familiar with them. To read Ovid is of course a shock to the uninformed modern reader, who suspects that those in the past once believed the world was flat. Ovid, written before the time of Christ, obliterates that conception, as does Plato's *Timaeus*, written even earlier. Studying the medieval source material helps us discover that the real ignorance comes from modern projections onto the past.

Lewis looks at other classic texts with influence on medieval literature. Among these is Cicero's *Somnium Scipionis*, *The Dream of Scipio*, which influenced Lucian, Boccaccio, and Chaucer with its theme of man's immortality. Scipio's postdeath, out-of-body experience reverberates with frequency throughout medieval literature.[30] Lewis suggests that many of Boccaccio's characters as well as Chaucer's *Troilus* are able to laugh "at the littleness of all those things that seemed so important before they died."[31]

Other books noted by Lewis include Statius's *Thebaid* and Claudian's *De Raptu Porserpinae*. In *Statius* he notes that nature is portrayed as mutable, not eternal.[32] In Claudian nature is "the demiurge who reduced primeval chaos into cosmos."[33] In other words, the cosmos is ordered and therefore purposed. Lewis sees much less influence of classical literature on the medieval model as it relates to the concept of nature as he traces the development of that concept.

The Middle Ages were the mythopoeic age. *Muthos*, from which comes our English word *myth* is the Greek word for "story"; *Poieo* means "making," a word meaningful to Lewis as well as to his close friend and collaborator, J. R. R. Tolkien. It was the mythmaking or story-making age.

Understanding, meaning, and significance were all advanced by means of story. Further, personifications were important to the medieval mind and liking.[34] The sky was masculine: father sky. The earth—nature—was feminine: mother nature. As Lewis writes, "The marriage relation between Father Sky (or Dyaus) and Mother Earth forces itself on the imagination. He is on top, she lies under him. He does things to her (shines and, more important, rains upon her, into her): out of her, in response, come forth the crops—just as calves come out of cows or babies out of wives. In a word, he begets, she bears. You can see it happening. This is genuine mythopoeia."[35] It is an expression of the realizing imagination.

Lewis also wants his readers to see that "The Medieval Poets...believed from the outset that Nature was not everything, she was created."[36] Being created, she has purpose; all creation implies intention. She is as intended as the design of the potter is intended to be worked into the clay. In a universe of mutability, purposes can yet be realized. Change makes digression possible and also development.[37] Further, this development has its source in the divine will, for as Boethius says, "All perfect things are prior to all imperfect things."[38]

Lewis notes the influence of Apuleius's *De Deo Socratis*. He sees in Apuleius the introduction of the daemons "between" us and the gods. Socrates believed he was guided by one of these spirits, who told him only the negative, what he ought not to do, never the positive. Lewis then sees developing from this a morphing medieval belief of the objective daemon (or *genius*) to guide as "an invisible, personal, and external attendant." Over time, this becomes one's true self, and then merely one's cast of mind, and lastly, among the Romantics, one's own literary or artistic gifts. Lewis observes, "To understand this process fully would be to grasp that great movement of internalization, and that consequent aggrandizement of man and desiccation of the outer universe, in which the psychological history of the West has so largely consisted."[39]

Boethius, *The Consolation of Philosophy*

One of the greatest influences on medieval thought was the work by Boethius (430–524), *De Consolatione Philosophiae*.[40] Lewis devotes sixteen pages to set forth the argument of *The Consolation*. He says it "was for centuries one of the most influential books ever written in Latin."[41] No other book in *The Discarded Image* gets such a lengthy treatment. Boethius was accused of being part of a plot to overthrow the Gothic king, Theodoric, whom he had served as advisor. While no evidence has ever come to light to prove his involvement, he was incarcerated nonetheless. His brother-in-law was involved in the actual plot, and Boethius was considered guilty by association.

As book 1 begins, a woman appears to Boethius in his cell as the personification of philosophy. "Boethius then passionately demands an explanation of the contrast between the regularity with which God governs the rest of Nature and the irregularity He permits in human affairs."[42] The discussion between Boethius and Lady Philosophy follows along through five books. In book 2 the discussion turns on the topic of the wheel of fortune and the fates. Book 3 is a discussion concerning misfortune and suffering. The topic of book 4 is the quest for happiness and the resulting frustration that occurs when a wrong route is taken in an attempt to find it. But book 5 may be the most significant section of *The Consolation* when it comes to the realizing imagination.

In it the doctrine of divine providence comes to the fore. If providence "foreknows my actions, how am I free to act otherwise than He has foreseen?"[43] Lewis summarizes the argument found in this section of *The Consolation*. He explains that "eternity is quite distinct from perpetuity, from mere endless continuance in time. Perpetuity is only the attainment of an endless series of moments, each lost as soon as it is attained."[44] Lewis rightly clarifies that

> God is eternal, not perpetual. Strictly speaking, He never *foresees*; He simply sees. Your "future" is only an area, and only for us a special area, of His infinite Now. He sees (not remembers) your yesterday's acts because yesterday is still "there" for Him; he sees (not foresees) your tomorrow's acts because He is already in tomorrow. As a human spectator, by watching my present act, does not at all infringe its freedom, so I am none the less free to act as I choose in the future because God, in that future (His present) watches me acting.[45]

The difficulty of reconciling God's foreknowledge and human free will seems to evaporate while reading Boethius. Perhaps the real problem was not with the paradox but our neglect of the old wisdom. We have failed to understand the giants who preceded us. A return to some of the old texts may provide a necessary spark to rekindle the realizing imagination.

All of these literary sources cited by Lewis as contributing to the medieval worldview are significant to the development of a realizing imagination. This exercise of the imagination is rooted in the past as a fruit tree is rooted in good soil. Out of this soil grows the fruit. When cultivating a realizing imagination, while seeking to understand one's place in the world today, we need to remember that the practice does not occur in a vacuum. It requires this sense of rootedness in texts as much now as it did then. The better-read person is more skilled in exercising the realizing imagination.

The Construction of the Medieval Image of the Universe

After discussing these influential texts, Lewis pieces together that great work of art: the medieval model of the universe. He speaks of what was known of the universe as the heavens were described and imagined in the medieval texts.[46] He writes of their operations[47] and movements as well as their inhabitants, both supernatural and human.[48] There were the Longaevi (or "Longlivers"), beings who inhabited the regions between the heavens and the earth.[49] On earth there were the beasts[50] and humans who possessed souls.[51] The medieval model did not stand with Plato when it came to the soul of humanity. Lewis notes that "the doctrine of pre-existence (in some better world than this) was firmly rejected in the scholastic age."[52] Lewis explains that "Rational Soul . . . is created in each case by the immediate act of God, whereas other things mostly come into existence by developments and transmutations within the created order."[53] Lewis also writes of the medieval model, "It was fundamental to his thought that no infinite series can be actual. We cannot therefore go on explaining one movement by another ad infinitum. There must in the last resort be something which, motionless itself, initiates the motion of all other things. Such a Prime Mover he finds in the wholly transcendent and immaterial God. The *Primum Mobile* is moved by its love for God, and, being moved, communicates motion to the rest of the universe."[54]

Oxford University Professor Basil Mitchell once wrote, "It is possible to make sense of fresh experience only if one is equipped with a conceptual scheme adequate to the task."[55] For the Christian, that conceptual scheme is rooted in the love of God. Lewis wrote, "Every Christian would agree that a man's spiritual health is exactly proportional to his love for God."[56] If we know we are loved and forgiven, then we have the freedom to fail, which is the freedom to grow and get better. This too is essential to the realizing imagination. Additionally, we will be more likely to extend to others the same graces we are so eager to receive.

The foundation undergirding any solid growth on any topic is benefited by the love of God. Lewis writes that the medieval model held that the love of God moved the universe "as an object of desire moves those who desire it."[57] The realizing imagination is encouraged by a worldview informed by the love of God. It was in this context the seven liberal arts, made up of the trivium (grammar, dialectic, rhetoric) and the quadrivium (arithmetic, mathematics, geometry, music), came to be. These subjects combined the development of mind and heart as the student sought via the realizing imagination to both know and love God better.[58]

The Influence of the Model

In the epilogue to *The Discarded Image*, Lewis discloses two important perceptions. First, he tells his readers that he was delighted by the medieval model of the universe.[59] Second, he acknowledges that the model wasn't true![60] Nevertheless, he says it was beautiful as a work of art. And it was an important link in a developing grasp of the universe of which we are still participants.

Lewis sees the future as he examines the past. Just as the medieval worldview had to become a discarded image, so too our worldview must give way to a new picture of the world. And, if Lewis is right, and our own worldview does give way to something more responsive to the universe as it actually is, then this book will become Lewis's greatest Christian apologetic. It testifies to the fact that the universe is big and we are small; we must always account for more and that more will continue to point us to God.

The Discarded Image is a book of emancipation, setting those who read it free of some of the prejudices of both the past and the present. It makes one equally free to engage without fear in the discovery of new things. Lewis sees that the medieval model was an unfinished work of art, but then so is the worldview of any culture or age. He writes,

> I hope no one will think that I am recommending a return to the Medieval Model. I am only suggesting considerations that may induce us to regard all Models in the right way, respecting each and idolizing none. We are all, very properly, familiar with the idea that in every age the human mind is deeply influenced by the accepted Model of the universe. But there is a two-way traffic; the Model is also influenced by the prevailing temper of mind. We must recognize that what has been called "a taste in universes" is not only pardonable but inevitable. We can no longer dismiss the change of models as a simple progress from error to truth. No model is a catalogue of ultimate realities, and none a mere fantasy.[61]

At the end of the day, we must remember: reality *is* iconoclastic. Reality invites the curious to perpetually engage the realizing imagination. We should never despair when a current model of the universe needs modification or reform. With anticipation like that of a child on Christmas morning, we should expect surprises. God's universe is big, and God is enormous. Every day, as we look, and listen, our minds and hearts should gain a more robust sense of awe and wonder at each new discovery.

Part 2

Imagination and the Literature of the Heart

Chapter 6

Narnia and the North

Penetrating Imagination in *The Horse and His Boy*

The penetrating imagination excavates below the mere surface of life to discover and reveal hidden depths in order to widen our grasp on truth. It invites us to accept other viewpoints so we might achieve a fuller understanding of reality. This imagination enables us to see more robust meaning in the world around us. This meaning is what gives value to our sense of being and purpose to our work. In *The Horse and His Boy*, we will examine Lewis's vivid delineation of the penetrating imagination.

Shakespeare and Saving the Appearances

Imagine putting on an enchanted ring, sipping a magic potion, or donning magical glasses that transform your daily realities into forms or meanings you could never have imagined. When carefully examined, you discover that these realities contain ever deeper meanings, like peeling the leaves of an artichoke to get to the heart. Humans are made for meaning. It is intrinsic in human nature to search for it in the world around us: our relationships, our work, and our interests. It's why most job-hunting books tell you to do what you love. We do what we love because we find a deeper sense of meaning.

We are always questing for what fulfills us. Meaning remains an integral part of this search. We desire not just superficial meaning but meaning that flashes forth its significance over time as we perform an activity repeatedly. It's one reason why people read certain works of literature again and again. Each time they are reread, a new significance that was not caught before rises to the surface. For example, the repetition of a liturgical church service each week gives worshippers a sense of deepened meaning over time. It's why scientists hunger to understand the atom, the quark, the smallest particle, the realms of outer space, or the ocean depths. This need for significance and meaning in our reality, for delving more and more deeply into life, for seeing what we didn't see before, is basic to human beings. The penetrating imagination performs this function. It explores depths and complexities in a particular thing by looking beyond the surface and the familiar to discover new territory. In short, it seeks to find the truth of a matter, the elusive glowing core.

In matters of truth, however, we never get a last word about anything. Yet this doesn't mean we cannot get a sure word about *some* things. We must not forget that any truth we know can still be plumbed more deeply, applied more widely, and understood in coherent relation with other truths. Yet any understanding of reality must be provisional. At any time, new data may show us that a previous understanding must be discarded or revised.

Therefore, when we seek the truth of a given thing, we must do so in a way that Lewis calls "saving the appearances." This is an expression borrowed from his friend and fellow Inkling Owen Barfield. Any explanation of truth or reality must save or preserve the appearances or phenomena it deals with, in the sense of getting them all in, in doing justice to them.[1] Lewis asks us to consider an individual gazing at the stars and observing their movements in relation to each other as well to himself. The observer's understanding or theory of the stars will then be based on his observations. In this respect, this simple theory will have saved the appearances, because it will have included all the apparent motions of the stars from the observer's vantage point.[2]

However, these observations may not be accurate, and so our idea of this particular reality must be augmented. It is guided by the theory that the understanding that employs the fewest possible assumptions saves the appearances. For example, Lewis says that in attempting to understand the bad parts in Shakespeare, two theories will equally save the appearances. The first states that the poorly written parts of Shakespeare were added by others. The second states that Shakespeare wrote them when he was not at his best as a writer. We know that Shakespeare existed, and we know that writers have bad days. Therefore, we provisionally accept the second theory because it explains the reality with the fewest possible assumptions.[3] Clearly, this process of provisional reality is much more concerned with accounting for the truth of factual assertions and far less concerned with the meaning of works of fiction or of art. But any understanding of truth must seek to save the appearances at some level.

Lewis references Shakespeare in connection with the penetrating imagination. Understanding Shakespeare's expert use of it will provide greater insight into the main work of this chapter, *The Horse and His Boy*. Shakespeare was adept at plumbing truths deeply. He attempted to communicate what he saw in his mind by darting at his target from many angles, like a school of fish attacks bait dropped in a pond. In the essay "Variation in Shakespeare," Lewis describes Shakespeare's process.

> Shakespeare behaves rather like a swallow. He darts at the subject and glances away; and then he is back again before your eyes can follow him. It is as if he kept on having tries at it and being dissatisfied. He darts image after image at you and still seems to think that he has not done enough. He brings up a whole light artillery of mythology, and gets tired of each piece almost before he has fired it. He wants to see the object from a dozen different angles; if the undignified word is pardonable, he *nibbles*, like a man trying a tough biscuit now from this side and now from that.[4]

Lewis provides an example from Shakespeare's *Macbeth* to further develop this idea of variation:

> Methought I heard a voice cry "Sleep no more!
> Macbeth does murder sleep," the innocent sleep,
> Sleep that knits up the ravell'd sleave of care,
> The death of each day's life, sore labour's bath,
> Balm of hurt minds, great nature's second course,
> Chief nourisher in life's feast.[5]

Here are six metaphors for sleep. Why does Shakespeare use this many? Partly it is to create poetry out of an abstract concept or idea, where one metaphor or descriptor would not do. But partly it is an attempt to get at the heart of a truth, to make us see precisely what the poet wants us to see. To ensure that we see it, he tackles it from many angles. One image may resonate with one person, allowing understanding, but another might not connect with that particular image. Here we have enough descriptors and images for everyone. Such an array can help each individual penetrate more deeply into these metaphors and understand more viscerally. The point of variation is not to needlessly multiply metaphors but to add them in a way that illumines rather than occludes.

Shakespeare's use of variation shows how the penetrating imagination can help us get nearer and nearer to the reality of a feeling, emotion, abstract concept, or spiritual reality that words in and of themselves cannot necessarily describe. The penetrating imagination enables us to view something from many angles in order to understand it, enumerate it, illuminate it, and to effectively "save the appearances."

Dante, Analogy, and Abdication

Shakespeare's similes are one way to achieve this, but Lewis offers another: through analogy. He turns to the similes of Dante Alighieri, the thirteenth-century poet and author of *The Divine Comedy*. Lewis suggests that this work was the ultimate example of the masterful use of simile in poetry, of meaning piled on meaning such that spiritual realities that could not be captured by definition could be captured by analogy. Definition means *of the finite*. We define things by their limitation (they can be distinguished from other things and are small enough that we can wrap words around them) and their function or purpose. But how does one define God, who defies definition and limitation? If God is infinite, God shatters the category of mere definition. Talk about God requires analogy, as medieval scholastics such as Dante and Edmund Spenser understood.

Richard Weaver defines the source of this type of argument as similitude; those who argue from it invoke "essential correspondences," that is, close equivalencies or similarities, to establish probability or to demonstrate something. Thus they are also likely to think analogically, because analogy expresses similarity. And it follows that analogical thinking, as Weaver states, expresses belief in a oneness or connectedness of the world, causing these correspondences to be seen as demonstrating or proving a particular truth.[6] In an eloquent speech in Lewis's *The Great Divorce* about knowledge of the eternal fate of all things, George MacDonald says, "Ye *cannot* know eternal reality by a definition."[7] Thus we require analogy to bring us closer.

Such analogies or similes in Dante do not fall into the category of mere comparison, for example, "Such a thing is like such another thing." In the work of many other poets, these more simplistic comparisons between unlike things would not even be capable of life outside the context of their poems. But Lewis states that the longer one looks at the likenesses in Dante's similes, the greater and more fruitful in interesting thoughts they become. "They don't fade as you come awake. They can stand daylight. We are made to dream while keeping awake at the same time."[8]

Lewis describes a simile from the first canto of the *Paradiso*. Beatrice, gazing at the sun, causes Dante, who is gazing at her, to gaze also at the sun. The production of Dante's gaze via Beatrice is compared to reflection, where one beam creates a second. The second beam is compared to a pilgrim desiring to return. Here's where it gets tricky. Those are the stated similes. But what Beatrice and Dante are doing is itself a response to light, and the relation between the two of them and the sun resembles the relation between the two of them. The desire of the beam to return home mimics the desire as well as the action of Dante and Beatrice at the moment.[9]

Of these similes Lewis writes, "The whole of Christian Aristotelian theology is thus brought together. Every idea presented to the mind, as in a figure, repeats the subject in a slightly different way, and suggests further and further applications of it."[10] These are incredibly dense layers of meaning, allowing us to appreciate the complexity and the manner in which Dante conveyed spiritual truth.

Another, subtler facet of the penetrating imagination exists. Lewis calls it abdication. In attempting to define reality, we may use variation or analogy, but the self must be removed as far as possible from the equation. Often the self, with its opinions and biases, interferes with the proper definition or understanding of reality. Again, Dante serves as the model for Lewis, who attributes the excellence of *The Divine Comedy* to the poet getting himself out of the way. To Lewis, the whole art of poetry is abdication. It is attained "when the whole image of the world the poet sees has entered so deeply into his mind that henceforth he has only to get himself out of the way, to let the seas roll and mountains shake their leaves or the light shine and the spheres revolve, and all this will *be* poetry, not things you write poetry about."[11]

In this structure, Dante's worldview is not his own; it is shaped and influenced by the thought of his contemporaries and of others who came before him. Thus, his primary job is to build the imaginative structure, then remove himself and let this worldview inform and flesh out that structure. Lewis believes that parts of the *Divine Comedy* essentially wrote themselves. All Dante had to do was give gentle guiding touches now and then. But the poet is not a primary figure in truth telling. The work has transcended the poet. He is only gently marshalling the energies that are naturally grouping themselves into a harmonious whole. Somehow, greater imaginative freedom, and thus greater analogical truths can be communicated when the self is all but removed from the picture. Lewis understands this to be a paradox.[12]

It would appear that this extremely subtle underlying assumption by Lewis is that what is happening in the poem is a supernatural occurrence, in the sense that it is occurring outside the confines of human ability. One possibility is that God breathes life, truth, and meaning into the imaginative structure in a manner the poet never could have accomplished. As God is a creator, so we are cocreators with God. God's presence imbues any work of creation. And while any piece of truth telling may be inspired, it is not inspired as Christians believe the Bible to be inspired, as the very breathed-out words of God (2 Tim 3:16). Nevertheless, these works can be inspirational in the sense we have described.

But here we encounter a blockade. No one knows where the realm of inspiration exists, but we know that it *does* exist. We don't know how one moment an entire poem springs into the mind, fully fleshed (as has happened to Mark once), and all we have to do is transcribe it. Every artist has a similar story. We must certainly acknowledge that our experience and imagination in that moment serve as the structure to which flesh is added in a way that we cannot understand and in which our selves hardly figure at all. It is hard not to imagine that this supernatural, even spiritual, occurrence might be at the root of what Lewis was thinking when he stated that once the poet got himself out of the way, this would *be* poetry, not just the things that we write poetry about. Yet it seems that Lewis did not fully support this view, even though he couldn't give a clear answer to the mystery himself. In *The Personal Heresy*, he writes about this poetic consciousness:

> The objects, then, which we contemplate in reading poetry are not the private furniture of the poet's mind. The mind through which we see them is not his. If you ask whose it is, I reply that we have no reason to suppose that it is any one's. . . . A mind which habitually saw as synthetically—which saw each single object with so vast a context—as we are made to see for moments by poetry, would be as far removed from us as we are from the brutes. It would not, indeed, be the Divine Mind, for it apprehends only the *what* and ignores the *that*; whereas God must be a permanent philosopher no less than a permanent poet. But it would be a mind, none the less, greatly beyond the human. The ancients called it the Muse.[13]

Whatever it is and wherever it resides, this consciousness is perhaps the purest essence of the penetrating imagination; though difficult and elusive to attain, this pure poetry, with the human element well in the background, might just be the clearest way of communicating spiritual realities. And it is this pure poetry that enables us to be fully immersed in the work of art, to pass through the words to the eternal meanings that can potentially go even deeper than what the poet has envisioned.

The Donegalities of *The Horse and His Boy*

The fifth Chronicle of Narnia is set during the reign of the four kings and queens of Narnia: Peter, Susan, Lucy, and Edmund. However, it takes place entirely outside that land. It tells the story of Shasta, the supposed son of a poor Calormene fisherman named Arsheesh. Shasta finds out that he is to be sold into slavery, so he escapes on a talking horse named Bree, who is likewise a slave. Their goal is to reach the free land of Narnia. The story describes their adventures on the way and also tells of their meeting with another pair of runaways, the horse Hwin and the girl Aravis. They are fleeing an unwanted arranged marriage and slavery to find freedom in Narnia. The group makes the treacherous journey through the city of Tashbaan, the heart of the Calormene Empire, only to confront the seemingly endless desert. Here they must race a band of warriors across the desert to warn a king of an impending attack. And here Shasta learns his true identity. But before delving into how the penetrating imagination is woven into this story, we must examine its overall characteristics.

As previously mentioned, Lewis sought to include the quality of immersion in his own work. We suggest this is another way to apprehend the penetrating imagination. Examining this quality will give us a framework upon which to further build an understanding of the penetrating imagination in *The Horse and His Boy*. In *Planet Narnia*, Michael Ward has written extensively about the hidden meanings in the Chronicles of Narnia and the arrangement of the seven books around the seven planets. In providing context for these assertions, Ward examines the ways in which Lewis, similarly to Dante, prized the indirect approach. Primarily important to Lewis was the essence or quality of a story and the ability of the reader to imaginatively inhabit it; indeed, for him, this was its main attraction.

Ward describes this essence by appropriating the term *donegality* as used by Lewis. In writing about why we return again and again to stories we love, Lewis states that it "is like going back to a fruit for its taste; to an air for its...what? for *itself*; to a region for its whole atmosphere—to Donegal for its Donegality and London for its Londonness."[14] Ward defines *donegality* by suggesting it "denotes the spiritual essence or quiddity" of a work, its "peculiar and deliberated atmosphere or quality," and again, its "pervasive and purposed integral tone or flavour."[15] In citing a passage from *The Lion, the Witch, and the Wardrobe*, Ward writes, "What the narrator is after is something far deeper, something beyond the limited time-frame of human life and human memory. He tells us that the waves break 'for ever and ever,' as if they belong to an eternal realm; and this is indeed what he is wanting to evoke, what the whole book has been intended to evoke: a glimpse of supernatural reality, a window onto an aspect of the divine nature."[16] Lewis is creating hidden meanings or a "quality" in *The Horse and His Boy* that will lead the reader into depictions of spiritual realities that are impossible to communicate with words alone; the words become merely the gateway. In attempting to understand how a poet can do this through the inadequacy of words, Ward writes,

> A poet has no other medium. However, through the technique of donegality a poet can deploy that medium in a way which approaches wordlessness. He can marry "thing with thought," not by frontal assault on his readers' conscious minds, but by embracing their whole reading experience with the thing he means to make them think. He can communicate his theme through participatory cognition, Enjoyment consciousness.[17]

Lewis desires these qualities or hidden meanings to remain hidden. Flagging them would cause a reader to do what Lewis terms looking *at* the beam. In his essay "Meditation in a Toolshed," he relates the experience of standing in a dark toolshed and seeing a beam of sunlight shine through a chink. Looking *at* the beam, everything else was dark, but the beam itself could be seen clearly. When he put his eye in the beam and looked *along* it, not only the beam but the whole shed vanished as he saw tree leaves and the sun outside the shed. It is the idea of contemplation versus enjoyment, or describing versus experiencing.

The qualities that Lewis attempts to communicate in *The Horse and His Boy* help us look along the beam. To fully experience these qualities, the meanings, explanations, or descriptions must remain hidden. The words have captured a state of being, but the state exists beyond the words. It is Dante all over again, and the true poetry that results when the poet gets himself out of the way. It is an attempt to communicate truth at the most visceral level, through a feeling or essence, rather than through words. The self, however, plays a slightly different role here. It is abdication in the sense of letting go of the need to understand (looking at the beam). It is immersion in the sense of letting the work of art communicate spiritual realities through its total essence (looking along the beam). We should not think that the two are incompatible. They are two sides of the same coin.

Lewis uses this essence or penetrating imagination to go beyond mere language in *The Horse and His Boy* and give us a picture of spiritual realities. Ward states that the inadequacy of language to address God is why we see the particular responses to the Christ figure, Aslan (the great lion). Words can never adequately address God in prayer because they cannot define God. God is infinite, breaking the category of definition. God's realities are too concrete and definite for language, so *being*, in this sense, is more vital than *saying*. According to Ward, when Aslan encounters the children and horses, they are "speaking" at the highest pitch of articulacy; their selves are irradiated with meaning and their responses are physical actions, not words.[18] After the walk along the mountain pass from darkness into light (which we shall discuss shortly), Shasta takes one glance at the lion's face and drops off his horse to the ground. "He couldn't say anything but then he didn't want to say anything, and he knew he needn't say anything."[19] Similarly, after Aravis and the two horses encounter Aslan in the hermit's enclosure, their response is not to talk, but to move away to different places to be alone and think.

This silence inspired by Aslan should not be understood as wordlessness but as thinking or simply "being" without language. This is similar to what Ransom and Merlin experienced in Lewis's *That Hideous Strength*, when they sat in the Blue Room and felt the influence of the gods descend into their inmost beings. One might almost say that instead of thinking, they were "being thought." Again,

Shasta's response of wordlessness, the desire for silence on the part of Aravis and the horses, and the response of silence and stillness by the group at Anvard after the judgment of Rabadash all point to Lewis's use of the penetrating imagination at this deeper and more difficult level. Lewis writes of this last example "There was a short silence and then they all stirred and looked at one another as if they were waking from sleep. Aslan was gone. But there was a brightness in the air and on the grass, and a joy in their hearts, which assured them that he had been no dream."[20] One might almost say they had waked to the real life in those moments, and died to the old life.

Aslan: At the Back of All the Stories

Lewis's depiction of Aslan in *The Horse and His Boy* is most reflective of the penetrating imagination. When Shasta is describing to Aravis the remarkable events that led to his reunion with his father and twin brother, he remarks that Aslan seems to be at the back of all the stories. And indeed, he is the prime mover and motivator behind this story. Though he appears only a few times in the narrative, we understand that there is an explicit and implicit Aslan. The explicit appears from time to time in the flesh. The implicit resides at the back of the story as a driver and shaper of the narrative. We cannot see this second Aslan, but something of his presence and influence hangs over the whole tale. At critical points, he appears briefly. The fact that this awareness exists as we read, that we feel as if Aslan might at any moment appear, is again the result of that Lewisian element of creating an atmosphere to communicate a reality.

Lewis himself used Shakespeare's method of variation to communicate the multifaceted reality of Aslan in *The Horse and His Boy*. Once we grasp Lewis's use of variation, we will see more clearly the implicit Aslan, with twelve distinct attributes of his character revealed. Recall that Shakespeare's use of variation darts at the subject from many angles to achieve a deeper understanding. Lewis does the same in setting forth the penetrating imagination in the following attributes of Aslan that capture the complex elements and revealed wonder of this lion.

> **Strategizer:** Aslan forced Shasta to join with Aravis in the forest so that they might benefit each other in their shared quest to reach Narnia. This is the Aslan that sees all ends and arranges the means to meet those ends. He is swift of foot and appears to be in many places at once. It is also the lion that guided to shore the boat in which the abducted child Shasta lay, to be received by the wakeful fisherman Arsheesh.

Comforter: He provided companionship and comfort for Shasta in the form of a cat while he was waiting for Aravis and the horses among the houses of the dead outside the city gates of Tashbaan.

Protector: Aslan drove the jackals away while Shasta slept near the tombs. This is also the lion who walked with Shasta along the mountain pass toward Anvard in the dark, protecting him from stumbling over the precipice.

Enabler/Motivator: He chased the horses outside the hermit's enclosure to instill fear into them for a last burst of speed, so that Shasta should reach King Lune in time to warn him of the impending attack of Rabadash on Anvard.

Loving Judge: He tore Aravis with claws to punish her for the drugged sleep she cast on her stepmother's slave and the subsequent beating the slave received.

Peacemaker: Aslan offered Rabadash two chances to accept the mercy of King Lune after he was taken prisoner in the battle at Anvard.

Reconciler/Confronter: He disabused Bree of his erroneous notions about who and what Aslan was by appearing to him in the flesh and revealing that he was a true beast, that he had an embodied as well as a spiritual being.

Devourer: The horse, Hwin, on first meeting Aslan face to face, says something odd. "Please," she said, "you're so beautiful. You may eat me if you like. I'd sooner be eaten by you than fed by anyone else."[21] This concept of devouring is not new as a depiction of Aslan. It is mirrored in *The Silver Chair* when Jill finds herself confronted by the lion on the Mountain of Aslan and asks him if he eats girls. His response: "I have swallowed up girls and boys, women and men, kings and emperors, cities and realms."[22] Shasta, on three separate occasions when he thinks he is about to be attacked by a lion, wonders what it will be like to be eaten. This fear drops away from him once he meets Aslan on the mountain pass.

Long Sufferer: Aslan described himself as one who had waited long for Shasta to speak. He also tells Hwin that he knew she would not be long in coming to him.

Deliverer: Bree describes Aslan as the lion that drove away the witch and the winter. This story is found in *The Lion, The Witch, and the Wardrobe.*

Originator: Aslan is the one at the back of all the stories, as described by Shasta. All the stories involve him at some level. Even if he doesn't appear in the narrative, you get the sense that he is the driving force behind it.

Threefold Being: On the mountain pass, Shasta asks Aslan who he is. The reply: "'Myself,' said the voice, very deep and low so that the earth shook: and again 'Myself,' loud and clear and gay: and then the third time 'Myself,' whispered so softly you could hardly hear it, and yet it seemed to come from all round you as if the leaves rustled with it."[23] Ward sees this as the most explicitly trinitarian moment in the whole Narniad.[24]

This list, once again, reveals Lewis's use of the penetrating imagination, for each of these images helps us understand the significance and meaning of Aslan. And these attributes of Aslan are not limited to *The Horse and His Boy*. If we had space, we could trace them throughout the rest of the Chronicles of Narnia and find their continuity in each book.

Similarly, the nineteenth-century American poet John Godfrey Saxe wrote an amusing poem in which six blind men approach an elephant.[25] Each, touching a different part of the elephant's body, gives his opinion of what an elephant is like. One feels the side of the elephant and likens it to a wall. Another feels the tusk and likens it to a spear. Another likens the trunk to a snake, a leg to a tree, an ear to a fan, and a tail to a rope. In a sense, each blind man represents the value of a different metaphor, a different manner of expressing the reality in order to arrive at the truth about the elephant. So too, we are offered a different perception of Aslan's character in each of these events or circumstances. It is Lewis's way of helping us to "see," of giving us a fuller understanding of a personality that remains mostly covert in *The Horse and His Boy*.

The Transformation of Shasta

Lewis also uses the penetrating imagination in the Shakespearean manner to convey how Shasta's experiences shape and transform him during his escape to Narnia. Each of these experiences is a dart (fish-like) to show us more fully and deeply Shasta's transformation. To begin with, Shasta doesn't have many advantages or experiences growing up as the son of a poor fisherman. His outlook is provincial, he is uneducated, he doesn't travel, and his days are consumed in chores related to mending nets and keeping house. One quality Shasta does possess is curiosity to know what is at the top of the grassy hill that leads up to a ridge in the north. So far, however, all his experience has taken place in the south. This curiosity exists partly from the fact that no one ever goes that way and that he is never allowed to go there himself.

The visit of a great Calormene lord changes everything. Shasta simultaneously discovers he will be sold as a slave to this great lord and that the lord's horse can speak in the tongue of men. Here he learns what is ultimately over the hill to the north: the land of Narnia, to which the horse plans to escape with Shasta. On the first day of his escape, he views, for the first time, the sea from a cliff. Down by the fisherman's hut, he had only one perspective on the sea. Now he acquires perspective on its vastness as well as its varied and colorful beauty. He sees "the coast stretched away, headland after headland, and at the points you could see the white foam running up the rocks but making no noise because it was so far off."[26] He also realizes this is the first time he has breathed air without the scent of fish in it. In this moment of transformation, Shasta begins to understand the value of multiple perspectives.

For weeks, he and Bree are solitary companions, until they meet fellow travelers Aravis and Hwin. Shasta must reckon on having them as companions for the rest of the journey. While he has learned much from Bree, he has not had to account for another person. His own ignorance and limitations are revealed many times in the face of Aravis's cultured and privileged upbringing. And he learns the value of working with a team to accomplish a worthy goal, even if at first he does so stubbornly. Back home, he probably didn't find value in his work mending nets or his relationship with his "father." His life had been little better than slavery, and he hadn't loved Arsheesh the fisherman. Shasta is now discovering value in life and relationship.

Soon after this meeting, the horses and children arrive at the edge of Tashbaan. Shasta's first glimpse of it at nighttime, with its thousands of twinkling lights, frightens and overwhelms him. He has no idea what a big city is like. But when he sees it at dawn the next day—with its pinnacles and palaces and rivers and gardens—he is nearly dazzled, declaring it a wonderful place. Entering and experiencing this city, he begins to acquire empathy; he sees and experiences a foreign way of life through the eyes of its inhabitants.

Perhaps his most transformative experience happens when he meets the Narnian lords in the streets of Tashbaan and is mistaken for another boy whom he closely resembles. When Shasta first catches sight of the Narnians in the street, he recognizes his own race of people in the fair skin and fair hair. He also sees how attractive and different their manner is from the olive-complected Calormenes, among whom he has grown up. They aren't bound by societal conventions. They dress in bright colors and walk freely. They chat, laugh, and whistle. "You could see that they were ready to be friends with anyone who was friendly and didn't give a fig for anyone who wasn't. Shasta thought he had never seen anything so lovely in his life."[27]

One can tell that in this vision, he gets a new taste of beauty, freedom, and perhaps an unnamed longing. Afterwards, he is made much of by the Narnians, given plenty of good food to eat and a soft bed to lie on. Again, this experience is completely new: "Nothing like this had ever happened to Shasta in his life before."[28] Shasta's awareness of beauty is growing, and we see transformation in his reactions to his experiences.

Once through Tashbaan, while waiting for his traveling companions to arrive, Shasta must spend an evening alone on the edge of the desert among the burial places of the kings. Here he is forced to confront his fears of being alone among the houses of the dead and at the mercy of wild animals. Luckily, he has a stray cat for a companion, who comforts him during the long night. In the morning, after bathing in the river, he sits gazing at the city and marvels at its strength and splendor. But now he also is aware of its dangers. This deeper awareness has come to him because of his brief stay in Tashbaan, perhaps an awareness of the difference between good and evil.

Once his companions return, they make the grueling trek across the desert to the mountains. When they are exhausted and thirsty beyond telling, they finally arrive at a small waterfall and pool. Shasta sticks his head right under the waterfall and "it was perhaps the loveliest moment in his life."[29] Lewis has added many of these small, seemingly insignificant moments to show us what it would be like to experience the pleasures most of us take for granted for the first time.

In the company's last flight to the hermit's enclosure en route to warn King Lune of an impending invasion by the headstrong prince of Tashbaan, Rabadash, Shasta discovers a new degree of courage. He throws himself off the madly galloping Bree in an attempt to stop a lion from killing Aravis. To his surprise, it works. Though Shasta is exhausted, the hermit says that he alone must continue to run over the mountains to warn King Lune. Though Shasta finds this extremely unfair, he does it anyway. "He had not yet learned that if you do one good deed your reward usually is to be set to do another and harder and better one."[30]

This could not have been the act of the poor fisherman's boy at the beginning of *The Horse and His Boy*. Only after the experiences of this journey could he have grown into this place of acceptance in the face of extreme hardship. After warning the king and mounting a horse to ride back to the castle, he gets stranded on a mountain pass in the dark. As he is feeling sorry for himself, he realizes he isn't alone and that something he cannot see is quietly pacing alongside him in the dark. This frightens him, but he plucks up the courage to address it. It responds by asking Shasta to tell about his sorrows. As Shasta comes out of the darkness into the morning light, he meets Aslan, who has kept pace with him during the night. This experience works the final transformation in Shasta, resulting in an act of worship and love, the one experience to which all the other experiences on his journey were leading.

Experiencing Reality through Many Lenses

In the transformation of Shasta from an ignorant boy to the son of a king and the enumeration of Aslan's various attributes, Lewis has masterfully used the penetrating imagination to point to the deeper realities that each represents in *The Horse and His Boy*. These realities not only point to truth but also to meaning. Even though we were made for meaning, and we search diligently for it, we often do so in ways that prevent us from finding it. We become too distracted, or we simply don't have (or are unwilling to have) the eyes to see. But we can consciously cultivate the penetrating imagination by earnest truth-seeking in all matters.

To accomplish this, we can work to enable ourselves to view reality through numerous lenses—not distorting lenses, but those that allow us to see the truth of a matter more clearly. This takes empathy and humility to develop a stance of openness toward the viewpoints of others, not being quick to criticize another's understanding. We must be willing to change our own viewpoints as the data shift and enlarge our understanding.

Thus, the penetrating imagination not only looks at a thing deeply but also does so in community. Developed in community, it allows us to transcend our own particularity. It reconciles us to a larger universe, where meaning is greater than our own individuality. It increases our capacity to be truly human and to empathize with and share the experiences of those with whom we interact. Then we will see aspects of reality to which only others with their own unique experiences can add. The more open we are, the more we are caught up into the grand story of life. That is why we need Lewis, Dante, Shakespeare, and others to help us. Our own views are narrow and hobbled; we need others' visions and views to shine their brightness into our darkness; those places we have not seen nor possibly even imagined.

Chapter 7

A Passionate Sanity

Material Imagination in *The Voyage of the Dawn Treader*

The material imagination seeks to accurately depict the material world through vivid description that resonates with our senses. Lewis chose the poet Christopher Marlowe as the master of this particular imagination, and it was Marlowe's genius to enable us to experience the material world rather than simply observe it. Additionally, the materials that artists or writers use to create works of art influence what the work will become. In and of themselves, these "made" things are worthy of contemplation apart from any psychological or philosophical musings they might suggest to our minds. They, too, are products of the material imagination. But above all, the material imagination, guided by a transcendent value, attempts to tell the truth about the material world and acts as a corrective to enable us to avoid its dangers. In order to experience his imaginary world, we will examine how Lewis engages the material imagination in *The Voyage of the Dawn Treader*.

Cupid's Burning Arrow: Christopher Marlowe and Making Holiday from Facts

The power of the material imagination is manifest in its accurate description of the material world, that world we apprehend through our senses. Lewis identifies sixteenth-century English poet Christopher Marlowe as the great master of the material imagination. Says Lewis, "He writes best about flesh, gold, gems, stone, fire, clothes, water, snow, and air."[1] It would be simplistic to say that all description of the material world is therefore a reflection of the material imagination and my description of stone, fire, and clothes will serve as well as Marlowe's. This imagination finds its fullest expression within defined parameters.

According to Lewis, Marlowe's particular genius, "the work he was born to do," is found in his ability to write erotic epyllion, a short form of epic poetry, with the flesh as its subject. Marlowe's poem *Hero and Leander* tells of an exceptionally beautiful young man and woman who meet, fall in love, and have a sexual encounter. The power of the material imagination is found in its *accuracy* in describing material objects, so we must try to understand what makes Marlowe's poem accurate in its depiction and what that accuracy attempts to achieve.

As regards *Hero and Leander*, Lewis describes Marlowe's masterful ability "to make holiday from all facts and morals in a world of imagined deliciousness where all beauty was sensuous and all sensuality was beautiful."[2] In other words, Marlowe chooses to show us something objectively without judgment, moral or otherwise. We are not observers of the lovers Hero and Leander from the outside in. Instead, Marlowe places us at the center of their passion and we see the world transformed through the lovers' erotic vision. Here we are given what we might call "interior vision," an important facet of the material imagination. We look *out of* rather than *at*. We experience rather than observe.

As a writer, Marlowe had always struggled to bring humanity accurately and believably into his works. Here he didn't have to. Thus, there is a quality of hardness to the poem, writes Lewis, that precludes human tenderness. It is dehumanized partly because this is Marlowe's *métier*, but also to increase its accuracy. We find that love is deaf and cruel, Leander woos Hero like a "bold, sharp sophister," the god Neptune tries to ravish and then kill Leander, and Hero is compared to diamonds. This poem describes a love separated from kindness, camaraderie, or friendship.[3]

Lewis states that if female spiders (who eat their male counterparts after breeding) wrote poetry, it would be like Marlowe's. This type of poetry, if it is to be bearable, must be heartless in order to succeed artistically. Marlowe keeps reality and humanity out of his poem, and so, in this vision, we "bid goodbye to the world of sober experience." While it is not morally pure, it has purity and integrity of another sort. There is no pretense that lust is anything other than lust. Lewis writes that the poem is a purity of form, color, and intention. He argues that it is necessary to separate tenderness and sensuality in poetry. He believes that if a poet attempts to do both, the poem becomes cloying and disgusting and we turn from it in contempt. In order to be endurable, it must be one or the other, never both. But this is just how the material imagination functions, and Marlowe shows us an accurate depiction of lust as perceived by the senses.[4]

Furthermore, says Lewis, Marlowe must be realistic enough to keep us in touch with the senses because his subject is the flesh. Marlowe's excessive use of hyperbole serves to strengthen this function, where at first glance these words might seem to be excessive ornament. These hyperboles contribute to "build up something like the world as the world appears at a moment of wholly unrestrained passion."[5]

Again, we are not mere spectators of the passion but of what the passion thinks it sees. The poet gives us interior vision. This is an important point, which an excerpt from the poem will serve to illustrate. This excerpt describes Hero (a young woman who vowed chastity in the service of the god Venus) in the moment of falling in love with Leander. During their conversation, she is suddenly shocked to find that an invitation for him to come and visit her slips unaware from her lips. As a virgin in the service of Venus, this is forbidden. Nevertheless, she is conquered.

> And suddenly her former colour chang'd,
> And here and there her eyes through anger rang'd;
> And, like a planet moving several ways
> At one self instant, she, poor soul, assays,
> Loving, not to love at all, and every part
> Strove to resist the motions of her heart:
> And hands so pure, so innocent, nay, such
> As might have made Heaven stoop to have a touch,
> Did she uphold to Venus, and again
> Vow'd spotless chastity; but all in vain
> Cupid beats down her prayers with his wings'
> Her vows about the empty air he flings:
> All deep enrag'd, his sinewy bow he bent
> And shot a shaft that burning from him went;
> Wherewith she strooken, look'd so dolefully,
> As made Love sigh to see his tyranny;
> And, as she wept, her tears to pearl he turn'd,
> And wound them on his arm, and for her mourn'd.[6]

As stated, Marlowe's vision for this poem was erotic. The seemingly overwrought hyperboles are authentic and accurate description if we take them as being characteristic of what the world might look like to a lover, as Lewis says, "from a moment of wholly unrestrained passion." It might really seem that heaven would want to stoop to touch Hero's pure hands, or that her tears seem turned to pearl. What's important to note here is that the description of the material world is true to the vision of the poet. Though we might initially scoff at such clearly fulsome description, through an effort of the material imagination to place ourselves within that interior vision, we can see how such description becomes, in a sense, accurate.

The Artist's Materials

The material imagination functions in yet another way. The vision of poet, writer, or artist is shaped by elements of the material world, which in turn affect accuracy of artistic depiction. Lewis writes in the *Arthurian Torso* that the material of anything only possesses potential until form is imposed upon it and it is transformed into the actual: a chair, a table, and so on.[7] So it is with a poem, a piece of literature, or a work of art. How do an artist's materials begin to shape and influence the work of art? How do the materials of stone, clay, or marble influence what the sculptor will do with each? Would Michelangelo's *David* have had the same accuracy and impact if it were carved out of oak rather than marble?

The material of a story or poem influences the author or poet, similarly to how paint or clay shapes a watercolor or sculpture. Lewis remarks elsewhere that the man who writes a love sonnet must not only love the beloved but must also love the sonnet.[8] Within the poet are the raw materials: experiences, thought, and so forth. A form is then imposed upon these materials. Marble more accurately portrayed truth in Michelangelo's sculpture than oak ever could have, just as Marlowe's epyllion was the perfect vehicle for *Hero and Leander*. A sonnet simply would not have conveyed the erotic passion appropriately enough for us to deeply understand it or see the world transfigured through the eyes of lust.

Lewis was a great advocate of the work of art as art. Apart from anything that it means or communicates to us, it is valuable simply for itself, for the way the materials of its construction are ordered and organized with precision. Lewis believed that we should enjoy a work simply for its "thingness." This will be discussed in more depth when we examine *The Voyage of the Dawn Treader*, but it should be noted that this is another primary function of the material imagination.

In addition, just as the physical material an artist chooses affects the form his work of art will take, so too the material features of an *imagined* physical object influence the way an artist describes it. Marlowe had to perform this exact function, imagining what it was like to exist in the material bodies of a young boy and girl with all hormones straining toward one another at the highest pitch of feeling.

Realism of Presentation and Accurate Description

As previously discussed, in *An Experiment in Criticism*, Lewis develops the particulars of accurate description in his distinction between realism of presentation and realism of content in works of fiction. Realism of content makes a work of fiction probable or true to life. In such a work there is no suspension of disbelief. We can imagine that this is just what would happen in the real world. It deals with what can be analyzed and felt, with life as it really is, as we know it.

On the other hand, realism of presentation is "the art of bringing something close to us, making it palpable and vivid, by sharply observed or sharply imagined detail."[9] It requires close-ups, things that can be seen, heard, tasted, touched. In short, it requires descriptions that can be apprehended with the senses. Lewis writes that the taste in much of the literature of the age is for realism of content and that, though it hasn't become a principle, there is some danger of realism of content coming to be the accepted and only way of telling a story. That is, if it isn't true to life, then it can't be worth reading. Lewis felt that the literary discussions and critics of his time assumed that this was the case and showed this assumption by neglecting the romantic, idyllic, or fantastic in literature, even though up until modern times, nearly all stories were based on realism of presentation.[10]

A distinction must now be made between accuracy and reality. The material imagination, in being accurate, does not therefore necessitate extreme realism such that we may never suspend our disbelief. We can and often must suspend it. But this does not mean that the material thing is not being accurately described. Marlowe makes it happen, though *Hero and Leander* is in almost no way "true to life" and requires constant suspension of disbelief. As Lewis wrote, Marlowe makes holiday from facts. Nevertheless, he accurately portrays the material and physical aspects of lust. Just because a material thing is described in an imaginary world doesn't necessarily make it more prone to inaccuracy.

On the other hand, use of the material imagination can be completely accurate, realistic, and factual while not requiring suspension of disbelief. There may be some tendency to lump this into Lewis's category of realism of content, but recall that this defines a work that is lacking in description of physical things, not one that accurately and realistically describes these things.

Take, for example, the role of description in classical education. An awareness of the nature of the material imagination and its importance in oration was an integral part of classical knowledge. We might safely assume that Lewis, in his extensive reading, was aware of the fourteen *Progymnasmata* described by fourth-century Greek rhetoricians Aphthonius and Libanius of Antioch. The progymnasmata are a set of rudimentary exercises intended to prepare students of rhetoric for the creation and performance of complete practice orations and were a crucial component of classical and Renaissance rhetorical pedagogy.[11] Christopher Marlowe was probably aware of them and possibly may even have been educated with them.

One of the fourteen exercises is description, the bringing of material subjects clearly before the eyes. This is very close to Lewis's definition of realism of presentation. The general term for employing this description is *ekphrasis*, which aims at vivid, lively description. The various types of description, termed as a whole *enargia*, are broken down into many categories of description, almost all aiming at description of the physical world and many of which are very specifically targeted: *anemographia* for a description of the wind or *dendrographia* for a description of a tree.[12]

Such description in this method follows a logical sequence as each element builds on the next to employ the senses and portray the clearest possible picture. Libanius provides many examples of description ranging from a harbor and an infantry battle to a painting and a description of spring. The description of spring is especially noteworthy for its attention to accurate, sensory detail.

> I love spring more than the rest of the seasons, and I wish to describe what it is like. For it releases people from winter as if from prison and reveals a day very different from the night; for it frees the sun's rays from the clouds. And at that time the sun is bright and gentle and delightful to our bodies, striking us more warmly than during the winter. . . . And to one lying awake there comes a spectacle most sweet: the night sky, adorned with various colorful impressions. The earth brings forth what comes from it, and crops at that time are green. . . . People resemble those who have returned to life, spending most of their time in the marketplace, but also going to the country and living luxuriously among the songs of birds and the smells of flowers. The swallow sings in spring and the nightingale also sings. . . . Spring leads people out to these and makes them recline and lavishly entertains them, delighting in wine, delighting in garlands.[13]

Libanius's use of the material imagination enables us to feel what it is like to experience spring through the senses. There is the feel of sun on the skin, the vision of the night sky and green, growing crops, the sound of birds, the scent of flowers, and the taste of wine. This type of description was Marlowe's genius. Despite the fact that he clothed his description in fantastic shapes unlike the restrained description of *ekphrasis*, we see in *Hero and Leander* the ability to render material descriptions accurately. He makes us see the material world for what it *actually* is. And it may be, that in some cases, we see it more accurately for its peculiar and fantastic clothing.

Truth and Transcendence in the Material Imagination

Though accurate, unbiased description of the material world is the goal of the material imagination, it also allows one to see the good as well as the potential evil in the materials of the poem, story, sculpture, or painting. If proper use is to be made out of the materials, one must be guided by a transcendent value. The material itself cannot be the source of determining how it *ought* to be used.

Accuracy is not merely representational but seeks to look beyond mere description to get to the descriptive truth or essence of a material thing. A true statement about a thing may not be pleasant or enjoyable and we may be tempted to condemn it on moral grounds, as Lewis says of Marlowe's *Hero and Leander*, but it is nevertheless still true. Therefore when we see the intense erotic vision in Marlowe's poem, we are seeing beyond mere depiction. We are inside the truth of eroticism and seeing a moment of the world transfigured.

Accurate truth telling is itself a transcendent value. The emphasis is on *accurate*. Human nature will often try to obscure the truth to make it more convenient, palatable, safe, or to render it less frightening. We do not often tell or hear truths easily, especially if they are difficult truths. We have all manner of devices and means to avoid and construct fortifications to hold the truth back. Biblical narrative is full of human wiliness and the hard splendor of God's penetrating truth. But God's truth is transcendent because it is thankfully not contingent on human weakness. Therefore, we believe all art should seek to tell truth in this way, and good art ultimately does.

In truth telling, there is certainly room for being offensive, and the line has to be drawn somewhere. The English poet William Blake writes that

> the great and golden rule of art, as well as of life, is this: that the more perfect the work of art, and the less keen and sharp, the greater is the evidence of weak imitation, plagiarism, and bungling. What is it that distinguishes honesty from knavery, but the hard line of rectitude and certainty in the actions and intentions? Leave out this line and you leave out life itself; all is chaos again, and the line of the Almighty must be drawn out upon it before man or beast can exist.[14]

Just because something exists as a truth or reality does not always mean that an artist should attempt to depict it. Pornography is a telling example. It is what we would call a misjudgment of the material imagination in which bodies are only useful for sexual excitation. Its advocates would say it is a form of art; after all, what is the difference between pornography and the voluptuous female nudes painted by the great masters hanging in every public art museum for all to see? Just as Blake suggests, intention comes into play here. What is the artist's true intent? Does the pornographer really just want to show us what the naked human form looks like? In and of itself, nudity is not shameful or offensive. But the artist's intent will determine how the work is received. Accurate description must be tempered by sensitivity. Recall that Lewis made a similar observation about *Hero and Leander*; he described its purity as that of form, color, and *intention*.

In this sense, the material imagination becomes far broader than simply describing what something looks like. It is seeking to accurately describe the essence of a material thing without value judgments about that thing or its realism. An artist doesn't want to give a prefabricated judgment on the work of art. The reader is left to make judgments and, as a result, to develop moral sentiments. Material imagination is also guided by the desire to show a thing for its essence, but is tempered by sensitivity and intention. Most of us tend to make value judgments when describing, especially if it is something that we love or hate or that excites or bores us. We will tend to embellish the thing in a way that will predispose others to judge it similarly for themselves. Marlowe could have been far more graphic in the details of the amorous encounter between Hero and Leander, but though he told the truth about sexual desire in very clear colors, he was not gross or offensive.

Dragon Lust, Gold, and the Book of Enchantments: Material Imagination in *The Voyage of the Dawn Treader*

The Voyage of the Dawn Treader, the third chronicle in the Narniad, relates the adventures of King Caspian of Narnia and his crew aboard the sailing ship *Dawn Treader* in their search for seven missing Narnian lords. Two of the Pevensie children, Edmund and Lucy, as well as their disagreeable cousin Eustace, are spirited by magic through a painting into Narnia to aid Caspian in his quest.

This delightful tale offers an ample canvas on which to examine the material imagination. As stated earlier, just as the physical materials an artist uses influence accuracy of depiction, so too the material features of an *imagined* physical object, unencumbered by moral judgments, influence the way an artist describes it. It provides the data for the reader to make his or her own judgments. Lewis provides several excellent examples of this aspect of the material imagination in this book. The work essentially represents Lewis's category of realism of presentation; it is not "true to life," but it contains sharply defined description accessible to our senses, so we know that Lewis is using the material imagination to bring us close to his imagined world.

The first setting is a fierce storm at sea. Driven to find harbor, the *Dawn Treader* anchors off an unknown island where Eustace wanders off by himself, becomes lost, and falls asleep in a cave on a mound of what he later discovers is dragon-hoarded treasure. When he wakes, he finds he has turned into a dragon. In his dragon state, Eustace tries ineffectually and with great frustration to communicate to his shipmates by writing in the sand on the beach of the harbor.

Lewis describes how the dragon claws, muscles, and nerves had never learned to write and were not meant to write anyway. And as Eustace tries to write in the sand, he keeps accidentally blotting out words with his tail or stepping on them.

As Lewis imagines what it is like for Eustace to be embodied in dragon flesh, the very material features of the dragon influence his imaginative development of the story telling and make that world more believable. Marlowe has to perform the same function, imagining what it is like to be in the material bodies of a young boy and girl in love for the first time with all the attendant sexual tension.

Similarly, we are given a glimpse, or interior vision, into the material world as perceived by a dragon. First of all, Eustace enjoys eating dragon flesh, as is evidenced by his automatic response to the dead dragon he finds outside the cave where he fell asleep. Lewis is placing himself into that interior vision when he writes, "There is nothing a dragon likes so well as fresh dragon."[15] Eustace has retained the mind of a human, but his tastes and digestion have become dragonish. Next is the fact that he likes his food raw and can kill it with one swipe of his tail, but because this is messy he eats only when he is alone. Then, being a dragon, he is able to shed his skin, which he does when he meets Aslan in the "undressing" scene by the pool. He also has great physical strength, which enables him to pull a great tree up by the roots and fly with it from a distant valley to his shipmates so they can fit a new mast on the *Dawn Treader*, damaged after the storm at sea. Last, he loses all sense of fear, because now he is fear embodied. All of these instances point to Lewis using the material imagination to enable us to understand the story from Eustace's point of view.

It may seem odd that Eustace did not know what to expect in a dragon's lair. But Lewis writes that he "had read only the wrong books. They had a lot to say about exports and imports and governments and drains, but they were weak on dragons."[16] This is because Eustace only enjoyed reading books that contained realism of content. If he had read books containing realism of presentation, as the Pevensie children certainly had, he would have known very well what a dragon's cave contained.

Remember that realism of presentation deals with sharply drawn details that can be apprehended by the senses. It is characteristic of most of the world's literature up until the modern period, including stories of the fantastic. Realism of content deals with the way things are, their trueness to life. Thus, Eustace, whose reliance on realism of content makes him ignorant of the truths contained in realism of presentation, cannot make an accurate judgment of the material world by employing the material imagination; therefore he falls prey to the dragon spell.

In another adventure, the company land on a tiny island to weather a storm. With great surprise, they discover a small mountain lake that turns to gold whatever objects are placed in its waters. Caspian, who is king of Narnia, falls under its spell and claims the island forever for the land of Narnia, naming it Goldwater, and binds the others to secrecy on pain of death. Edmund claims that he will not be bound in any such fashion because he is one of the ancient high kings. It nearly comes to single-handed combat between the two until a sight of Aslan, slowly pacing on a far hilltop, interrupts them. They recover their senses and are enabled to make an accurate judgment of the material value of the water (but really of material wealth), realizing it is under a curse. They name the island Deathwater instead and sail away from its shores.

In this example, Lewis uses the material imagination to give us the interior vision of what the world might look like from the perspective of someone who has suddenly received great wealth. First is the onset of cupidity, the eager avarice for wealth and the possessiveness that accompanies it. Then selfishness appears as Caspian swears the others to secrecy and claims the wealth for himself. Alienation and division follow. Caspian refuses to share the secret with Drinian, one of his closest companions, and attempts to challenge Edmund in combat. Edmund responds in jealousy, also preparing for combat, because he believes he has an even higher claim to the wealth.

Finally, if these emotions unravel to their logical ends, we see betrayal, war, and death on the near horizon. And it is a telling touch that when the adventurers return to the ship, they appear to their fellow shipmates to be under a spell. This is the natural outworking of how wealth can exert power over the hoarder and confuse the mind, rendering it unable to make accurate judgments of the material world.

A similar scenario occurs on the Island of the Voices, another port to which the *Dawn Treader* sails. After landing and exploring, the company discovers that the island is peopled by invisible warriors. These warriors require a young girl (Lucy) to break the spell of their enchantment and make them visible again, or they will put everyone to death. So Lucy alone goes upstairs in an old house where a magician, who hasn't been seen in years, supposedly resides. She navigates a long, dark, sinister hallway with many doors (behind which might be anything) and somehow stumbles upon the magician's spell book.

She then begins leafing through it to locate the spell that makes hidden things visible. But she encounters another spell first. It is "An infallible spell to make beautiful her that uttereth it beyond the lot of mortals."[17] Lucy is strongly tempted to say the spell, especially as she has lived all her life in the shadow of her sister Susan, the avowed beauty of the family. As she gazes at the book, pictures begin to appear in the margins, making the manuscript illuminated. She sees herself saying the spell. Then more and more pictures materialize, depicting the events following the transformation of herself into the woman beautiful beyond the lot of mortals.

It is here that Lewis uses the material imagination to give us the interior vision necessary to see the world transfigured from the viewpoint of ultimate beauty. First, Lucy sees the picture of her alter ego, as it were; the beautiful woman she has become grows larger until it is as big as she is. Ultimate beauty now has an inflated estimation of itself as pride arises. Next is a picture of the world's noblemen, kings, and princes fighting for her beauty; wars and countries and economies are decimated as a result of the jealousy and possessiveness of those fighting for her favor. Alienation from her family is the natural outcome, as no one is any longer interested in Susan but only in Lucy. And ultimately she must sacrifice the real Lucy in order to be beautiful beyond the lot of mortals.

Realism of Presentation in *The Voyage of the Dawn Treader*

In addition to showing us the material world transformed through the eyes of beauty, wealth, or the imagined world of a dragon, Lewis also utilizes realism of presentation, one of the elements of the material imagination. Perhaps the most powerful is his description of the last days of the *Dawn Treader*'s voyage to the utter East, in which he invokes nearly all five senses to bring that experience close to us. We pick up the story where the ship is sailing through the Last Sea or the Silver Sea, an endless expanse of lilies, stretching as far as the eye can see.

The farther the ship sails, the larger the sun becomes and the more the ship's company are able to bear the incredible brightness, with the result that "they could look straight up at the sun without blinking. They could see more light than they had ever seen before. And the deck and the sail and their own faces and bodies became brighter and brighter and every rope shone."[18] In this enchanted place, they pulled up "dazzling buckets of water from the sea, stronger than wine and somehow wetter, more liquid, than ordinary water, and pledged one another silently in deep draughts of it." The farther they sail, the less they are inclined to speak. "The stillness of that last sea laid hold on them."

There is also much to see. On the waters of the Silver Sea are endless leagues of lilies, the whiteness of which is like the Arctic, "shot with faintest colour of gold," except for the lane of open water behind the ship "that shone like dark green glass." The open sea far behind them "was only a thin rim of blue on the western horizon." And the lilies have a wild smell, "a smell which Lucy found it very hard to describe; sweet—yes, but not at all sleepy or overpowering, a fresh, wild, lonely smell that seemed to get into your brain and make you feel that you could go up mountains at a run or wrestle with an elephant."[19]

Lewis accurately describes what he is imagining. Of course we must suspend our disbelief, but just because it isn't realistic or true to life doesn't mean the accuracy of Lewis's description is any less genuine. We must always be careful to make this distinction. Using the material imagination, Lewis is giving us an accurate depiction of what author Michael Ward calls "a growing spiritual wisdom"[20] in those journeying aboard the *Dawn Treader* through the Last Sea. We see how the world might appear to those who have been given new eyes and are steadily growing in knowledge of the infinite. Lewis has helped us to experience it rather than simply observe it. We have been able to imagine ourselves on the ship, partaking in the splendor of the Last Sea.

Logos and Poiema: *The Voyage of the Dawn Treader* as a Made Object

One other aspect of the material imagination to consider when thinking about *The Voyage of the Dawn Treader* is what Lewis calls its *poiema*. He writes that the work of literature is something made (poiema) as well as something said (logos).[21] Again we recall that the material of the story influences the writer's depiction of the world, and as Lewis says elsewhere, the poet who writes a love sonnet not only loves the woman, but also loves the sonnet.

The poet Scott Cairns writes about those writers fixated on expression, elevating *what* is intended over *how* it is articulated:

> Unduly enamored of intention, thus focused on some *prior* purpose, they fail to find how the *act* of writing—poring over words, phrases, and sentences as they are pressed to the page—is itself the means of the artist's discovering new matter to share. The rule holds for all the arts—writers must love language, painters must love pigment, sculptors must love iron and stone, and musicians must delight in song; in this way, each medium duly attended becomes itself the agent of revelation.[22]

According to Ward, the poiema of *The Voyage of the Dawn Treader* and of all the Narnia Chronicles was deeply rooted in Lewis's love of the medieval cosmology and his working out of that model into many aspects of the story. Particularly relevant to this tale is the solar influence, the sun as the fourth planet in the pre-Copernican model of the universe and its influence on the characters and events in the story. You will recall the many references to gold in this story: the scene we have already examined on Deathwater Island, the golden appearances of Aslan, Eustace and the dragon hoard, the preeminence of the sun toward the end of the story and its effects on the characters, the gold and gilding on the ship itself.

These are a few of the larger depictions; Ward catalogs a great many others that we won't go into here.

The point is that the story exists as a made object as well as a said object. It is beautiful in and of itself, dense and packed with hidden meaning, if we believe Ward's explanation to be credible. Lewis took the raw materials in his mind and imposed a form upon them through use of the material imagination. We do know for a fact that Lewis loved to combine pagan and Christian elements in a syncretistic jumble that somehow worked. We aren't too jarred when we find Father Christmas appearing in *The Lion, the Witch, and the Wardrobe*, or the pagan Roman god Bacchus and his Maenads appearing in *Prince Caspian* during the glorious parade following Aslan, an explicitly Christian figure. This was a distinctly medieval characteristic: harmonizing disparate figures, stories, and myths into a whole.

The shaping of the story using these particular materials creates something greater than simply the message, or *logos*, we might assume the author is attempting to communicate. For Lewis, as Ward argues, the created poiema, its quality or tone, is actually the more important of the two. And Lewis himself argues that "lovers of romance go back and back to such stories in the same way that we go back to a fruit for its taste; to an air for...what? for *itself*."[23] Thus the story exists as something desirable quite apart from any allegory, symbol, or metaphor we want to make of it or impose upon it. Lewis has used the material imagination to help us see and value a work of art in this respect. It has become, as Cairns writes, an agent of revelation.

In *An Experiment in Criticism*, Lewis provides an explanation of the work of art as poiema that we believe can also act as a helpful framework with which to explain one way to cultivate the material imagination.

First is the confusion between life and art: the failure of some to allow for the existence of art at all in the sense that it is first and foremost a made object. They only want to know what it means or says or how it is reflective of reality, writes Lewis. They want to use it. And Lewis makes a clear distinction between users and receivers of literature.[24] He writes, "We are so busy doing things with the work that we give it too little chance to work on us."[25] Thus, the concept of intention outlined earlier is important to a right use of the material imagination. This is where Caspian and Lucy make the wrong choice. If they had cultivated a right use of the material imagination, they would have seen gold and beauty for the beautiful objects/things they were. Instead they were thinking only how they could use these things, versus receive them: Caspian for the wealth, and Lucy for power. Their intentions were in the wrong place.

Second, art isn't reality. It selects from reality what it needs for its art. Life provides the raw materials, and art proceeds by selection, patterning, and isolation of those raw materials, writes Lewis.[26] The visions of wealth and beauty given to Caspian and Lucy are not true to their real lives. They are simply additions to life, beautiful additions if one takes them properly, and destructive additions if one doesn't. Again, the circumspection inherent in the right use of the material imagination will allow one to make a proper distinction.

Finally, Lewis writes that a work of art is saturated with the wisdom, experience, and knowledge an author or artist has; it will also be saturated by the flavor or feel actual life has for him or her. Done well it allows us to feel what Lewis terms "a passionate sanity." We are experiencing the work as it was meant to be: as a made thing. This is where the importance of realism of presentation comes into play. These are the carefully crafted details that arouse our senses to the material world. We may find psychological truths and profound reflections, but these only come to us as the spirit of the work. To make this into a philosophy or to think that the work itself is a vehicle for this philosophy is an outrage to the work the author has made, says Lewis.[27] This is where we are tempted to make misjudgments of the material world and find things there that were never meant to be.

Looking *out of,* not *at,* the thing the artist has made will help us to see the world with the flavor the artist saw; we inhabit or are immersed in the work, without judgment, just as Lewis writes that an examiner reading a student's writing that he violently disagrees with will nonetheless give it high marks if it is genuinely well-crafted.[28] The point is to experience rather than observe. Looking *at* will make us want to understand how to use it for our own ends. Lewis writes elsewhere that "to see things as the poet sees them I must share his consciousness and not attend to it; I must look where he looks and not turn round to face him. I must make of him not a spectacle but a pair of spectacles. . . . I must *enjoy* him and not *contemplate* him."[29]

Rumpelstiltskin and the Alchemists: Dangers and Correctives of the Material Imagination

Most of our examples in *The Voyage of the Dawn Treader* have been instances of the material imagination as Christopher Marlowe used it: to depict what it might be like to be a dragon, or how untold wealth might change the world, or incredible beauty cause destruction and desolation. Lewis has briefly showed us how the world might look as it is transformed from within these viewpoints. But there is a darker side to the material imagination that we have already touched on. Most of these examples resulted from an inability to make an accurate judgment of the material world, which is the primary danger of the material imagination. Fortunately, correctives exist to counteract this. Misapprehensions of the material world are common throughout all literature, and a brief thumb through a copy of *Grimm's Fairy Tales* will yield a good sampling. We will limit our selection to those that contain a golden or solar theme similar to that of *The Voyage of the Dawn Treader.*

In *Rumpelstiltskin*, a poor man falsely brags to the king that his daughter can spin straw into gold, and the king demands the poor girl to spin increasingly larger rooms full of straw or else die. *The Golden Goose* attracts several greedy daughters who, in the attempt to pluck its golden feathers, are caught fast. *The Golden Bird* tells the tale of a king who, finding one golden feather of a bird that is worth more than his whole kingdom, greedily decides he must have the whole bird and so sets in motion a series of events that ends in the death of his two eldest sons. Each of these tales illustrates a misjudgment of the material imagination, and demonstrates an inability to relate properly to gold and wealth. Though these are tales of fiction, follies with gold are not limited to fictional realms. Plenty of examples exist throughout history.

Those who practiced alchemy throughout the ages sought to create gold and silver out of common, or base, metals as well as find the "elixir of life" that would confer unending youth and immortality. In her work *The Philosopher's Stone*, Allison Coudert writes of the alchemists in this way:

> In their quest for wealth, spirituality and eternal life, in a word for perfection, alchemists went beyond the bounds of convention, science, religion and even reason.... They were attracted to alchemy through the intoxicating notion of inexhaustible wealth and eternal youth. More often than not they dissipated their wealth and embittered their lives fruitlessly seeking to transmute base metal into gold and old flesh to youthful suppleness.[30]

Their misjudgments were no different than the characters in the fairy tales, for they sought endless wealth as well as to extend indefinitely the limit of human life. Thus we see that not only greed and self-serving motivations, but also plain ignorance can be at the root of misjudgments of the material world.

Such ignorance may be willful, but it may also be inadvertent. Take, for example, a man who claims to struggle with lust when really he is simply experiencing normal sexual desire. Sexual desire is a normal expression of our physical, material nature. It isn't lust any more than hunger is gluttony. The man was not misjudging the proper use of the physical urges he was experiencing, in the sense that he was using them inappropriately or excessively. Rather, he was conscientiously concerned that he might be misusing them. Ignorance is ignorance regardless of motive and may lead to tragedy of one form or another, but we would not put the alchemists and the man in the same class.

So what is the corrective for the misuse of the material imagination? We have mentioned that our understanding of this imagination must be guided by a transcendent value. In order to make proper estimations of the material world, we have to follow Blake's hard line of rectitude and certainty in our actions and intentions. But we think Lewis gives us at least a partial key to the correct use of the material imagination in *The Voyage of the Dawn Treader* during the adventure on Deathwater Island. Though the characters at first are tempted to misjudge the material world (endless wealth from the enchanted water), a transcendent value (the sight of Aslan) allows them to see a material thing for the proper use that might be made of it. This includes both its potential for good and for evil. It also allows for accurate and objective description or truth telling (naming the island *Deathwater* rather than *Goldwater*) and then enables them to act accordingly (walk, or in this instance, sail away). Ultimately and ideally the material imagination imparts not only truth through depiction and a transcendent value but also wisdom, allowing one to avoid misjudgments and ultimately, tragedy.

On the other hand, author Philip Yancey writes, "A brilliant depiction of reality will lead to despair unless the artist can also offer up a new vision."[31] Again, what is the role of the artist in the use of the material imagination? The material imagination offers up depictions of truth such that they allow us to more accurately perceive the material world around us through our senses. But we also believe that there must be a transcendent value for judging and implementing this type of imagination. And because we also require a corrective to misjudgments, we can agree with Yancey that the material imagination must not offer mere depiction only but also some kind of transcendent vision through the depiction, just as a work can contain a logos as well as a poiema: some glimpse of deeper truth caught through the words of description or the use of a particular material in a work of art.

In the last few pages of *The Voyage of the Dawn Treader*, Lucy, Edmund, Eustace, and Reepicheep have arrived at the end of the world and are standing before a high, fixed wave at the end of the Last Sea. During their journey, their eyes have become so strengthened by the waters of the Last Sea that they can look steadily at the rising sun and not only see it clearly but suddenly also see things behind it. They see a far, green country and a range of impossibly high mountains. With the vision come a sound and a smell for which they have no description. The closest they could get to describing it was to say that it would break your heart. They know they are seeing into Aslan's country. They are seeing a new vision through the current reality they are caught up in; it points to something transcendent before the vision is taken from them, something they cannot name. And Lewis gives us this transcendence through a sound and a smell, both physical senses. In the same way, the material imagination acts as a corrective when it points to something beyond itself. That is its ultimate and difficult task.

Chapter 8

Discovering New Worlds

Primary Imagination in *Out of the Silent Planet*

The poet Samuel Taylor Coleridge acknowledged that the five senses consisted of sight, sound, smell, taste, and touch. These sensory gates make it possible for humans to gather data from the objective world. But sensory data come without meaning attached. These data are simply a disordered batch of raw information. For the data to make any sense, one must sort through and organize it into meaningful and useful information.

As you read this book, many things present themselves to your senses. Odors may be wafting through the room. Noises may be coming from others talking in the distance. There are colors all around that compete for your attention with the letters on this page. You feel the smooth texture of the book or mobile device as you hold it and the hardness of the chair on which you are sitting. You may even have just had a sip of coffee or tea, and the taste remains on your tongue. And yet, with all of this teeming data, you can still concentrate on the words you are reading.

How are you able to do this? Coleridge suggested that you have capacities that transcend the mere sensory data gathered from your five senses. This capacity to make sense of the data is not another sensory gathering capacity; it is an ability to synthesize the data and make sense of it. It is the ability to bring all of the data into a common experience and understand your place in the complex sensory world. This common sense makes it possible to minimize distraction and yet maximize all that may inform your grasp of a given event. Coleridge, and Lewis after him, believed this ability to sort out the sensory data was an imaginative exercise. They refer to it as primary imagination.[1]

The very idea of common sense or primary imagination seems to strongly indicate that humans are not merely material creatures; we are immaterial as well.

Common sense, a capacity that transcends mere material sense, suggests that humans have what some call a soul. Coleridge was not the only one to suggest such a thing. William James made a similar observation: "Without selective interest, experience is an utter chaos."[2]

By contrast, John Locke said that the mind was like a blank tablet and that experience writes across it. Lewis, of course, disagreed.[3] Lewis believed that if the mind were merely a blank tablet, it would remain one even after having some kind of experience. Before any experience occurs, something such as memory must be present if any sense is to be made of it. How else would the experience ever be recalled and later compared or contrasted with other experiences?

With memory also comes the capacity to differentiate between various other memories, sorting them and distinguishing them from one another. The ability to sort, select, and identify by means of the superlative (big, bigger, biggest; small, smaller, and smallest; etc.) is necessary for the experience to be retained in a meaningful way. A movie screen is a blank tablet, so to speak, and it retains nothing of what has been projected on it because it lacks the capacity for retention. This capacity for retention suggests there is something beyond mere material existence for humans that allows us to make sense of our experience.

Out of the Silent Planet is the first of Lewis's science fiction trilogy, which also includes *Perelandra* and *That Hideous Strength*. In the first two, Ransom, the main character, takes journeys to Mars and Venus. Each world provides an array of new sensory experiences out of which he must make some kind of sense. His primary imagination is stretched to nearly full capacity as he sorts all of the data of his five senses. This chapter will explore the use of primary imagination as it relates to Ransom's visit to Malacandra, or Mars. But first more background is required.

Human Immateriality

Lewis wrote his autobiography, *Surprised by Joy*, very aware of the idea of primary imagination. He subtitled this work *The Shape of My Early Life*. Certainly this was the shape he gave to his early life according to his rhetorical purposes, as he told the story of his conversion to Christ. Lewis's life, like anyone's, was full of experiences, but his design for the book in some ways dictated which experiences he would discuss. He selected the data that enabled him to best tell his story.

All storytelling, in this way, has a bit of the "Once upon a time…" element to it. The storyteller chooses those elements important to what he or she wants to say. This is very much like the artist who picks a particular bit of landscape for his or her painting, chooses the paint that best represents the colors visible in the scene and then, when the work is done, surrounds the picture with a frame. The capacity to group and frame ideas into a coherent display transcends materiality. The artist is selecting to make a point, or to highlight something in particular. He or she wants others to see this same thing from this unique perspective, too. Using the will, choosing what to highlight, is also a capacity exercised by some immaterial function of one's humanity. This use of primary imagination is ontological: it is essential and actually embedded in what it means to be human. It is a use of the imagination we need to make sense of our experience.

In *Miracles*, Lewis argues that a materialist's presuppositions have an embedded contradiction. The materialist says that humans do not have souls. All that appears to be a function of immateriality, this view says, can be explained by materiality. Intangibles such as thought and justice and love do not, for the materialist, indicate the existence of something immaterial. Lovers don't actually love. The materialist would say they merely look at another and the picture of the other is projected on the retina of the eye. The optic nerve sends a message through a series of electrical impulses until it stimulates the brain. This causes a response of the secretion of particular hormones that the so-called lovers call love.

Lewis reminds readers that the materialist wants others to believe that this assessment *is* accurate. Unfortunately for the materialist, if he or she is right, this has not merely explained away the love of the lovers as mere chemistry, but explained away the explanation. He or she cannot have it both ways. And if the materialist is right, he or she could never know it, for no explanation can carry significance. While it is true the brain has certain neurological functions that can be observed, monitored, and tested, much remains for which the firing of neurons in the gray matter cannot account. Lewis noted in *Miracles*, "Reason is something more than cerebral bio-chemistry."[4]

On the other hand, this contradiction embedded in materialism does not occur when one believes in the existence of the soul. The immaterialist can accept the existence of certain physiological occurrences that can be monitored to a degree. Yet he or she also knows these cannot account for the existence of reason itself. Belief in the existence of the soul appears to be far more coherent than materialism. And the existence of common sense, or primary imagination, as Coleridge and Lewis understand it, has merit.

We try to make sense of our experiences. Whether or not we attend to the process, we actually do sort through the data supplied by our senses in order to understand our world. And the exercise is not one of futility. Sense can be approximated.[5] Knowledge can be gained of the real, objective world that exists independent of our thoughts about it. And those thoughts have significance. The data supplied by empirics can be sorted, synthesized, and understood. This is an imaginative exercise, an example of primary imagination.

Others besides Coleridge, Lewis, and William James held similar views. The French mathematician and philosopher Blaise Pascal observed, "It is impossible that our rational part should be other than spiritual [i.e., immaterial]...there being nothing so inconceivable as to say that matter knows itself."[6] Observes Benjamin Jowett, master of Balliol College, Oxford, and the great English translator of Plato and Hegel: "A first principle of knowledge is prior to experience." The capacity to know must precede any given experience if sense is to be made of that experience.[7]

Plato realized the problem and sought to solve it by speculating about the possibility of prior existence. He knew that something must exist in humans that makes it possible for them to make sense of their experience; he believed this was an ontological necessity. The Christian resolution of the problem attributes this capacity as a gift from God that is unique to humans: "And the LORD God formed man of the dust of the ground, and breathed into his nostrils the breath of life; and man became a living soul" (Gen 2:7 KJV). If this is so, then it is fair to infer that the imagination is also a gift from God.

We have evidence from science that suggests the existence of the soul and therefore the existence of common sense or primary imagination. In 1961, Dr. Walter Graves Penfield discovered that individuals have a self-identity operating independent of their bodies. Penfield opened the cranium of an epileptic patient. While the patient was awake and alert, Penfield touched the cerebral cortex with a probe. The patient jerked his arm into the air. Penfield asked, "Why did you move your arm?" The patient responded, "I didn't; you did." At that moment Penfield realized this patient had a self-identity separate from his physiology. Such observations have driven the mind-body debate in philosophy.

George MacDonald, in *Annals of a Quiet Neighborhood*, wrote that we do not *have* souls. He suggested that we *are* souls, and we *have* bodies. Tell a child he has a soul and he may think he could be separated from his soul. He begins to think that when he dies, his body will go to the grave and his soul will fly off somewhere else. But MacDonald says we ought to tell a child he *is* a soul, and when he dies, he goes to heaven and leaves his body behind, like clipped hair on the floor of a barber shop, or like clothes discarded after growing out of them.[8]

What makes up the soul? Traditionally we say it has a choosing capacity (the will), a thinking capacity (the reason), and a feeling capacity (the emotions). Of these capacities, it appears that the reason is by far the weakest. For example, when we make bad choices, our will marshals reason to make excuses for what we have done. In other words, reason is employed by the will to rationalize and justify bad choices. Aristotle called this *akrasia* in the *Ethics*.[9] The word literally means "without command." This is the characteristic of the compromised soul;

it loses "command" of its moral life when it makes excuses for its bad acts and remains in a state of moral blindness. Aristotle writes in the *Ethics* that "vice is unconscious of itself."[10]

Lewis indicates his awareness of this idea in *A Preface to Paradise Lost* when he says that "continued disobedience to conscience makes conscience blind."[11] Similarly, the Apostle Paul writes in Romans 1:18 that we "silence the truth with injustice." The weakness of reason is also manifest when it is marshaled by the emotions to keep hurt feelings suppressed rather than process them and forgive the offender. Consequently, offenses linger longer than necessary. Bitterness sets in, hurts remain unforgiven. Emotional toxicity morphs into emotional blindness. We have lost command; our souls drift toward a state of chaos.

By contrast, Lewis wrote that dogs lacking common sense or primary imagination live in a world of facts without meaning or rational understanding. For example, dogs do not understand pointing. A piece of food may fall to the ground. The dog owner points to the food, but the dog does not understand what the pointed finger signifies. He comes and smells or licks the finger but has no inclination to look for the food to which the pointed finger is directing his attention.[12] It is a human characteristic to want to make sense of experiences. When we fail to do this, something is wrong. We live beneath our capacities as humans. Similarly, John Polkinghorne, the Cambridge physicist and theologian, says if you ask the scientist why water is boiling, he or she will say it boils because the burner agitates the water molecules. But Polkinghorne notes a person could also say that the water boils because someone wanted a cup of tea.[13] The second answer is as valid as the first. Both explanations are valid; but to suggest that only the first has validity puts common sense at risk. The former explanation accounts for the facts but not the meaning of the boiling water. It reduces the matter to the merely measurable features. It cannot take you to the meaning behind the kettle being on the burner in the first place.

The desire to make imaginative sense of our experience is ontologically significant. Ontology is the study of being and existence. It begins with the assumption that something is there, that something exists. Ontology is the attempt to understand what is there and why it is there. In a universe of contingencies, if anything exists, something must be eternal and necessary. What is eternal and can account for the existence of other things? The materialist says matter is eternal. But, as we have seen, matter cannot explain itself. So saying that something immaterial is necessary and eternal bears no inherent contradiction. Lewis, in his book *Miracles*, argues in support of supernaturalism that God exists and has created humans with a soul and the soul has the capacity of common sense.

Chapter 8

Out of the Silent Planet

A Summary of the Plot

Out of the Silent Planet allows readers an opportunity to enter a world unknown and begin engaging the primary imagination as if for the first time. A summary of the story will show us how this is so.

Elwin Ransom, a Cambridge philologist, is kidnapped by two wicked men. One is Devine, a man full of avarice, looking for ways to make a fortune without care for the welfare of those he may have to exploit while feathering his own nest. The other is Weston, a physicist, who believes man is at the apex of the survival of the fittest. He believes therefore that he has license to dominate any and all in order to extend his own kingdom. One lusts for riches and the other for power. Weston has developed a means of interplanetary travel. He has been to Mars with Devine. Devine has discovered an abundance of "Sun's Blood," the Martian word for gold, and he wants as much of it as he can gather. Weston, for his part, desires to colonize Mars, called *Malacandra* by the Martians.

However, these men's plans run aground when the Martians tell them they must leave and cannot come back unless they bring another person with them. Weston and Devine believe the Malacandrians want to sacrifice the other human.

They kidnap Ransom for this supposed sacrifice. Once he arrives on Mars, Ransom manages to escape from the nefarious duo and has his own Malacandrian experience. The Martians are made up of three races: Hrossa, the poets; Soroni, the philosophers; and the Fifltriggi, the engineers and craftsmen. Ransom's first awkward encounter is with Hyoi the Hross. After some initial fear and shyness, an acquaintance occurs. Ransom discovers that the races of Mars are rational and have language. Being a philologist, Ransom shortly is able to decipher the language. He begins engaging in rudimentary conversation and develops friendships with the Hrossa. Learning much about Malacandrian culture, Ransom becomes Hyoi's friend.

Weston and Devine, meanwhile, are looking for Ransom. Finding him with Hyoi, they shoot Ransom's new Malacandrian friend with the rifle they've brought to Mars. Ransom escapes and is told by the Hrossa that he is wanted by the Oyarsa, the ruler of that world. At this point, one of the Seroni, Augray, befriends him. Ransom learns more of the Martian ways as Augray takes him on a journey to the Oyarsa. Ransom discovers that the planet is full of eldilia, nearly invisible to human eyes, equivalent to angels. He also discovers that the Oyarsa is like the archangel of that world.

Finally meeting the Oyarsa, Ransom is queried about Earth, a planet the Malacandrians call Thulcandra, the Silent Planet. During this encounter, Ransom discovers that Malacandra is an ancient world, slowly moving toward extinction. Nevertheless, it seems untouched by anything like the fall of humanity on earth. Avarice, pride, and self-interest are foreign to these very sophisticated but unspoiled beings. Ransom also discovers that Thulcandra, because it is the fallen planet, is silent due to its disharmony with the rest of the planets of the solar system.

Ransom tells the Oyarsa of the evil designs of Devine and Weston. At this moment, Weston and Devine are also brought, now as captives, before the Oyarsa. They have killed three Hrossa and now must give an account of their evil acts. In the end, the Oyarssa sends all three earthlings back to their own planet, never to return. He has discerned that Ransom is not like the other two, and so he manages to protect Ransom from harm during the return voyage.

Ransom and the Primary Imagination on Malacandra

Ransom's use of primary imagination allows him to begin to make sense of his experiences. All the data coming to him empirically must be interpreted. Ransom grows through his experiences. His early friendship with Hyoi allows him to correct any misunderstanding and clarify his developing grasp of Malacandrian language, culture, and history. Further exposure to the Seroni, the Fifltriggi, and to Oyarsa himself allows for increased clarity. On the other hand, Weston and Devine are caught in their own interests and cannot develop because their outlook is all projection. They are too hard-hearted and stiff-necked to learn about the real world, preferring to believe only what they want to believe. By virtue of these two differing approaches, Lewis can exhibit for his readers the benefits of primary imagination and the dire consequences of failing to cultivate sensitivity to the realities of the world presented to our senses.

Lewis's Ransom becomes the embodiment of primary imagination. He is in a world utterly new to him. Everything that comes to his senses—the sights, sounds, aromas, textures, and tastes—is new. How will he adjust to that world? Much of the book contrasts Ransom's growth of understanding with the truncated development of Weston and Devine. Ransom's nemeses have no interest in understanding that world; they are utterly utilitarian and seek merely to colonize and exploit. By contrast, every new experience for Ransom is an opportunity to accommodate himself to this strange world.

Lewis writes, "The moment of his arrival in an unknown world found Ransom wholly absorbed in philosophical speculation."[14] His natural curiosity, very much a part of his earthly life, has not ceased simply because he has been transported. And, even before he has vocabulary to describe the specifics, the reader is told, "Before he knew anything else he learned Malacandra was beautiful."[15] His senses are at work, but what does this new world mean? How is Ransom to make sense of it? "He gazed about him, and the very intensity of his desire to take in the new world at a glance defeated itself. He saw nothing but colours—colours that refused to form into things. Moreover, he knew nothing yet well enough to see it: you cannot see things until you know roughly what they are."[16] His heart is freighted with wonder, and this wonder is a prequel to discovery.

Lewis also makes Ransom's experience believable, for once he escapes from Devine and Weston he is not without fear. He knows nothing of this world. He knows nothing of its dangers, its inhabitants, and if the environment is friendly or hostile. He has only overheard in the space capsule while traveling to Malacandra that Weston and Devine planned to hand him over to some other beings. From their talk, Ransom took no comfort in what might happen. Having escaped, he is then faced with the reality of his aloneness. His sanity at this point is rooted in that which keeps him linked to reality.

Lewis writes, "He was quite aware of the danger of madness, and applied himself vigorously to his devotions and his toilet."[17] He must not sink into himself and his fears. He must orient himself to this strange outside world, the world present to his senses. At that point, the continued collection of sensory data allows him the material for the operations of primary imagination and the discovery of meaning.

Ransom begins with what is near. That which made sense to him in the world from where he came becomes the starting point of making sense of things in this new world. His toilet, washing up in the morning: one can imagine him brushing his teeth and combing his hair. Ransom also did his devotions: his Bible reading and prayers. Lewis is no materialist. Ransom makes sense of things by orienting himself spiritually. But Lewis is no gnostic, either. Ransom finds it necessary to tend to his bodily needs. The union of these two opens the door for Ransom to begin making common sense, bit by bit, of the spiritual and material realities of Malacandra.

Ransom's First Encounters with Malacandrians

Ransom first meets a Malacandrian inhabitant through a chance encounter with the Seroni. It occurs after he has escaped from Weston and Devine. These creatures are much taller than any he has met on earth. Both their bodies and heads are elongated. Being so different from what he knows in his world, he is afraid. Fear informed his first observation due to his remarkable lack of understanding of what or who they were.[18] In part, his fears emerged because he lacked the language to make sense of his experience. His fright leads to flight. He has projected wrongly onto his experience and will later discover he has misunderstood.

Shortly after his escape, Ransom meets Hyoi, the Hross. "Then something happened which completely altered his state of mind.... The creature was *talking*. It had a language."[19] It is a moment of great disequilibrium for Ransom. This is not what he expected. He is encountering a rational creature in another world. Present conceptual frameworks that are no longer able to make sense of one's experience must give way to something better and more robust. To avoid making changes in the face of fresh evidence prohibits the growth necessary to make sense of new experiences. It fails to benefit from the resources of primary imagination. Ransom discovers this creature can make articulate sounds, and these sounds have observable patterns. As a philologist, Ransom is elated at this discovery. He suspects that he might be able to accelerate his understanding of his environs. Lewis writes,

> The love of knowledge is a kind of madness. In the fraction of a second which it took Ransom to decide that the creature was really talking, and while he still knew that he might be facing instant death, his imagination leaped over every fear and hope and probability of his situation to follow the dazzling project of making a Malacandrian grammar. *An Introduction to the Malacandrian language—The Lunar verb—A Concise Martian-English Dictionary...*the titles flitted through his mind. And what might one discover from the speech of a non-human race? The very form of language itself, the principle behind all possible languages, might fall into his hands. Unconsciously he raised himself on his elbow and stared at the black beast. It became silent. The huge bullet head swung round and lustrous amber eyes fixed him. There was no wind on the lake or in the wood. Minute after minute in utter silence the representatives of two so far-divided species stared each into the other's face.[20]

Slowly the two representatives of two different rational species begin to trust each other and learn language from each other. As they do, they gain sight and with it understanding. The data supplied by the senses are organized into knowledge and sense. Ransom gains knowledge about Malacandrian food.[21] As trust between the two develops, he gains insight into Malacandrian religious beliefs.[22] At this time he finds out there is gold on Malacandra, and this feeds his suspicions about Devine's greedy interest in the planet.[23] All of this is part and parcel to Ransom's making sense of his Malacandrian adventures.

In his own creative way, Lewis allows the primary imagination in *Out of the Silent Planet* to be portrayed at least two different ways. Understanding develops among the Hrossa as well. We see this first when an eldil, or Malacandrian angel, appears. A young Hross sees it, but Ransom sees nothing. The young Hrossa responds, "'Hyoi!' said the cub, 'the *hman* cannot see the *eldil*.'"[24] Like the ghosts in Lewis's *The Great Divorce*, Ransom, being fallen, is not substantive enough to see the spiritual realities of Malacandra any more than the ghosts in *The Great Divorce* can accommodate themselves to the realities of Heaven. Ransom must learn more about the eldila if he is to continue to organize his thoughts of that world.

Ransom's entire experience on Malacandra is one of learning, of making ever enriched and meaningful discoveries. He soon learns of the three races of Malacandra. He is surprised to learn that they never go to war with each other or have disputes among themselves.[25] Indeed, Ransom discovers this planet is untouched by any kind of fall. The inhabitants are wise but also possess a sort of innocence. They are not merely unspoiled; they have progressed through Malacandrian time and history cultivating the kind of character that breeds moral fiber and girth.

For example, Ransom wonders about their reproductive practices. He notices that the period for reproduction among the male and female species is very short. Ransom wants to know why the Hrossa don't want the opportunity to practice sex more frequently than they actually do.[26] He is told that the act and the memory are, in their culture, one. While the reproductive period is short, there is pleasure in the remembering. Hyoi informs Ransom, "A pleasure is full grown only when it is remembered. You are speaking...as if the pleasure were one thing and the memory another. It is all one thing."[27] Here Lewis, through Ransom, allows his readers to enter a world far more complex, and perhaps far more sane, than their own. The data has given way to primary imagination. Ransom also leans that among the *hrossa* promiscuity does not exist.[28]

Evil Comes to Malacandra

While Ransom is seeking to understand this new world, Weston and Devine come upon them and shoot Hyoi. As he dies, Ransom, grieving, tries to explain to his new friend the fallenness of Thulcandra. "'We are all a bent race. We have come here to bring evil on Malacandra. We are only half hnau—Hyoi...' His speech died away into the inarticulate. He did not know the words for 'forgive,' or 'shame,' or 'fault,' hardly the word for 'sorry.' He could only stare into Hyoi's distorted face in speechless guilt."[29] Since the Hrossa have no experience of the fall, they have no language to describe wickedness and the constellation of topics surrounding it.

Ransom is told he must go to the Oyarsa, the archangel of Malacandra, to give warning of the evil in their world.[30] On his way, Ransom is sent to the sorn, Augray, to aid him as he travels. He is grieving, but the encounter with another of the Malacandran races gives Ransom further opportunity to learn about the mysteries of this planet.[31] Augray tells Ransom, "To us the eldil is a thin, half-real body that can go through walls and rocks: to himself he goes through them because he is solid and firm and they are like cloud. And what is true light to him and fills the heaven, so that he will plunge into the rays of the sun and refresh himself from it, is to us the black nothing of the sky at night."[32]

As Ransom talks with Augray, new data flood his mind and inform his experience. This must also be filtered through the grid of his primary imagination. Things are not as they seemed. When Ransom first saw the sorns, he thought they were like a race of ogres; now he thought them more like titans or angels. Ransom realized it was his own vulgarity that prevented him from seeing things as they truly were.[33] But the learning is two way. Augray also learns as Ransom speaks of earth. So too, when they prepare to meet with the Oyarsa and are joined by other Malacandrians, "They were astonished at what he had to tell them of human history—of war, slavery and prostitution. 'It is because they have no Oyarsa,' said one of the pupils. 'It is because every one of them wants to be a little Oyarsa himself,' said Augray."[34]

At a gathering of the Malacandrians, Ransom also finally meets a pfifltrigg, Kanakaberaka.[35] Many Malacandrians have gathered with great pomp and pageantry for the council with the Oyarsa. When Ransom meets the Oyarsa, he cannot say exactly what he was like, for the experience was new and unique. There was a greatness about him that overwhelmed Ransom's vocabulary.[36] He has learned from Augray that the Oyarsa are swift moving like light. But he also discovers, to his surprise, that the Oyarsa is curious about Thulcandra, Earth, the silent planet. He knew that earth had an Oyarsa, but this one did some evil act, and Thulcandra has gone silent. The Oyarsa of Malacandra knew that the Oyarsa of earth became bent. The Oyarsa also knew that Maledil, or God, accomplished certain things on Thulcandra into which the Oyarsa long to look.[37] Even this unfallen angelic being uses something like primary imagination as he seeks to understand Ransom's world.

The tribunal is about to occur as Weston and Devine are brought into the presence of the Oyarsa, along with the remains of the three Hrossa they have killed. These two, so bent in their self-referential ways, cannot see the objective world of their surroundings. Their assumptions projected onto that environment minimize their capacity for sight. In the end they are perceived as fools. The judgment against them is that they shall never return to Malacandra or they will perish. The Oyarsa, recognizing the difference between Ransom and the other two, arranges for Ransom to be protected as they journey back to earth.

Further Observations about Primary Imagination

The adventures of Ransom on Malacandra become a place where common sense is embodied in Lewis's fiction. As on Mars, so here on Earth, data are always before us. Every glance at our own world gives clues to its meaning and significance. A composite police sketch of a criminal is made from multiple eyewitness accounts. No one description tends to be enough to make the image clear. Each witness notices a particular detail or two. But the composite drawn from all the descriptions proves to be remarkably accurate once the criminal is captured. In a similar way, the data supplied by the senses make up a sort of composite sketch of the world presented to our senses and then arranged in a meaningful way in our own minds. Lewis has imaginatively set something like this before his readers in Ransom's travels to Malacandra.

But the composite is just one element in the story. Ransom is fallen, true, but he is far less affected by the avarice and lust for power that have so polluted Weston and Devine. Consequently, Lewis shows that the conditions of the heart can go a long way toward enabling one to see and gain full use of the primary imagination.

Perhaps an image from classical literature will clarify the point. In the *Theaetetus* by Plato, Socrates compares the mind to a block of wax. He says perceptions of this world are like impressions that might be made on the wax. The condition of the wax dramatically affects the integrity of the impression. If the wax is too cold and hard, no impression is made. If the wax is too hot, no impression is retained, for the heat keeps melting the wax and it returns to the form it had before the impression was made. So too, if the wax is filled with impurities and pollutants, every impression made on the wax lacks integrity and is compromised. So it is with the primary imagination.

We also learn that this capacity, while giving one the ability to make sense of the world, also calls the perceiver to the responsibility to maintain moral integrity in order to see rightly. The contrast Lewis makes between Ransom and the other two characters opens a window on this truth. Lewis also can show by this contrast the relative lack of imagination in those who seem irreparably bent, like Devine and Weston. Exercising the primary imagination makes us more fully human in our experience of reality, just as we were created to be.

Chapter 9

The Magician's Bargain

Generous Imagination in *That Hideous Strength*

For Lewis, the generous imagination is manifested in the blind estimation or deification of an idea or thing to the point that it borders on adoration or vilification.

Simply put, it seeks to embellish a thing beyond what it deserves. Its effect is to weaken the self and narrow the soul. It is not a positive use of the imagination, as we will discover in the examination of Lewis's *That Hideous Strength*.

The Semantic Thread

An exploration of the generous imagination as Lewis understood it is best begun with his book *Studies in Words*. Lewis wrote this work to help facilitate the accurate reading of old books but also to encourage a sense of responsibility to the language and ways that words change meaning over time. Lewis examines a number of words, including *life*. This word and ultimately its implications for the generous imagination as embodied in *That Hideous Strength* is the one that we want to scrutinize most carefully.

Lewis discusses at least thirteen different senses, or meanings, of the word *life* as manifested in literature and common usage throughout the ages. However, it is life in its modern biological sense that matters for the generous imagination. Lewis characterized this as *Life (biological)*, which we will hereafter shorten to *Life (bio)*.

These changes in meanings, Lewis writes, bear witness to the rising emotional temperature of the word, caused by its semantic halo. This is defined as the emotion derived from one sense of the word leaking into and infecting all its other senses. The word *gentleman*, for example, used to be defined simply in terms of a social class. It then acquired an ethical sense, in which a gentleman is anyone who behaves in a certain way. This second sense became closely associated with the word but without emptying it of its original meaning, thereby causing confusion. Lewis believed a similar increase in temperature was affecting the word *Life (bio)*.[1]

According to formal logic, *Life (bio)* is in the same position as any other universal, that is, it is a term abstracted from particulars: generally, what is common to all organisms or specifically, organization, nutrition, growth, reproduction, and so on. Therefore, it cannot be a thing as individual organisms are things.[2]

However, it was not always so. Plato propounded that Justice or Beauty were not only as real as just acts and beautiful things but much more so. Plato gave the name *eidos* to this transcendent entity. To modern *logical* thought this is completely alien. We are no longer dealing with an abstract universal. However, writes Lewis, we can come close to understanding what Plato was doing because the modern *common* usage of *Life (bio)* has taken on this same *eidos*. This is, in great measure, what has contributed to the rising temperature.[3]

Lewis gives examples of the *eidos* surrounding *Life (bio)* as exhibited by several modern writers, and shows how these usages are not logically possible. His last example is a George Bernard Shaw quote that personifies *Life (bio)*: "Evolutionary biology is 'the science of the everlasting transmutations of the Holy Ghost in the world.' Creative Evolution is 'the religion of the Twentieth Century.' This religion has as its great commandment: 'Life must not cease. That comes before everything.'"[4]

The logical problem with this statement, Lewis suggests, is that the ordinary name for the preservation of life above everything is *terror*.

> We feel that some lives should be preserved at the expense of others. We call this *love*. We want them to live because we love them, not because they are specimens of *life*, he writes. So do we logically really feel that *Life (bio)* should be preserved above everything else? In order to follow the model of Shaw, we will have to step outside of "all that instinct or experience has taught us to desire and learn to desire, to love 'before everything' an invisible, unimaginable object."[5]

As it relates to the generous imagination, this is ultimately the problem we will need to examine in *That Hideous Strength*.

So how did we get to this understanding of *Life (bio)*? Because we naturally think about biology in terms of this earth's biology and not the common biological situation that would arise if life began on any other planet, we have understood that all organisms are connected and descended from one another. Keep in mind we are speaking of the general popular view held in Lewis's time, not of individual views. Lewis likens this unity to a family tree. He describes a hypothetical English family called the Postlethwaite-Joneses who so venerate their family name that they elevate the "blood" of their family above all else. This is an instance of the *eidos*. They have turned the blood from something abstract into something that is almost a distinctive reality. Preserving the blood becomes more important than the people who possess it.[6]

This popular picture of evolution, which differs from the scientific, "is one that must deeply move any generous imagination," writes Lewis. The same feelings we have for the family can go out to *Life (bio)*, similarly to Shaw's view. There are two reasons for this. First, it

> begins as something very weak and humble with all the odds against it. Nevertheless it wins. It becomes Man. It conquers inanimate nature. It aspires to be the ancestor of super-Man. The story thus embodies one of the great archetypal patterns: the Ugly Duckling, the oppressed but finally triumphant Cinderella, the despised seventh son who outshines the six others, Jack the giant-killer. So moving a tale must not be that of a mere abstraction. It invites us first to reify, then to personify, finally to deify, *Life (Biological)*.[7]

Second is the fear of our own death and the death of those we love. Therefore, *life* has a rich, warm connotation because we think of it as the opposite of death. However, Lewis posits that the opposite of life is not death but the inanimate. So our understanding rests on false premises after all. Both of these reasons align with Plato's model, the *eidos*. It is also the beginning of an understanding of what the generous imagination seeks to do; embellish a thing far beyond what it deserves, far beyond the bounds of logic. The implications of this embellishment are far-reaching.

Just how far-reaching, we will see in *That Hideous Strength*. We maintain that the philosophy that rules Belbury and the N.I.C.E is the result primarily of a semantic situation in which *Life (bio)* has acquired such a significant halo that it leads its members to enact their philosophy in dark and dangerous ways. We will see how this semantic thread unwinds throughout our study.

We've examined how the misunderstanding and deification of a word or concept can lead to the generous imagination. We must now ask how such words come to be deified in the first place and how the generous imagination can be intentionally cultivated for purposes of control through the use of rhetoric, and especially rhetorical terms, or *words*. Oftentimes, it is the *misuse* of rhetoric that ignites the generous imagination, causing it to flare up and express itself in ways unsupported by reality.

God Terms and Charismatic Authority

In *The Ethics of Rhetoric*, author Richard Weaver states that the art of rhetoric, rightly practiced, aspires to the highest good, the truest objective, the ultimate term. Rhetorical terms work like links in a chain stretching to the master link (or ultimate term), or "the good," which in turn transfers its influences down the chain.[8] Thus, in any piece of rhetorical discourse, one term supersedes another only by being closer to the term that is ultimate. These ultimate terms are also known as "god terms."

Weaver writes, "Rhetoric at its truest seeks to perfect men by showing them better versions of themselves, links in that chain extending up toward the ideal, which only the intellect can apprehend and only the soul have affection for."[9] Thus, terms like *justice* or *love* might be god terms, the highest good toward which a rhetorician is trying to move an audience or the highest terms that a particular culture or society values. And of course, this definition of the right-thinking rhetorician does not preclude the fact that base (or evil) rhetoric is practiced as well, and that nothing prevents a base rhetorician from defining evil as the highest good.

In our recent past, such terms as *progress*, *science*, or *American* have functioned as god terms.[10] And today, *technology* is one of our god terms. People don't necessarily attach any negative connotations to these terms; however, they may tend to inflate them and view them blindly, or speak of them with devotion bordering on adoration or groupthink. They have used the generous imagination to set up these terms and the ideas behind them as the highest good that humans can attain.

The problem with groupthink is that it produces the illusion of invulnerability and facilitates the loss of independent thinking. Consider how we look to technology, especially digital technology, as a sort of savior. There are very few dissenting voices or independent thinkers questioning whether we really need more devices or faster connections or yet another social media platform. We tend to blindly accept these changes as they arrive. We have deified the idea of *technology* or *progress* beyond what it deserves. We have succumbed to the generous imagination. This is, of course, not the goal of rhetoric. Yet rhetoric, used wrongly, even without ill intention, can produce the generous imagination.

Weaver also identifies another type of ultimate term, "charismatic terms." While god terms come into being through identifiable derivation or referents, charismatic terms have somehow broken free of any derivation and operate without any connection to something we understand. Thus, they are irrational, rhetorically speaking. Weaver explains their existence as the result of a "spontaneous general will." Words such as *freedom* and *democracy* fit into this category.[11]

But there is a darker aspect. Charismatic terms can have their authority forced upon them. This authority is simply the intentional appropriation of lesser terms in the rhetorical chain, which are then forced into the position of ultimate terms.

We see this especially in political discourse. Weaver suggests that any number of truncated terms such as *FBI, FDIC, NPA,* or *NEP* represent the efforts of government to force charismatic authority on them. As long as we can identify the terms and what they stand for, we know the world we live in. Once the terms become abstractions by being truncated, they lose any correlation to rational rhetoric because they divorce the word from the meaning and the import. During World War II, terms such as *defense* and *war effort* became for a time charismatic terms. These terms often become ultimate in times of crisis, but they still serve as base rhetoric to manipulate people's feelings and control the way they think about a certain situation. It's important to note that charismatic terms function in such a way that all of life can be defined in relation to them.

Charismatic terms are forced into ultimate positions intentionally in order to foster an environment in which the generous imagination can multiply. Thus, we see another facet of this imagination: the desire to manipulate. And, as Weaver states, any group determined to have control will first look to appropriate the sources of charismatic authority. We see this time and again in history. We've seen it in the rise of the Third Reich and the blind estimation of Hitler and his ideas. We see it wherever totalitarian regimes are flourishing in the world today. We see it in the Middle Ages in the use of the term *infidel.* Wherever such rhetoric is being used, the generous imagination is sure to be present.[12]

Holding a Pistol to the Head of the *Tao*

Before turning to *That Hideous Strength* we must examine its philosophical foundations upon which the generous imagination is built, in *The Abolition of Man.* It was Lewis's occasional practice to write one book in propositional form, and then follow up with its counterpart in imaginative form. Such was the case with these two works. In *The Abolition of Man,* Lewis describes a passage in what he calls *The Green Book,* a work on education by two schoolmasters. He takes issue with the fact that the authors appear to make the claim that all value statements are only about our feelings and are therefore unimportant. Lewis calls this "debunking." The authors may attempt to fortify their pupils' minds against emotional propaganda with this reasoning, but they also may believe that human emotion is contrary to reason. They may claim to be "cutting away the parasitic growth of emotion, religious sanction, and inherited taboos, in order that 'real' or 'basic' values may emerge."[13]

However, writes Lewis, humanity through the ages has always believed that emotional reactions could be either congruous or incongruous to any given object, that indeed things *merited* certain responses. But such emotional reaction is not innate; we must be trained into it. Lewis calls this doctrine of objective value the *Tao*. It states that certain attitudes about the universe and about ourselves are true while others are false. These attitudes bear a strong affinity to reason because, under the *Tao*, emotional states can be in harmony or out of harmony with reason.[14]

But the *Tao* presupposes a standard that is lacking in the claims of *The Green Book*, says Lewis. Our responses can only be reasonable or unreasonable given a standard. Thus, from an educational perspective, the duty of those within the *Tao* is to train appropriate responses in the pupil. But the duty of those from without is to remove all sentiment from the mind of the pupil or to teach certain sentiments that have nothing to do with their intrinsic congruity. If this is the case, they are "creating in others by 'suggestion' or incantation a mirage which their own reason has successfully dissipated."[15] While the old method of education initiated, the new merely conditions. It makes its pupils what it wants for purposes that the pupils know nothing about. Thus, we have arrived at propaganda, an important function of the generous imagination.

"Without the aid of trained emotions," writes Lewis, "the intellect is powerless against the animal organism."[16] As in Plato, the reason must rule the appetites through sentiment; the head rules the belly through the chest. This is why an education via *The Green Book* produces what Lewis calls men without chests; that is, sentiment has been debunked and devalued and is no longer a ground for action.

Once we imagine the idea of sentiment being stripped away to get at a more real value, Lewis suggests there are only two ways in which we can proceed. One would be from factual propositions. The example given is the preservation of society. The authors of *The Green Book* couldn't get anyone to accept this through an appeal to emotion, because emotion is what they are debunking. A refusal to sacrifice oneself would be just as rational.

Therefore, says Lewis, you cannot draw practical conclusions from propositions about fact alone. "This will preserve society" cannot lead to "do this" except by "society ought to be preserved."[17] So either you must decide that what you call sentiment is actually rationality itself or you must find some other more rational core of value.

The real question, he asks, is this: Do we even have this instinct? Most people don't desire the preservation of people in far perpetuity. They desire to preserve the people around them: their sons, daughters, wives, or mothers.

Again, Lewis asks a question. By what authority do people accept some things, such as the continuation of the race, and reject others? Ultimately, these concepts are all derived from the *Tao*. There is no ground for the preference. The *Tao* is the only source of value. Reject it and you reject all value, writes Lewis. There can never be any new system of values. New ideologies are simply pieces of the *Tao*, engorged and isolated by those using them.

This is vitally important to understand in terms of the generous imagination, not only in the context of rhetoric but because this imagination seeks to embellish beyond desert. "The rebellion of new ideologies against the *Tao* is a rebellion of the branches against the tree: if the rebels could succeed they would find that they had destroyed themselves."[18] This is the situation at Belbury in *That Hideous Strength*, to which we shall shortly turn.

Lewis analyzes what happens to the society that has stepped outside the *Tao* altogether and can decide for itself what man ultimately is to become. This is the rejection of value altogether. He writes of "man's conquest over nature" and proves this to be simply the conquest of some men over other men with nature as the instrument. Thus, for example, contraception is the power of one generation to use "nature" to deny or shape the existence of another generation.

We are finally shown an eerie world in which one generation has acquired the power to make its descendants what it pleases. This would be an age most liberated from tradition, from the *Tao*. It would be rule of the few over the many. Since these few, or conditioners, as Lewis calls them, have stepped outside the *Tao*, they can make decisions about the rest of humanity only based on their own pleasure or impulses. Good and bad do not apply to them. All sentiment has been debunked, thus only "what I want" remains.[19]

Human conquest over nature turns out to be nature's conquest over humanity. Things are reduced to the level of mere nature in order to conquer them. The price of conquest is to treat the conquered as mere nature. At first this is a loss, not only for us but also for the thing itself. Something in us vanishes or dies, that something in the *Tao* that makes us uniquely human. Once we reduce the human species to this level, humanity has been abolished.

We think that by giving up our souls we can attain power, but really we become the puppets of our dehumanized conditioners, who will manipulate us at their own whim, by appetite, by mere nature.[20] It is this reduction, writes Lewis, that allows us to change our language to reflect it. "Once we killed bad men: now we liquidate unsocial elements. Virtue has become *integration* and diligence *dynamism*."[21] In the case of *That Hideous Strength*, the word *sanitation* must be examined through this lens as it underlies the whole philosophy of Belbury.

Throughout this brief study, we have first looked at the deification of the word *life*, then at the misuses of rhetoric for control, and finally at the philosophy that leads to the abuses of power to manipulate men. Over all these three, the generous imagination flies like a standard unfurled. We must now connect them all as we examine *That Hideous Strength*.

The Empty Hand of Clotho: The Generous Imagination in *That Hideous Strength*

That Hideous Strength is the third book in Lewis's space trilogy. It follows the story of Mark and Jane Studdock and their respective adventures with the heroes at St. Anne's and the villains at Belbury. An organization called the N.I.C.E. has taken over the university town of Edgestow. Its stated aim is to apply scientific principles to create a better society for its citizens. What is really at stake is a dark and dangerous battle for the survival of humankind.

Previously, we said that the philosophy ruling Belbury is primarily the result of a semantic situation in which *life (bio)* has acquired such a significant halo that it leads its members to enact their philosophy in dark and dangerous ways. The whole tale of Belbury hangs upon this semantic thread, woven throughout. To discover the beginnings of this thread, we must now turn briefly to the first work in the space trilogy, *Out of the Silent Planet*. Indeed, Lewis's study of the word *Life (bio)* is the perfect key to unlocking chapter 20 of this book, which we now examine. Though Weston does not figure as a character in *That Hideous Strength*, his ideas are the foundation for the atrocities of Belbury.

Recall that *Out of the Silent Planet* details the adventures of Weston, Devine, and their captive Ransom in a journey to Malacandra, or Mars. The scientist Weston explains why he has come to Malacandra in his "trial" before Oyarsa, the ruler of this planet: to put the race of humankind finally beyond the reach of death. His mission is to conquer it when earth is no longer habitable. Thus, the human race may continue, conquering new worlds each time a world becomes uninhabitable. In this way, he hopes to stay one step ahead of the final extermination of the race. It is the pursuit of human immortality. He has made generous assumptions of both his self-importance and the idea that the human race is to be preserved at all costs, even at the cost of the morality that gives value to human existence.

We see how his misuse of the word *Life (bio)* has led Weston to the folly of believing that he has found the secret to the eternal continuance of the species. Oyarsa silences Weston with simple logic: What will happen when all the planets have been conquered and there is nowhere left to go? Weston has forgotten that there is a balance between life and death. As long as there is one, there will always be the other. His misinterpretation of the word *Life (bio)* has led him to ascribe to it associations to which it is not logically entitled—for example, as a counter to a fear of death.

Weston lacks the absorbing imagination[22] but he has the generous imagination in abundance. He is enacting what Lewis described in *Studies in Words*. Using the generous imagination, he has inflated the importance of the continuance of *Life (bio)*—similar to the blood of a family—assuming that it must go on at all costs. He has created an *eidos*, a concrete reality out of an abstract concept, and deified it beyond anything it deserves. The celestial being Oyarsa recognizes this at once.

Oyarsa then describes Weston's problem. He shows Weston how he cares for none of the laws of what in that world is called *hnau* (that is, all reasoning creatures including humanity and the Malacandrian inhabitants), which make them rational. He cares for only one law, the love of one's kind. He says that the lord of the silent planet (Earth) has so bent this idea that it has become like a god or idol in Weston's brain, and he will break every other law to serve this one. And a bent man has more capability for damage than a broken one. He has torn the concept straight from the *Tao* and inflated it out of all proportion.

This lord of the silent planet has bent humans with a fear of death and a desire to flee from what eventually none can escape.[23] This connects Lewis's idea of the generous imagination—essentially an *eidos*—to precisely the reasons we deify *Life (bio)*: because we fear death. The halo on *Life (bio)* is burning very brightly. And it is ironic that this brightness masks the deep darkness of the generous imagination.

The Abuses of Power, Control, and Groupthink at Belbury

In *That Hideous Strength* the generous imagination is extended to its logical limits as described in *The Abolition of Man*. Here we will explore Belbury, and exclude St. Anne's, primarily because Belbury is the ideal model for the generous imagination.

Belbury is the headquarters of the N.I.C.E. (National Institute of Coordinated Experiments) and is founded on the philosophy that objective value does not exist. Those who ultimately control it have stepped outside the *Tao* and are no longer ruled by systems of value. Because they have figured out how to fashion humanity into what they want, they have begun to see humanity as mere nature, to be experimented on and manipulated at will. As previously stated, to do this they must suspend their value judgments about humanity and see it as a thing, as mere matter.

This is perhaps the very reason Frost is able to propose to the prisoner Alcasan that his severed head will be kept alive after his death. It is why Belbury chief of police Fairy Hardcastle can burn Jane Studdock with the lighted end of a cigar and "do things" to the prisoners at Belbury without any qualms. In order for this philosophy to flourish, it must be converted to an ideology.

The ideology of Belbury is based on Weston's deification of *Life (bio)*. As Lewis writes, "What purport to be new systems or (as they now call them) 'ideologies,' all consist of fragments of the *Tao* itself, arbitrarily wrenched from their context in the whole and then swollen to madness in their isolation."[24] To enact this ideology, they must also deify *Life (bio)* by using the generous imagination. They do this with words.

In a meeting with his college colleagues Feverstone, Busby, and Curry, the protagonist Mark Studdock comments on what the N.I.C.E. will supposedly do for society: "The real thing is that this time we're going to get science applied to social problems and backed by the whole force of the state, just as war has been backed by the whole force of the state in the past."[25] Lewis says elsewhere that the generation that achieves this ability to make man what it wants will have enormously increased power through the state and an "irresistible scientific technique."[26] Belbury has assumed this power and backing, making it the perfect setting in which the generous imagination can flourish to enact its ideology in the wider culture.

The advancement of the N.I.C.E. ideologies doesn't come without a heavy cost internally. For this philosophy to be successful, several elements must be in place. Since the true conditioners are the "men" at the center of the organization, everyone else who works for the organization must be controlled and manipulated by them, but without knowledge of such manipulation. They must be led to believe that they are being drawn further in. This is why there are inner circles and circles within circles at Belbury. Mark's great motivation in joining the N.I.C.E. is not because he approves of their program, but because it offers him a place in what he thinks is the inner ring of the organization. All his life, he has longed to be on the inside and has seriously sacrificed his personality to do so. We can infer from this the secret he has repeatedly reinforced within himself all his life: that he is stupid and unintelligent. If he can just be part of the inner ring, perhaps he can show others just how intelligent he is and thus silence, at least for a time, that nagging inner voice that tells him otherwise.

What he finds is an atmosphere of incredible vagueness. Nothing is defined and no one understands what the organization is doing. But the institute is purposely vague and elastic, as befits those who have stepped outside the *Tao*. It is an environment in which anything can change at any moment. This is the natural outcome of stepping outside the *Tao*, writes Lewis. "When all that says 'it is good' has been debunked, what says 'I want' remains. It cannot be exploded or 'seen through' because it never had any pretentions. The conditioners, therefore, must come to be motivated simply by their own pleasure."[27]

It would then make sense why Belbury is always shrouded in secrecy. Even the conditioners don't know what action they will take next because they are relying only on impulse, having debunked value. Thus we get the ludicrous situation in which everyone wants to be in on what's happening, yet no one really knows what's happening. And no one will admit that they don't know what's happening, but will make believe that they do. They are simply puppets on strings dancing to the music of the conditioners.

Fear and anxiety naturally abound in that environment. Everyone knows there are circles within circles and are all trying to break into the innermost circle to discover a pseudosecurity. All the while, they project to others the pretense that they are already insiders. Yet, though each has, at best, only a vague understanding of its designs, everyone employed there has become deluded to believe that the N.I.C.E. is at the cutting edge of societal change and reform, and they have all bought into its schemes without even knowing what drives its machinations.

Each personality has merged into one single organism with false notions of the intentions of the N.I.C.E. No one wants to dissent, because everyone wants to be on the inside. No one really cares what the organization does, just so long as they can belong to the inner ring. So they sacrifice their individuality and devalue critical thought within their own paradigm, thereby achieving groupthink. And groupthink is nothing more than deifying some concept at the expense of all else through use of the generous imagination.

Mark discovers this loss of individuality when he catches himself compromising moral good by ceasing the attempt to understand what he is supposed to be doing. This is why he can so easily be persuaded to perpetuate lies and propaganda without any moral qualms through the writing of false news stories. The organization's will has become his will. From this position, the use of base rhetoric and charismatic authority to control thinking and actions is quite a simple and logical step. This is perhaps the highest cost of the generous imagination: the loss of individuality, creativity, and independent thinking.

The puppeteers at the center of this stage of power and control are of course John Wither and Augustus Frost. These men are examples of those who have stepped outside the *Tao* and rejected the idea of objective value; hence Wither's annoying vagueness and Frost's icy detachment. It is no accident that Lewis used these particular names for his conditioners. The use of the generous imagination to take Weston's ideal and deify *Life (bio)* out of all proportion has involved them in rejecting value altogether so they can do what they like.

Thus Frost can say in his interrogation of Mark, "That is why a systematic training in objectivity must be given to you. Its purpose is to eliminate from your mind one by one the things you have hitherto regarded as grounds for action. It is like killing a nerve. That whole system of instinctive preferences, whatever ethical, aesthetic, or logical disguises they wear, is to be simply destroyed."[28] Frost and Wither have engaged in a Faustian pact and exchanged their souls for power and are forcing Mark to do the same. It is ironic and perhaps intentional on Lewis's part that when Mark reaches the coveted innermost circle of Belbury—that which he has longed and sacrificed for all his life—he is a captive.

Contraction: Rhetoric and Propaganda at Belbury

The N.I.C.E. was organized, at least to the minds of the greater public, to solve social problems and improve the quality of life. But as we observe the organization from inside through the eyes of Mark, we see just how the N.I.C.E. uses rhetoric to inflate its own estimation of itself and the world as well as to deceive; that is, it engages in the generous imagination.

The acronym supplies sufficient evidence to confirm the fact that the organization is appropriating sources of charismatic authority. And indeed we find two terms that are far down on the rhetorical chain, being forced into ultimate positions, or god terms. Recall that charismatic terms have broken free of derivation and operate with no connection to anything we understand. Thus, rhetorically speaking, they are irrational. They divorce the word from the meaning and the import, which in this case they would do, since "meaning" is a holdover from the *Tao*.

These two terms are *sanitation* and *man* or *mankind*. As stated, the greatest good for the N.I.C.E. has become the continuance or evolution of mankind, and sanitation is the means to that end as well as the clarion call for the institute's ideology. Our semantic thread of *life (bio)* is here clearly shown as the ideological impetus running through Belbury and affecting its rhetoric and controlled engagement with the wider community through words—in this case, charismatic terms.

Remember that all of life can be defined in relation to charismatic terms. Thus, *sanitation* is applied to wider and wider contexts where it has no business. The N.I.C.E. police are called *sanitary executives*, for example. And part of the institute's success in controlling the surrounding community is the result of appropriating these sources of charismatic authority.

Filostrato, a scientist working for the N.I.C.E., exposes the horrors at work behind the seemingly innocuous term *sanitation*: the eradication of all organic life. Humans are to evolve simply as mind, without the body, thus attaining eternal life. Filostrato says of the N.I.C.E, "This institute—*Dio meo*, it is for something better than housing or vaccinations and faster trains and curing the people of cancer. It is for the conquest of death: or for the conquest of organic life, if you prefer."[29] Recall that once we are able to truly see humanity as mere nature, our language—our *words*—change to reflect this. So it is here. Every act or atrocity is committed in the name of furthering this cause.

Given its philosophical underpinnings, it is perhaps inevitable that the organization should rely on propaganda as a means to achieve its ends. Charismatic terms often become ultimate in times of crisis, as Weaver writes, but they still serve as base rhetoric to manipulate people's feelings and control the way they think about a certain situation. And when the conditioners who make up the nucleus of Belbury have the ability to "produce conscience and decide what kind of conscience they want to produce,"[30] it is a simple matter, for example, to write news reports that seem journalistic, but are really telling people what to think, oftentimes about events that never existed or are simply manufactured, like the riot in Edgestow, drummed up by chief of the Belbury police Fairy Hardcastle.

When "my will" and "what I want" are the highest court of appeal for any given action, base rhetoric, in which evil is defined as the highest good, prevails. From a Christian perspective, evil or sin is to make my will the final end and to eschew God and the *Tao* from my life. All I can do then is follow my impulses. This is how Frost functions. An impulse, for him, is a justification for action. Wither simply wanders aimlessly around the halls of Belbury. Rationality has disappeared. There is no system of checks and balances because this notion is derived from the *Tao*. Thus, propaganda can flourish.

If we think about the situation at Belbury, both philosophically and semantically, it is nothing more than a great contraction, by which I mean a shrinking or narrowing of focus. Groupthink, base rhetoric, and propaganda all contribute to this effect. We are drawn into the contraction through the wider world of Edgestow and St. Anne's. This world contracts to Bracton University and its acceptance of the ideas of the N.I.C.E. The university kowtows and contracts to Belbury, which contracts to the inner rings, which themselves contract to the inmost ring, Frost and Wither, both of whom have stepped outside the *Tao*. Thus, what the two of them represent contracts to the loss of objective value, which contracts to randomness and Babel, which ultimately contracts to self-destruction and death. As Lewis wrote, it is the rebellion of the branches against the tree, and in succeeding they have destroyed themselves, which is literally the case at Belbury by the end of the story.

As Merlin orchestrates the destruction of the institute during the banquet scene, he calls in a "loud intolerable" voice, "They that have despised the word of God, from them shall the word of man also be taken away."[31] What ensues is the curse of Babel; gibberish prevails. It is fitting that the story of Belbury ends in this way. We have come to the end of our semantic thread. The deification of *Life (bio)* and the ideology that developed out of it have been destroyed, removing the ability to make sense out of words altogether. As the Gospel of John says, "In the beginning was the Word / and the Word was with God / and the Word was God" (John 1:1). We can hardly help associating what Lewis calls the *Tao* with this supernatural Word, and the destruction of Belbury is the only ending that could possibly have happened once reason and value had been discarded in favor of impulse. What is naturally left is nonsense.

The generous imagination, that is, overinflation, overestimation, and deification, in reality lead to self-repression, not self-expression and expansion. The soul withers as we move closer to the center of Belbury as everything is sacrificed to a blind ideal. Wither and Frost are the magicians who have shaken hands with the devil. They have given up their souls, what Lewis calls "the seat of magnanimity," and have become men without chests. It is an unnecessary sacrifice of soul and personal value.

Even Mark recognizes this when he is imprisoned in the cells of Belbury. All his life was defined by participation in activities so that he might be accepted or invited in, not because he actually enjoyed them. His whole life had been one great contraction of his world by deifying the idea of acceptance and status. Thus, in this sense, the entire structure or shape of Belbury and the N.I.C.E. is one of contraction or downward spiral, because its philosophy always ends at an inevitable and tiny "I." And this whole process began with words inflated by the generous imagination.

Or we can look at it another way. To return again to Lewis's example of Plato, the head (reason) rules the belly (appetites) through the chest, that is, the organ of magnanimity, of "emotions organized by trained habit into stable sentiments."[32] Belbury is a contraction of Plato's ideal, where everything is ruled through the gut or the appetites, rather than by the head and emotions trained into stable sentiments. Everything is ruled at whim, which would indeed be the case if our appetites were turned loose from reason and objective value.

Fried Eggs, Soap, and Sunlight: Cultivating the Just Imagination

The tiny "I" is perhaps the place where we must begin to counter the abuses of the generous imagination. This would involve the cultivation of a just imagination that would free one to embellish in a way that is coherent with his or her humanity and with reality.

The just imagination seeks to render a thing its due; no more and no less. This is simply another way of saying we are to remain within the *Tao*, within that system of objective value where everything merits an appropriate response. "The right defense against false sentiments is to inculcate just sentiments," writes Lewis. "By starving the sensibility of our pupils we only make them easier prey to the propagandist when he comes. For famished nature will be avenged and a hard heart is no infallible protection against a soft head."[33]

In Plato's *Republic*, Glaucon and his brother Adeimantus engage Socrates in questioning the nature of justice. The two brothers take the position of devil's advocate, stating that the practice of injustice is actually a greater good than practicing justice. They tell the story of Gyges, a shepherd caring for the flocks of the king of Lydia. After an earthquake, Gyges descends into the ground and finds a body with a ring on its finger. He takes the ring, and later, as he toys with it, finds that in turning the setting a certain way, he becomes invisible. He goes with the shepherds to give the king a report of the flocks and with the ring of invisibility seduces the queen and kills the king, becoming king in his place.

Glaucon maintains that even if there were two rings and one was given to a just man and the other to an unjust man, both would take advantage of the godlike power they possessed. The just man would not be able to stand fast and would end like the unjust man.[34] We can see that Gyges came to a similar end. He deified the powers of the ring and inflated its use so that he could manipulate the world around him. Only one with absolute wisdom can wield absolute power without compromise.

All of us operate with some levels of power. If we are loved, we hold power over the heart of the beloved. If we are an employer, we hold power over the employee. If we are a parent, we have dictatorial power over our children.

Even the limited amounts of power we have put us at risk. We will always try to justify bad behavior. We must not covet power such that we are willing to step outside the *Tao* and lose our essential humanity in a magician's bargain. It is because all are at risk of rationalizing bad behavior and engaging in the generous imagination that we must not isolate ourselves from community. It is in genuine community that we are reminded that we play only a part in a larger scheme, that our imaginings move toward the just imagination when they remember that to each must be rendered his or her due. The self is not isolated from the whole. True community is an antidote to the rationalizations of the generous imagination.

The ability to see the world rightly and to align the self with the world and with others is at the heart of cultivating a just imagination. So how does one cultivate this type of imagination? Lewis provides a key in his short essay "The Trouble with X." We all want to change certain people around us who have a particularly irritating habit, because they have a profound effect on our happiness or well-being. Yet, no matter how hard we try, we cannot change that other person. Now we can understand a bit how God feels, writes Lewis.

In the same way, God sees all people with their flaws. God has provided them with all good things, yet they consistently spoil all these things with their twisted natures. Now just as we never see the flaw that we ourselves have, the one that makes others miserable in the same way their flaw makes us miserable, so God sees not only others, but us as well. And despite that flaw, God loves others and us. This, says Lewis, is what we must do: when we find ourselves caught up in the morbid delight of dwelling on the faults of others, we must dismiss these thoughts and instead focus our energies on changing the flaw within ourselves. There exists in all of us a flaw that, unless changed, will separate us from God's power to keep us from being forever miserable.[35]

This is an antidote to the generous imagination. It locates the source of the trouble within us, which is the right place to begin looking. It also prepares us to function in community more holistically. A just imagination would first take an honest look within to find the flaw that might cause us to embellish others' flaws above and beyond what they deserve, or to fall prey to groupthink as Mark Studdock did, or to deify an idea or person beyond desert, as Weston and all of Belbury did with the semantic concept of *Life (bio)*. The generous imagination flourishes because we are unable or unwilling to see the flaw within ourselves, and it remains hidden from us. And the generous imagination atrophies when we do those things that make us just members of a larger community.

Mark finally realizes this in the Objective Room of Belbury. The problem with pursuing mere *Life (bio)* is that we are not actually after the life but what the life provides: wealth, fame, virtue, pleasure, godliness, and so on. These aren't valuable for the sake of life, but life is valuable, when at all, for the sake of these things.[36]

For Mark, the objective training has an effect opposite to the one Frost intends. The generous imagination he has adopted begins to fall away. He begins to see life for the sake of these things. As he falls in step with the *Tao*, he experiences ordinate feelings toward the way life is:

> As the desert first teaches men to love water, or absence first reveals affection, there rose up against this background of the sour and the crooked some kind of vision of the sweet and the straight. Something else—something he vaguely called the "Normal"—apparently existed. He had never thought about it before. But there it was—solid, massive, with a shape of its own, almost like some-

thing you could touch, or eat, or fall in love with. It was all mixed up with Jane and fried eggs and soap and sunlight and the rooks cawing at Cure Hardy and the thought that, somewhere outside, daylight was going on at that moment.[37]

Lewis offers one more way for us to cultivate a just imagination. He writes, "For the wise men of old the cardinal problem had been how to conform the soul to reality, and the solution had been knowledge, self-discipline and virtue."[38] This seems a return to the ideal of Plato's right-functioning human. We must rule our appetites with our reason, through our soul, our chest, sentiment, the part of us that makes us human. By reason alone we are only spirit and by appetite alone only animal. We must train our sentiments to be just, to be congruent to the thing the world is and the people we are. There is a very real sense in which they require it. It is all there, waiting for us in the *Tao*. To do anything less is to be less than human.

Chapter 10

The Hellish Nature of Projection

Transforming Imagination in *The Great Divorce*

As we have seen, not all forms of the imagination identified and defined by C. S. Lewis are positive. One example is the transforming imagination, as developed in *The Great Divorce*. Before looking at the text, we will define the term. Then we will flesh it out by looking at other examples in Lewis.

In a fallen world, any generalization about human beings is subject to falsification, hyperbole, and misunderstanding; even many of our suspicions about human untrustworthiness can be faulty. All personal abilities can be used for good because humans are made in the image of God. But they can equally be used for ill because we are fallen. Our lives are freighted with both dignity and depravity. The best among us can fall short and, at times, *will* fall. And yet, even the worst among us are capable of an occasional kind act. Aslan the lion, the Christ figure of Narnia, addresses the newly coronated King Caspian, "'You come from the Lord Adam and Lady Eve,' said Aslan. 'And that is both honor enough to erect the head of the poorest beggar, and shame enough to bow the shoulders of the greatest emperor in earth.'"[1]

Lewis recognizes that the imagination can be used for good or for ill. The transforming imagination is the proclivity to engage in what psychologists call projection. In *The Discarded Image*, Lewis observes elements of the transforming imagination in some of the work of the English Romantic poet, William Wordsworth.[2] Wordsworth, at times, projected onto nature the innocence he hoped to find there. He believed that youth is unspoiled. This he contrasted with his own growing sense that aging was making him become more calloused and jaded. He grieved the loss of his youthful innocence and longed to get back to the pure, the unspoiled, and the unadulterated. To some degree he idealized the innocence of childhood. Revolted by the growing pollution and problems created by industrialization, Wordsworth projected onto nature a notion that it was undefiled and pure, qualities it did not possess—at least, not without some qualification. Nevertheless, these projections revealed Wordsworth's own growing disappointments with himself and his culture. This tendency to project is bound to lead to disappointment with oneself, and certainly with others who do not meet the transforming imagination's inflated expectations.

The transforming imagination has a tendency to overidealize and project inflated expectations onto the objects of its affection. This limits the possibility to experience any kind of genuine fulfillment. The things idealized cannot do what is imagined of them. Whenever expectations might be raised by projection, not only do disappointments follow, but often, contempt is projected onto the very things we once valued. Lewis observes four phases of expectation, which he classifies into four stages of enchantment.[3] The first stage is to be unenchanted. Limited experience has not yet given rise to wonder and awe. We are, as of yet, unenchanted. We have still to notice any sunrises or sunsets. The wonder of first love is still in our future. Fascination with some hobby or interest has not yet occurred.

Then, something happens to us and we become enchanted. For Dante it was seeing Beatrice on the streets of Florence when he was only nine years old. For Lewis it was when his brother brought a toy garden arranged on the lid of a cookie tin, which awakened him to the presence of beauty. For some it happens when they notice the colors of a spring morning, when the buds of the trees have popped open after a long, dormant winter. For others it is the wonder of fireflies coruscating in the back garden on a humid summer evening, or the leaves of an autumn season bursting forth into a cornucopia of glorious color: reds, yellows, peach, maroon, salmon, and apricot. It is as if, through some particular event, one feels the imperious call of the transcendent, awakening wonder in the soul.

The temptation in the transforming imagination, however, is to imagine that the thing or event that awakened desire is the very object of one's longing. The transforming imagination seeks to transform the thing into the very object of one's longing. It is all projection.

Unfortunately, the thing awakening desire is seldom able to sustain the longing, and the heart crashes into disappointment, or, what Lewis calls disenchantment, the third phase of enchantment. Once disappointed the transforming imagination can begin to vilify and project hatred onto the very thing once held dear. Given time, the once desired object proves itself incapable of sustaining interest. It cannot live up to misdirected and inflated longings and expectations. Lewis recognized in himself this tendency to vilify what disappointed him. He wrote about it in the introduction to the second edition of his pre-Christian, narrative poem, *Dymer*: "Instead of repenting of my idolatry I spat on the images which only my misunderstanding greed had ever made into idols."[4]

Lewis identifies a fourth stage of enchantment, reenchantment. This is the moment one realizes that one's deepest longing is for some object that is never fully given, and the desire is redirected toward the true object. In such cases, one becomes *reenchanted*. Lewis wrote,

> If I find in myself a desire which no experience in this world can satisfy, the most probable explanation is that I was made for another world. If none of my earthly pleasures satisfy it, that does not prove the universe is a fraud. Probably earthly pleasures were never meant to satisfy it, but only to arouse it, to suggest the real thing. If that is so, I must take care on the one hand never to mistake them for the something else of which they are only a kind of copy, or echo, or image. I must keep alive in myself the desire for my true country, which I shall not find till after death; I must never let it get snowed under or turned aside; I must make it the main object of life to press on to that other country and to help others to do the same.[5]

If disenchantment fails to ripen into reenchantment, if it is freighted with contempt for the thing that awakened desire, then the imagination calcifies into the transforming imagination. In such cases, the projection is very negative and equally inflated in its hatreds. It still remains at a stage of projection, unable to see things as they truly are. From the creativity that crafts a healthy imaginative grasp of matters, the transforming imagination gives way to a kind of idolatry. Its inflated estimations, unchecked, lead to regrettable behaviors.

In this way, the transforming imagination can become rhetorical. In its contempt, it seeks to persuade others to join in its hatred of the given object. It can even cultivate a party whose very existence and identity is centered on its mission to destroy what it vilifies. Rational argument cannot rebuff the contempt because reason is not what drives the anger; it is rooted in the emotional disappointment. No injustice has occurred that needs to be righted. The offense is imagined and therefore very difficult to shake. The transforming imagination is not guided and shaped by reality at all. Rather, it seeks to shape reality for itself and for others.

Four Examples of the Transforming Imagination

Apart from *The Great Divorce*, Lewis provides his readers with at least four examples of the transforming imagination.

Historicism

In his essay "Historicism," Lewis points to a frequently used imaginative projection. He writes, "I give the name *historicism* to the belief that men can, by use of their rational powers, discover an inner meaning in the historical process."[6] The inner meaning, if it exists, would by nature be impossible to discover at a point in time. As history is unfolding, it is, therefore, not a story any mere mortal has seen to its end. Consequently, to suggest we have knowledge of the end is a projection.

Lewis recognizes that a misapplication of Hegel's philosophy of history could lead one to suspect that he or she can perceive the outcome of some unfolding of history. Lewis sees that this kind of projection can be engaged in equally by the secular as well as by the religious. Nevertheless, he warns, "We have no notion what stage in the journey we have reached. Are we in Act I or Act V? Are our present diseases those of childhood or senility?"[7] Not knowing with certainty what the future might bring, and with the inability to know what unexpected surprises might occur, anything suggested by advocates of historicism in any of its forms risks possible fear-mongering, abuse, and manipulation. This is the first of many warnings Lewis provides about the excesses of the transforming imagination.

The Great Myth

Lewis suggests that a kind of transforming imagination can begin to shape a false notion, mythology, or worldview, of a given culture. He writes the essay "The Funeral of a Great Myth," to warn against a myth he saw as the religion of evolution. Though Lewis himself held to a position of theistic evolution regarding human origins, he warned against this religion of evolutionism.

> I call it a myth because it is, as I have said, the imaginative and not the logical result of what is vaguely called "modern science." Strictly speaking, there is, I confess, no such thing as "modern science." There is only particular sciences, all in a stage of rapid change, and sometimes inconsistent with one another. What the Myth uses is a selection from the scientific theories—a selection made at first, and modified afterwards, in obedience to imaginative and emotional needs. It is the work of the folk imagination, moved by its natural appetite for an impressive unity. It therefore treats *data* with great freedom.[8]

Lewis recognized that this myth appeared in Western culture prior to the publication of Darwin's *Origin of Species*. It found expression in the culture's poetry and music—Keat's *Hyperion* and Wagner's *Ring* were examples. Lewis observes, "That, then, is the first proof that popular Evolution is a Myth. In making it, imagination runs ahead of the scientific evidence. 'The prophetic soul of the big world' was already pregnant with the Myth: if science has not met the imaginative need, science would not have been so popular. But probably every age gets, within certain limits, the science it desires."[9] This myth of evolutionism, that is, the religion of popular evolution, was for Lewis an example of the transforming imagination. Lewis was not antiscience, but he was opposed to those popular expressions of science that took on the quality of religious faith. Lewis observes, "In science, *Evolution* is a theory about *changes*: in the Myth it is a fact about *improvements*."[10]

Jeering

This example of the transforming imagination tends to project on facts whatever it wants those facts to mean. We find this in Lewis's *English Literature in the Sixteenth Century Excluding Drama.* Lewis writes about the Renaissance humanists, whose emerging worldview led them to look with disdainful condescension upon medieval forms of poetry. Consequently, toward those with whom they disagreed, Lewis writes, "They *jeer* and do not refute."[11] In other words, rather than engage in a dialectic with others that could produce light, they merely projected their contempt on others. This was little more than a fantasy and could no more stand up to scrutiny than a straw man argument can prevail against the truth.

Lewis opposed all tendencies in literary criticism that blindly projected their assumptions. Lewis saw in some a readiness to dismiss both the content of given texts, as well as the authors who did not hold the approved assumptions. At this point, Lewis might agree with the postmodernist practice of deconstructing texts to discover embedded assumptions. But Lewis equally would have wanted to remind the critic to be aware of his own assumptions regarding any given text. Lewis frequently announced his own Christian assumptions up front as he began a critique. He would have appreciated the same level of honesty and self-awareness from others doing literary criticism.

Bulverism

Lewis also warns against something similar to the transforming imagination in an essay titled "'Bulverism' or, The Foundation of 20th Century Thought." This fourth example of the transforming imagination Lewis defines as the projection of wrong on those we disagree with without any consideration of the reasons for their views. Lewis writes, "You must show *that* a man is wrong before you start explaining *why* he is wrong. The modern method is to assume without discussion *that* he is wrong then distract his attention from this (the only real issue) by busily explaining how he became so silly. In the course of the last fifteen years I have found this vice so common that I have had to invent a name for it. I call it Bulverism."[12]

Lewis was tempted to write an imaginary biography of Ezekiel Bulver and have him say, "Assume that your opponent is wrong, and then explain his error, and the world will be at your feet. Attempt to prove that he is wrong or (worse still) try to find out if he is wrong or right, and the national dynamism of our age will thrust you to the wall."[13]

Lewis observed that dominant worldviews of his day tended toward Bulverisms and expressed themselves, in various ways, in popular culture. Freudians—who say we exist as bundles of complexes—commit a Bulverism when they charge, "You are only saying that because you had a cruel father or over-nurturing mother." Marxists—who say we exist as members of an economic class—commit a Bulverism when they assert, "You are only saying that because of your bourgeoisie values and tendencies toward utilitarian treatment of the proletariat." Lewis warns, "You can only find out rights and wrongs by reasoning—never by being rude about your opponent's psychology."[14] Lewis reminds his readers, "The universe doesn't claim to be true: it is just *there*."[15] What we do in trying to decipher the meaning of the universe is an imaginative exercise full of assumptions. These imaginative assumptions can be helpful, but they also can be very wrong.

From these four examples we can conclude that the transforming imagination is an unhealthy activity. It is projective. It does not allow for any positive development of thought and understanding. This diseased use of the imagination is self-referential and utilitarian. It has a prejudice about the way things ought to be from the perspective of the imaginer and sets out to find what it wants. It ignores evidence to the contrary. It then becomes imprisoned in a dungeon of its own making.

Lewis describes hell as "the place where being is nearest to not-being."[16] A biblical understanding says that sin estranges us from God, from others, and even ourselves. Asserting one's will against the realities of God's claim on our lives as well as the inexorable demands of nature segregates us from reality. This assertion sets us up as a sort of final authority in disputable matters and leads us to take condescending attitudes toward others who do not see things our way. This is destructive. The imagination that transforms reality into what the imaginer wants, or projects to be, keeps that person isolated and diminished. He or she is unable to participate in community. This therefore is a hellish set of circumstances.

Lewis recognizes that in a fallen world the imagination can be used for bad as well as for good. As a warning against the bad uses, we turn now to Lewis's depictions in *The Great Divorce.*

The Great Divorce and the Transforming Imagination

The Great Divorce is a satire, borrowing much of its material from Dante's *The Divine Comedy*. As Dante is a character in *The Comedy*, so Lewis is a character in *The Great Divorce*. The book begins with Lewis wandering the streets of hell. No clue is given as to how he got there. The town is grey. There is a constant and steady drizzle of rain. The buildings are abandoned, the windows broken. Hell is a place of isolation and estrangement, and a deep sense of loneliness sets in. We read twice on the first page, "I never saw anyone" and "I never met anyone."[17]

Then Lewis comes upon a queue of people waiting for a bus. As arguments and fights reduce the number of those waiting in line, Lewis moves up, pleased that he has advanced. On board the bus and on his way to he knows not where, Lewis sees frequent fights break out among the passengers. After each jumble, he finds himself sitting next to someone new. In this way, he learns more about the "grey town" from each of these new encounters. He finds out that everyone in the town keeps moving farther and farther out and away from others with whom they cannot get along. Lewis learns that two men from the town traveled a distance of some two million miles to see Napoleon. When they returned, they said he was constantly pacing back and forth, blaming others for his demise. While there is undeniable humor in an Englishman's depiction of a Frenchman as one of the farthest out in hell, the account gives a sense of astronomical distances, not only separating the characters from one another, but from any form of reality.

Each seat mate Lewis encounters has a terrible story of injustices endured and offenses borne. Each portrays himself as a victim of circumstance. None readily admits to any actions on earth that might have led to his diminishment in hell. Lewis's descriptions reveal each as a despicable person. Nevertheless, just as the bus reaches the very threshold of heaven, a glorious light streams into the bus. Lewis looks down the aisle and sees his own reflection in the mirror up front by the driver. He must learn that he too is counted among the broken and despicable passengers.

As they disembark, several things are immediately obvious. Lewis notes that they lack substance; that is, they are mere phantoms.[18] Each can be seen through, like a ghost. They have no weight; the grass will not bend beneath their feet—it pierces like a bed of nails.[19] They fear that any rain will pierce their phantom bodies like bullets. One ghost tries to pick a flower, only to discover that its stem is, to him in his present state, as hard as diamonds. The threshold of heaven seems inhospitable. Who knows whether these ghosts could ever find themselves comfortable in heaven itself?

As in Dante, each of those arriving from hell receives a guide. The weighty substance of each guide, in contrast to the spectral state of the ghosts, is unmistakable. Lewis says, "The earth shook under their tread as their strong feet sank into the wet turf."[20] These guides come out of heaven to greet each passenger and encourage the letting go of whatever artificiality each holds onto in God's place. This is a strong example of the transforming imagination. Each ghost thinks what he or she holds on to in God's place will sustain, setting him or her apart from God and without consequence. Each engages in a false projection of himself or herself. Each imagines he or she is something very different, something better than the reality. Each is practiced at the transforming imagination. None seem to be able to see or hear of his or her real condition. None will let go of some tenaciously held falsehood in order to embrace truth that would set them free and make them solid and whole.

As Virgil the poet was Dante's guide, so George MacDonald, the man Lewis claimed was his unofficial teacher, is his guide. As Dante was deeply influenced by Virgil, so, too, Lewis owed a great debt to MacDonald, the Scottish Victorian novelist whose works Lewis said baptized his imagination. Lewis leans on MacDonald's arm in order to negotiate his way painfully across the piercing grass. The two encounter other ghosts challenged by the solid people who have come to greet them.

Lewis uses the dialogue between MacDonald and himself to state the core problem facing those in hell. MacDonald tells Lewis that "Heaven is reality itself. All that is fully real is Heavenly. For all that can be shaken will be shaken and only the unshakable remains."[21] Ultimate reality, as Lewis understands it, is spiritual, not spectral. Lewis's heavenly beings are more solid, more real than those who have traveled to heaven from hell. All who deny reality are, by that denial, diminished. Any truce with reality demands from the ghosts their full surrender. MacDonald draws on Milton's *Paradise Lost* to make his point. "'Milton was right,' said my Teacher. 'The choice of every lost soul can be expressed in the words, "Better to reign in Hell than serve in Heaven." There is always something they insist on keeping even at the price of misery. There is always something they prefer to joy—that is to reality.'"[22]

MacDonald says, "There are only two kinds of people in the end: those who say to God, 'Thy will be done,' and those to whom God says, in the end, 'Thy will be done.' All that are in Hell, choose it. Without that self-choice there would be no Hell."[23]

Many of these ideas appeared in *The Problem of Pain*, written earlier than *The Great Divorce*. There Lewis wrote, "I willingly believe that the damned are, in one sense, successful, rebels to the end; that the doors of hell are locked on the inside."[24] This idea is not new with Lewis. The story of Job gives a similar accounting. In Job 21:13-15 it says, "They spend their days contentedly, go down to the grave peacefully. They say to God, 'Turn away from us; we take no pleasure in knowing your ways; who is the Almighty that we should serve him, and what can we gain if we meet him?'"

Perhaps the gates of hell *are* locked from the inside. The foolishness of it is obvious. We reap what we sow. Sow barley, you will reap a crop of barley. Sow corn, you reap corn. If you sow wheat, you reap wheat. So, too, if you sow self, you will reap solitude, isolation, and estrangement. Lewis's depictions of the transforming imagination in *The Great Divorce* echo these comments in *The Problem of Pain*.

Lewis, writing in *The Problem of Pain*, says, "To enter Heaven is to become more human than you ever succeeded in being in earth; to enter hell is to be banished from humanity. What is cast (or casts itself) into hell is not a man: it is 'remains.'"[25] Nevertheless, all the ghosts have opportunity to let go of the thing they prefer over God. Selected examples show the transforming imagination in action.

The Foreman

The big foreman ghost epitomizes one form of the transforming imagination. This particular ghost is incensed that heaven has sent him one of his former employees, a man named Len. Len murdered one of their coworkers, Jack, who also is in heaven. Because of the murder, Len finally looked honestly at himself and repented. The foreman is angry. He feels he deserves better than having a murderer come to greet him. "I've got my rights," he says at least seven times. But he has an inflated sense of what he is entitled to. He keeps saying that he is a decent man. "I'm not asking for anybody's bleeding charity."[26] The foreman keeps saying he was a decent man. But Len must tell him, "It isn't exactly true, you know.... You weren't a decent man and you didn't do your best. We none of us were and we none of us did."[27] The ghost refuses to believe he wasn't the kind of man he thought he was. Len tells him that none of his men liked him or respected him. He adds, "I was the worst. But all the men who worked under you felt the same. You made it hard for us you know. And you made it hard for your wife too and for your children."[28]

This is a moment of disequilibrium for the foreman. He can accept the truth in the very context where love and forgiveness are available, or he can continue with the rationalized sense of self and think he is better than he actually is. Rather than look at the facts, the foreman is furious that a murderer has been sent to greet him. He feels he deserves better than that. He can see all that is wrong with others but cannot see the truth about himself. How often it is that, like this foreman, we can spot the injustices of others a mile away and miss the very incongruities abiding in our own hearts. We strain at gnats and swallow camels. So it is with this ghost. Ironically, he is diminished at the very moment he projects on the world his inflated sense of self.

Two things might clarify what Lewis is saying about the foreman's situation and ours. First, if we were honest, each of us must admit that none of us is gifted with the skills to thrive in life. Nobody is ever ready to get married. If we waited until we were, we would miss out on all the joys of marriage. Nobody is ever ready to have children. If we waited until we were, the human race would end with this generation. In truth, we are all awkward. A toddler learning to walk falls down and gets bruised. A five-year-old taking the training wheels off the two-wheeler for the first time falls down and gets a scraped knee. The adolescent trying to skateboard for the first time breaks a wrist or sprains an ankle. That first day in middle school, when we left the security of a single teacher in a single-room class, to enter the world of six teachers and six classrooms, and a five-minute passing period where we had to stop off at a locker that never seemed to work while bumping along through the corridors with a gazillion other people, revealed how truly awkward we are.

Every new experience in life reveals in fresh ways our awkwardness. If we are not awkward somewhere in our life, we are not growing. This awkwardness reveals our lack of life skill, or our propensity to make mistakes. We can fall into the unfortunate habit of making excuses for our mistakes. Of course, this increases the likelihood of our repeating them and perhaps blaming others for them. Pretty soon these mistakes do not qualify any longer as mere awkwardness. The excuses and rationalizations and justifications have nearly led to moral blindness. It is only *nearly*, however, because if someone else does something inappropriate to us, we can spot it a mile away. In that moment when we are upset at others, we show that we are condemned and without excuse. We all face various circumstances all of our lives, and, like the foreman ghost, they can lead to a rationalized, inflated sense of self, causing us to forget that we all need the "bleeding charity."

The second thing that might clarify the foreman's condition and ours may be seen in the following account. Years ago Jerry was asked to deliver a sermon. Church leaders asked him to answer a question asked by a member of that congregation: Would a tyrant who committed egregious acts of genocide and cruelty still go to heaven if he repented in his heart in his last conscious moment?

This wasn't an easy question for Jerry to answer. He wrestled with it for a couple of weeks. He didn't want to be flippant about such a freighted question. And he certainly prayed about it. Then an approach for addressing the question finally came. He began the message by recounting the question and saying as he attempted an answer that he wanted to give a short answer, then follow it up with a question, and then give a long answer. For his short answer he said, "Yes, if an evil, despicable, mass murderer repented in his last breath, regardless of his crimes against humanity, he would go straight to heaven after his death." Then he asked those in attendance,

> How does this make you feel? If you find yourself getting angry at the prospect of an evil person getting into heaven just by an act of confession of sins in his last breath, then you are still operating with some form of works righteousness. You still believe, at some level, that heaven is a reward for your good works and that someone who has not done what you have done should not get what you deserve.

At some level, we find ourselves belonging with this foreman ghost, who must have his rights.

As for the long answer, Jerry spoke of the grace of God that is available to all—not on the basis of our works or earned merits. This ghost says he is not asking for any bleeding charity. Len, the solid person who came from heaven to greet him, interjects immediately, "Ask for the bleeding charity. Everything is here for the asking and nothing can be bought."[29]

With Lewis, there is no equivocation. Nobody gets into heaven unless he or she surrenders and receives what cannot be earned but is freely given. What would ever keep an honest person from acknowledging that he or she is messed up and in desperate need of grace? It is either ignorance or an inflated sense of self, one that fails to see our true need.

This foreman ghost is a tragic figure. As he goes back to the bus and seeks to return to hell, he says to Len, "I'd rather be damned than go along with you. I came here to get my rights see."[30] Years ago someone once said to Jerry after a very nice thing occurred, "Jerry, you deserved that!" Jerry said, immediately, "Please pray I never get what I deserve; I desperately want mercy and grace instead." The foreman ghost failed to enter into the mercy because he projected onto himself the very false notion that he was just fine without it.

The Apostate Priest

Another ghost whose way is characterized by the transforming imagination is a cultured apostate priest. Clearly he was willing to give up his principles but not willing to give up his living. We see in this the pretense of his life. His theology is thin. He covers his lack of belief by means of new definitions and an inflated sense of his vacuous spirituality. He cannot see that he is in hell and calls it instead "that grey town with its continual hope of morning." As he has rationalized hell, so, too, his whole life is one great rationalization. He cannot admit, even in the face of the consequences of his choices, that he might have been wrong. He has come to rationalize the existence of heaven or hell and therefore lives in complete denial of any accounting for his life.

He is greeted by a fellow priest, a man named Dick. The two of them drifted substantially from orthodoxy during their lives on earth. But Dick regretted his apostasies and repented of them. The ghostly priest, employing the transforming imagination, makes excuses for his. He projects that what he did, as he drifted, was the courageous thing to do. He asks Dick, "Do you really think people are penalized for their honest opinions?"[31] Rightly Dick asks, "It all turns on what are honest opinions."[32] Implied is that the ghost's opinions were not honest. The pretense is becoming thick as the ghost is thinning. He says, "I took every risk."[33]

But Dick suggests he moved to apostasy and controversy to sell his books, to gain invitations to speak at various gatherings, and to gain the notoriety that would win him a bishopric. His convictions were rooted in inflated self-promotion. Dick challenges the ghost's notions of himself by saying, "Our opinions were not honestly come by."[34] These men denied the supernatural; they didn't want it to be true. They drifted gradually until they no longer believed. Lewis is communicating to his audience that such rationalizations of faith may lead to spiritual blindness. So it is with this priest. He prides himself on the questions but seems to have lost interest in finding the answers. He appears to enjoy his own self-referentialism over any form of true faith.

The solid person, Dick, says to the ghost, "Once you were a child...there was a time when you asked questions because you wanted answers...become that child again."[35] He has lost all interest in true questions, and certainly in true answers. The transforming imagination tends not to ask genuine questions, because truly honest answers may be less predictable. They may take us where we do not want to go.

Years ago, a father of one of Jerry's students asked, "Jerry, how is your soul?" Jerry says, "I like that question; it gets down deep quickly. We had the kind of friendship where the question was fully appropriate. I took stock and surveyed my life for a moment. Then I answered, 'I do not think I have had more questions about my faith than I do right now.' He seemed puzzled and a look came across his face as if to suggest he was thinking, 'I do not want my son in any more of his classes.' So I added, 'Let me clarify. I have never felt more loved by God than I do right now. And, I've never felt more in love with God than I do right now. I feel like a child in a perfectly safe relationship who can ask any question he wants with the confidence that it is a safe environment to do so. I feel like a child who feels loved and knows he will not be treated poorly, a child who believes that for asking the question, solid answers will be coming. And, if the answers do not come immediately, he trusts the one with the answers to give them at the appropriate time.'"

What has become of a subculture for whom to ask questions of and to feel loved by God seem to be incompatibles? Our questions of God should be as natural to us as the perpetual questions asked by a child in a safe environment. Dick, the solid one, says to the apostate priest that he should seek to reenter that childlike place. Unfortunately, the ghost will have it his way and can no longer hear anything to the contrary. He has given up on all questions where he is not in charge. The apostasy turns tragic when the ghost decides he must return to hell to read a paper to the theological society there.[36]

The Nagging Wife

Another encounter occurs between one of the solid people, named Hilda, and one of the ghosts. They are discussing the ghost's relationship with her husband, Robert. Hilda is hardly able to get in a word, for the ghost is continually talking. More accurately, she is continually justifying the way she nagged her husband all his life. Unaware of how she used him for her own ends, she rationalizes that it was all done for him: "It was all for his own good in the end."[37] Her interests were her own. She has grown blind to her selfishness and conniving. "I was doing it all for his sake," she explains, adding, "Every useful friend he ever made was one to me."[38] Even her understanding of friendship is defined by its usefulness. She used her husband; she used the people she selected to be his friends. In the end, this woman acknowledges that she is miserable in Hell; she has no one to control there. "I'm so miserable. I must have someone to—to do things to."[39] She cannot say to do things with. *Withness* is not a concept she can understand. It would require respect for the wishes of others, sensitivity to their needs and not merely her own. She wants someone to do things *to*.

Here again is the transforming imagination. It is all projection. The devaluation of another's personhood always comes with the high price of the loss of one's own humanity. The situation is tragic. And yet even here Lewis sees how laughable it is, in its way. He has the woman tell Hilda that she felt it was her duty to force her husband to get exercise, so she bought a Great Dane.[40] It gets worse. She continues by telling Hilda, "It's simply frightful down there. No one minds about me at all."[41] She is reaping what she has sown. The exaltation of herself over others has left her abandoned, isolated, and alone. In the end, she demands her husband, Robert, saying, "Put me in charge of him."[42]

The Controlling Mother

To match the nagging wife, Lewis looks at the transforming imagination from another angle. The reader encounters the ghost who was Michael's mother.

Lewis's character in the book describes it this way: "One of the most painful meetings we witnessed was between a woman's ghost and a bright spirit who had apparently been her brother."[43] The mother is incensed that her son did not come himself to greet her. She is told that currently she is not substantive enough to see her son. Some thickening needs to occur first. The mother, Pam, wonders what is expected of her.[44] She is told she will never be able to see Michael until she wants something else more than she wants him.[45]

Pam's inflated sense of self has led her to believe that she truly wants Michael's welfare. But she does not truly want Michael's good at all. She only wants what having Michael does for her. She has no real interest in Michael's welfare. She is told if she really wants Michael she must begin by wanting God. The angel clarifies, "It's only the little germ of a desire for God that we need to start the process."[46] It is too much. She begins demanding, on her terms, "I want my boy, and I mean to have him. He is mine, do you understand? Mine, mine, mine, for ever and ever."[47] She would rather have her son with her in hell than have him be happy in heaven. It is a ghastly picture of what self-referentialism can do and how destructive self-interest mediated through the transforming imagination can be. In *The Problem of Pain*, Lewis writes words that could easily sum up the themes of *The Great Divorce*: "The characteristic of lost souls is 'their rejection of everything that is not simply themselves.'"[48]

The Dwarf and the Tragedian

A majestic and glorious lady comes out of heaven with her entourage. Her name is Sarah Smith of Golders Green. Unheard of on Earth, her faithfulness is justly rewarded in heaven. "Every beast and bird that came near her had its place in her love. In her they became themselves. And now the abundance of life she has in Christ from the Father flows over into them."[49] Sarah Smith passes on the life of Christ to all she meets but one, her husband. Lewis describes Sarah as she approaches what looks like a giant tragedian actor attached by chain to a dwarf ghost. At first, Lewis thinks the actor is holding onto the chain. But closer observation reveals it is the dwarf who holds the actor on the leash. The actor is the pretense behind which the dwarf hides.

To Lewis's surprise, he discovers that Frank, the dwarf, was once, on Earth, Sarah Smith's husband. She appeals to him to let go of his false notions of self. At each denial of reality, Frank shrivels and the actor enlarges. Soon, the masculine singular pronoun *he* is no longer used for Frank; he has become an *it*. At last, he lacks even the minimal substance necessary to keep the chain from flopping about at the side of the pretense.

Remember Napoleon, two million miles out from the center of hell. At this moment it becomes clear. The size of hell is infinitesimally small. Its inhabitants are shrinking at such a rate it is merely their diminutive stature that makes the distances in hell seem so great. MacDonald observes, "All Hell is smaller than one pebble of your earthly world: but it is smaller than one atom of this world, the Real World."[50] The transforming imagination, as Lewis describes it, and then depicts it in *The Great Divorce*, is little more than a pretense. While the pretense may loom larger than life, all the while, the one doing the projection becomes diminished by his incapacity to connect with the world as it is, rather than how he would have it.

Chapter 11

The Grey Town

Controlled Imagination in *The Screwtape Letters*

Projecting one's self-seeking desires onto others is the primary component of the controlled imagination. This differs from the transforming imagination described in chapter 10, which attempts to change the world in order to accommodate it to the self. The controlled imagination seeks to project self in order to gain ascendancy over the world, and even more, to devour it. It is a negative type of imagination caught up in wish-fulfillment that places the self at the center of life. It can be either knowingly or blindly manipulative. It projects its self-serving wishes and personal interests onto the thing imagined. By means of the abuse of the imagination, it attempts to use others for its own ends. Lewis says that even one's beliefs of heaven and hell can be so affected. He writes of the controlled imagination either explicitly or implicitly in many of his books, but he embodies it most dramatically in *The Screwtape Letters*.

Free and Servile Activities of the Imagination

In *Reflections on the Psalms*, Lewis gives an example of the controlled imagination when writing about heaven. If we use heaven as mere compensation for bereavement, he writes, or simply as "a sequel to life's sad story," this can become self-serving. In this scenario, heaven does not exist for the glory of God but rather for human comfort. The controlled imagination turns it into a utilitarian fantasy by avoiding reality. It attempts to manufacture an imaginary world onto which we project our desires.

This abuse of the imagination, Lewis suggests, no longer sees heaven as the kingdom of God, the very sovereign to whom all owe their due. Rather, heaven is nothing more than a just compensation for our cleverness. It is little more than

God's obligation to us. It is the carrot at the end of the stick that keeps the donkey moving forward. As soon as this belief in heaven becomes compensation for something apart from God, we are using the controlled imagination, and deep down, we know it is our own imagination and not reality.[1] Those who interpret divine things in this way can quickly use the promise of divine, or diabolical, things to manipulate others. Delusion breeds delusion.

As for hell, Lewis describes how older divines would use the fear of hell to influence and frequently manipulate their hearers. He believed that sometimes these men, with their hell-fire sermons, could act out of their own self-centeredness. What was masked as prudence led to terror. Those manipulated would, in the end, be unlikely to have permanently changed behavior. Lacking intrinsic motivation, their conduct was extrinsically coaxed and coerced. The controlled imagination here is mere projection: the eclipsing of reality in order to achieve the wants of the imaginer.

Lewis writes of children who read fairy tales and school stories. Both arouse longings, the one to visit fairyland, the other to be the popular boy or girl. However, the second longing is different in a negative sense. Lewis says it is deadly serious: "Its fulfillment on the level of imagination is in very truth compensatory: we run to it from the disappointments and humiliations of the real world: it sends us back to the real world undivinely discontented. For it is all flattery to the ego. The pleasure consists in picturing oneself the object of admiration."[2] In the fairy tale, the reader takes pleasure in the desire the story creates. The difference is that the mere wish-fulfillment or realistic story focuses the mind on the self, while the fairy tale does not.

Lewis elaborates on this theme by describing two activities of the imagination, as outlined in *Selected Literary Essays*. These activities are called the free and the servile. Lewis describes them, respectively, as the daydream from which the self is absent, and the wish-fulfillment dream that sees the self as the great success and the center of attention. He provides some examples of his own free imagination: his imaginary village of mice called Snug Town, the unknown room in a house that he was always waiting to discover, a garden that existed partly in the west and partly in the past. The main point is that these imaginings are loved for themselves, not for how they can contribute to dreams of self-aggrandizement. The free activity also desires joy for all by seeking after God and his kingdom first. This kingdom utilizes the imagination in a way that embraces a larger world. Lewis saw that even a work of satire such as *The Screwtape Letters* could help open one's eyes to see more clearly the foibles of self-centeredness.

On the other hand, examples of the servile imagination flow out of the common daydreams we all have of being wealthy, powerful, beautiful, or famous. They revolve around us as the center of a throng of admirers, or around how people would behave toward us if we were suddenly wealthy beyond measure. The servility of the servile imagination is not to the object (as an artist to his muse). It is all projection. The things imagined are servile to the lusts of the imaginer. It is self-referential and utilitarian.

We all have both types of daydreams. Both can be the starting point for works of imagination or art, but each takes a different approach. The free imagination begins with a dream or the imagining of the artist and moves to what Lewis calls "elaboration." Here the artist seeks to improve the work of art by removing or replacing those portions that were self-seeking—in a sense, "cleaning up" the work and bringing it closer to the clarity of reality.

The servile work is not elaborated at all. Sensitivity to the work is sacrificed to the mere wish-fulfillment of the artist. In this case, the artist uses the servile daydream or imagination to get the work going, and then removes it when it is complete, as scaffolding is removed from a completed building. The products of the free imagination, says Lewis, are typically the fantastic, mythical, or improbable type of literature; those of the servile, the realistic type of literature.[3] Lewis also states elsewhere that the one type of activity is an *askesis*, a spiritual exercise, and the other a disease.[4]

The servile activity feeds directly into the generous imagination, fueling it with images and wish-fulfillment dreams that keep us locked within a fantasy world. Whenever self-aggrandizement is at the center of our thoughts and reality is sacrificed to lustful desires, we are perhaps closest to existing in hell. To understand this more clearly, we shall first have to examine the philosophy of hell.

George MacDonald's Vision of Hell

George MacDonald, who profoundly influenced Lewis, expresses the servile and diseased outlooks as characteristic of his vision of hell. In *Unspoken Sermons* he writes,

> For the one principle of hell is—"I am my own. I am my own king and my own subject. *I* am the centre from which go out my thoughts; *I* am the object and end of my thoughts; back upon *me* as the alpha and omega of life, my thoughts return. My own glory is, and ought to be, my chief care; my ambition, to gather the regards of men to the one centre, myself. My pleasure is *my* pleasure. My kingdom is—as many as I can bring to acknowledge my greatness over them. My judgment is the faultless rule of things. My right is—what I desire. The more I am all in all to myself, the greater I am. The less I acknowledge debt or obligation to another; the more I close my eyes to the fact that I did not make myself; the more self-sufficing I feel or imagine myself—the greater I am. I will

be free with the freedom that consists in doing whatever I am inclined to do, from whatever quarter may come the inclination. To do my own will so long as I feel anything to be my will, is to be free, is to live. To all these principles of hell, or of this world—they are the same thing, and it matters nothing whether they are asserted or defended so long as they are acted upon—the Lord, the king, gives the direct lie."[5]

This is a description of the extreme self-referential person who exists only to gratify his or her own desires at the expense of all others. As described here, hell is the curvature of the self back upon the self. The natural outcome of such thinking is what is seen in Lewis's *The Great Divorce*. In hell (the grey town as it is described in the story), people don't live clustered together in neighborhoods. They quarrel and then move farther and farther away, quarreling each time with new neighbors. Eventually, they have moved so far away that they are separated by light years from their nearest neighbors. The goal is total isolation, so one may focus entirely on self.

MacDonald hints that what unifies all of these statements about the self in hell are simply and only that selfish desires are acted upon. There is no thinking included in his definition of hell. It is all action and no introspection. Intellect does not exist in hell; it is merely activity—to do what I please when I please to do it, regardless of the outcome. There is no sense that any other self exists. All that matters is that we are the center of the universe. Thus, Napoleon, as described in chapter 10 has achieved what he desired. He has moved so far away and is so isolated from any other person that he does indeed exist as the center of a universe. And at that center is a little man pacing a room for all eternity...doing what? Not using his intellect for self-examination, but caught in a fantasy of being wronged where all he can do is blame others, projecting onto them all the reasons why things went wrong. The servile activity of his imagination is functioning in full force. The controlled imagination has entrapped him forever.

Charn and the Shoddy Lands

Let's look at two other examples of the controlled imagination. In Lewis's *The Magician's Nephew*, two children, Digory and Polly, are coerced into traveling to other worlds by means of magic rings made by Digory's misguided and avaricious Uncle Andrew. They arrive in an empty city called Charn. Through a series of strange events, they wake a sleeping queen named Jadis who tells them the story of the destruction of Charn.

Charn was a thriving city once, at a time when magic was still abroad in the world. Jadis's sister sat upon the throne, but jealousy awoke in Jadis and she demanded the queenship. Her sister refused, and so they made war on each other until at last every one of Jadis's soldiers had been killed. Now Jadis had learned by magical arts the power of the Deplorable Word. All the kings of old had bound with oaths all subjects in the kingdom never to seek—let alone ever speak—this word. For it gave to the one who spoke it the power to preserve one's own life at the cost of the destruction of all other life. Despite all warnings, Jadis, at great expense to herself, discovered the Deplorable Word and used it to destroy all living creatures in her world when it was clear she would otherwise be defeated.

Digory questions her indignantly about how she could kill the ordinary people who never did her any harm. With great arrogance she proclaims, "I was the Queen. They were all *my* people. What else were they there for but to do my will?"[6] Here is almost an exact echo of MacDonald's statement: "My own glory is, and ought to be, my chief care; my ambition, to gather the regards of men to the one centre, myself. My pleasure is my pleasure. My kingdom is—as many as I can bring to acknowledge my greatness over them. My right is—what I desire." This is the very philosophy of hell we will see in *The Screwtape Letters*. Jadis has used the controlled imagination to believe a reality that only her own wishes matter, and therefore she rationalizes the sacrifice of innocent lives to maintain her self-referential fantasy.

A second example is found in Lewis's short story, "The Shoddy Lands." Lewis, as narrator, is in his rooms at Oxford. One of his former pupils drops by for a visit, accompanied by his fiancée, Peggy. While they are chatting, the narrator has a strange experience. For a brief time, he is let into the girl's mind and can see the world as it exists for her. This world is a very dull and shapeless one, in which everything seems blurred and indistinct, prompting the narrator to apply the term *shoddy* to all he sees. However, he finds that certain realities are astonishingly clear: particular cut flowers, women's clothes in shop windows, men's faces, jewelry in stores, and so forth.

But everything else—trees, grass, and people—are blurry. Then he encounters the girl herself, lying on a beach, larger than life, and completely in focus. Lewis describes the scene this way: "At the centre of that world is a swollen image of herself, remodeled to be as like the girls in the advertisements as possible. Round this are grouped clear and distinct images of the things she really cares about. Beyond that, the whole earth and sky are a vague blur."[7]

Peggy essentially lives in MacDonald's hell, and she exists as the most real thing in that place, which has become her world. She retreats from reality around her as those in Lewis's grey town retreat to astronomical distances to avoid others. She has used the servile activity of the imagination to become the heroine of her daydreams. As Lewis describes, the products of the servile activity of the imagination are prosaic and seemingly realistic. The girl projects on life and the world only what she wants it to be and do for her. Clothes and jewelry simply function to attract the eyes of men and to fuel Peggy's idolatry. Even the desire, subjugated by self-worship, to be attractive to men has ceased to possess any value. And it is Peggy's idolatry of herself that is the only fully clear thing in the Shoddy Lands. She is Screwtape in another guise.

The Diabolical Canvas: Controlled Imagination in *The Screwtape Letters*

The Screwtape Letters is a collection of fictitious letters written by one devil, the Abysmal Sublimity Under Secretary Screwtape, to his nephew, a junior tempter named Wormwood. Screwtape is advising Wormwood how to tempt a human soul to a secure place in hell. The unsuspecting human psyche is the very canvas across which Screwtape paints his manipulative machinations using the controlled imagination as his *modus operandi*.

Throughout this work of satire, Lewis develops his most sophisticated expression of the controlled imagination. We can think of the devils as artists, the human soul as the canvas on which they create their work of art, and the temptations and manipulations of the devils as the tools or materials used. It should also be noted that God, not only the devils, is working on this canvas of the human soul to bring it into right relationship with himself. And it is within this tension that the devils seek to coax their subject by using the controlled imagination. Its goal is to take captive the soul of another so that its own designs might be accomplished. Remember that the servile imagination sacrifices all sensitivity to the work of art to the mere wish-fulfillment of the artist. And in the case of Screwtape this work is a heinous one. Of course, Screwtape in his devilry is a far cry from how the average reader would see himself or herself. Still, Lewis writes in such a way that honest readers catch a glimpse of themselves reflected in this mirror of both scorn and pity.

To understand this depiction of the controlled imagination on the diabolical level, we need to understand something of the philosophy of hell as embodied by Screwtape and Wormwood. This philosophy serves as the motive force behind their work as nefarious artists. According to Lewis's vision, devils require and feed on human misery, despair, and horror. They thrive on the distillation of fear as if it were a fine wine. Their goal is to lead the human soul into making choices that lead to eternal damnation. This outcome enables them to feast eternally on another soul's misery. The book depicts the domination of one will by another.

In one letter to his nephew, explaining how humans inhabit time and how this affects their constancy, Screwtape writes, "To us a human is primarily food;

our aim is the absorption of its will into ours, the increase of our own area of selfhood at its expense."[8] He goes on to elaborate the differences between what God wants and what devils want. "We want cattle who can finally become food; he wants servants who can finally become sons. We want to suck in; He wants to give out. We are empty and would be filled; He is full and flows over. Our war aim is a world in which Our Father Below has drawn all other beings into himself: the enemy wants a world full of beings united to Him but still distinct."[9]

In the preface to *The Screwtape Letters*, Lewis described his understanding of devils:

> I feign that devils can, in a spiritual sense, eat one another; and us. Even in human life we have seen the passion to dominate, almost to digest, one's fellow; to make his whole intellectual and emotional life merely an extension of one's own—to hate one's hatreds and resent one's grievances and indulge one's egoism through him as well as through oneself. His own little store of passion must of course be suppressed to make room for ours. If he resists this suppression he is being very selfish. On Earth this desire is often called "love." In hell I feign that they recognize it as hunger. But there the hunger is more ravenous, and a fuller satisfaction is possible.[10]

If we are honest, we have all experienced this desire to "digest" someone else, to make his or her life merely an extension of ours. This can be observed in the hero worship of sports figures and celebrities who dictate to their admirers how to look and behave. We find it in our desire to be like certain people we admire, to take on their traits, develop their sensibilities, see the world with their eyes. This desire extends beyond simply increasing our own vision of the world as the result of another's vision, which in itself is good. It comes at the expense of true selfhood. As Lewis states, God desires that we should all be united to God but still be distinct from one another. The absorption of one self by another, however, does not increase selfhood but dramatically decreases it. And this absorption is a result of employing the controlled imagination. By giving up our true selves, we end up living in a fantasy.

In another letter to his nephew, this time on sexual temptation, Screwtape enumerates eight principles of the philosophy of hell. This list is quite similar to MacDonald's view. It also reflects the idea of the absorbing of others just discussed.

1. One thing is not another thing

2. One self is not another self

3. My good is my good

4. Your good is my good

5. What one gains another loses

6. A self either thrusts other objects aside or absorbs them

7. Absorption is the sucking of will and freedom out of a weaker self into a stronger

8. "To be" means "to be in competition"[11]

If we could distill these principles of hell to just one concept, as seen in *The Screwtape Letters*, it would be Macdonald's "I am my own." Now the controlled imagination is projecting onto reality whatever it needs to satisfy its own self-referential desires. Thus Screwtape and his nephew are acting in perfect accordance with their philosophy as they maneuver the human soul to also begin adopting this same philosophy. As long as it resists, they cannot be fulfilled. The more the soul becomes like them, however, the more they can absorb it into their own nature. And this philosophy is also operative in hell itself, even between nephew and uncle. Self-aggrandizement is the ultimate will of each, and the absorption of the nephew by the uncle can be seen easily as the book progresses.

Despite all his work to win this assigned soul for hell, a mistake-prone Wormwood continues to slowly lose this soul to the "enemy" (the devils' name for God). In the final letter to his nephew, we learn that Wormwood has truly "lost" his charge. Screwtape, beside himself with rage, closes this letter with the ominous and telling lines, "Meanwhile, I have you to settle with. Most truly do I sign myself your increasingly and ravenously affectionate uncle, Screwtape." Here again we see the eager desire for that absorption, which is part of the philosophy of hell. The controlled imagination is depicted as one that manipulates for its own utilitarian interests.

Another characteristic of Lewis's hell as described in *The Screwtape Letters* is its false ideal of the real. Lewis understands that the servile (or wish-fulfilling) activity of the imagination produces what appears to be real. Its literature and art approximate real life; it is self-centered and makes one out to be the hero of the imagined world. And indeed, this is true of Screwtape. Speaking of the philosophy of hell, Screwtape says, "All that sustains me is the conviction that our Realism, our rejection (in the face of all temptations) of all silly nonsense and claptrap, *must* win in the end."[12] The wish-fulfillment or servile activity of the imagination arises out of our own very realistic desires for wealth, status, or renown. We reject anything that doesn't fall easily into definable and unambiguous lines because it is difficult to control; therefore, the characteristic products of this activity will be realistic. The servile activity seeks to put all things into its own kingdom. And because this self-centered world approximates the tangible and potentially accessible world, it looks real. But, in truth, it is a charade.

The controlled imagination pursues the absorption of others as well as the "treasures" that Jesus says are corruptible by moth and rust and are stolen by thieves. A large part of Christ's teachings calls for counterintuitive thinking and action. The logic of heaven seeks to give life, not devour it. It gives to receive, dies to live, loves when unloved, and forgives when wronged. Screwtape knows nothing of this. Hence, we understand the devils' revulsion of "the enemy's" manner of securing souls. It simply doesn't fit into a philosophy that begins and ends with self. Therefore, the controlled imagination centered in this way is not free. It is imprisoned and attempts to imprison others.

Returning to the analogy of the artist, Lewis reveals that it is the goal of devils to create out of the human a canvas on which they can project all the desires of hell. But their work is not creative. They are to creativity and originality what the first case of leprosy was to smooth and healthy skin, the first appearance of bitter water was to a fresh spring, or what the first murder was to a whole and active life. The controlled imagination will not be satisfied until it can project on all others its hellish desire. The devils are utilizing Lewis's servile activity of the controlled imagination to subject their dreams to their lusts and desires, thus producing a characteristically realistic work of diabolical "art" that destroys the soul. They are using the controlled imagination to sustain the grand lie that exists as the very philosophy of hell. They do this through manipulation of the human soul and by twisting perfectly good impulses, thoughts, and actions to self-serving ends.

Most of *The Screwtape Letters* is not about how the devils get the human soul to do evil things. It is about how they get the soul to do good things in a twisted way. It is especially about how they keep the soul from ever thinking about or suspecting its own motives. We call it "nobbling the mind," and keeping it in the dark about what is really happening. And, really, the devils are attempting to inculcate the controlled imagination in the mind of this soul. Not only does the devil manipulate, but the adversary seeks to reproduce manipulators who do not suspect to what depths they are falling. When we refuse to examine our own motives and desires, we exist essentially in the dark because we have chosen to accept blindness over reality. If we continue, we become victims of the controlled imagination, which requires us to believe the lie that we are somehow the center of the universe. And let us not get this pseudoreality in any way connected with the real world. The controlled imagination conceives of itself as genuine and logical but rejects everything that counts against its refined rationalizations.

In order to maintain this blindness and lack of self-examination, Screwtape and Wormwood must carefully craft a battle strategy, one so insidious that we do not recognize when we have fallen prey to it. We must now gain intelligence of this strategy.

Battle Tactics of Screwtape

Reading every chapter of *The Screwtape Letters* with a tactical eye, we see a pattern begin to emerge. Each chapter contains a specific formula by which the devils plan to produce the controlled imagination in the humans. For example, the first several chapters deal with tactics to keep reason and logic from awakening, to prevent growth by reinforcing old habits, to create a devotional mood that keeps one from real prayer, to make the world an end and faith a means, and so on. These tactics comprise four general, overarching strategies: *diversion, inflation, substitution,* and *inversion.*

> **Diversion:** Seeks to divert the attention from what must or needs to be examined in order to grow, to something external. For example, it keeps a man or woman from living in the present or eternity by fixing his or her eyes on the future or makes petitionary prayer seem absurd and ineffective.

> **Inflation:** Inflates the importance of one thing over another. For example, using a person's sexuality to his or her own undoing or reinforcing the thought that Christianity is an inner ring (a clique of self-serving interests) and all who don't belong to it are really quite silly.

> **Substitution:** Attempts to substitute one thing for another in order to denigrate it. Examples include substituting fashion for faith in order to stultify faith or corrupting spirituality by focusing attention on the historical Jesus rather than the real Jesus.

> **Inversion:** Takes seemingly paradoxical elements of life and flips them. Thus, this strategy would cultivate a self-conscious unselfishness or produce gluttony of delicacy rather than of excess.

These four main strategies and ultimately all of the tactics used to achieve them work toward one end for the devils: keeping humans from ever giving any thought to what they are thinking or doing, and encouraging reaction rather than introspection. It is total blindness. Lewis outlines the ultimate goals of the devils in another letter of Screwtape to his nephew.

> Think of your man as a series of concentric circles, his will being the innermost, his intellect coming next, and finally his fantasy. You can hardly hope, at once,

to exclude from all the circles everything that smells of the Enemy: but you must keep on shoving all the virtues outward till they are finally located in the circle of fantasy, and all the desirable qualities inward into the Will. It is only in so far as they reach the will and are there embodied in habits that the virtues are really fatal to us.[13]

This can perhaps be best represented pictorially in the following diagram:

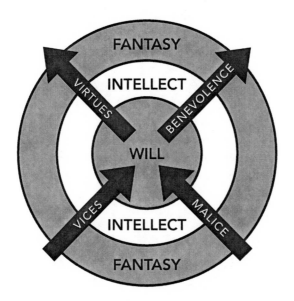

This is the intelligence of Screwtape's battle plan that we were seeking. It shows the human fully in the grip of the controlled imagination. Diversion, inflation, substitution, and inversion all keep one caught up in the self and the manipulation of the world for self-serving ends. Because we operate out of our wills, it is simple, as Lewis writes, for our benevolence to operate in the realms of fantasy. For example, we may feel benevolent toward the poor in a foreign country suffering an economic depression. But they are also removed from us. Therefore, projection is operative because we are engaging in "benevolence" toward objects that really are only being used to inflate a sense of self-righteousness or self-satisfaction.

But it is another story to feel benevolence for the people one knows, one's family and neighbors and friends who are right at hand, whose faults we know all too well and who often irritate us. This is why it is simple for the devils to inflate the vices and push them into the will; they seem far more real than the benevolence we feel toward those who are distant and whom we do not know at all. But, again, it is a benevolence that operates in the realms of the imaginary. And of course what seems real will often seem right, though in reality, this is just another form of projection.

Thus our malice will seem like an appropriate response to those we know, but in reality it will simply be a self-centered excuse for not using benevolence in the realm where we are actually called to use it. Instead we will focus on how we are right and the other person is wrong and how he or she must change. In both instances we are maintaining a delusion with the controlled imagination. We have moved to another neighborhood in the grey town because we have quarreled with our neighbor. Lewis describes this process elsewhere and reverses it by suggesting that we must see ourselves the way that we see others. If some trait in my neighbor irritates me, I can be sure there is some trait in myself that irritates my neighbor.

Lewis's devils want to make sure that the virtues bypass the circle of intellect altogether. Their goal is to keep the human from ever engaging the reason to question his thoughts and behavior. This avoidance allows the controlled imagination to flourish.

Moving Away from the Grey Town: The Diminishing of the Controlled Imagination

If the great and diabolical goal of the evil one is to keep the mind diverted by all manner of tactics, we have an insight into how we can respond to the controlled imagination. We must simply engage the intellect at all levels of life, to question why we behave a certain way or think within a certain paradigm. This necessary questioning would turn our gaze inward, not that we might be the center of the universe but that we might see and remove what keeps us from stepping off the throne. Because, paradoxically, while the definition of hell is "I am my own," this philosophy does not require any self-examination. Insofar as we are thinking at all, we are thinking only about how we can utilize others for our own ends. In a sense, to be in hell is never to look too closely at oneself.

We must constantly be aware of the ways in which our virtues are pushed into the realms of the imaginary and how our vices are brought right into our wills. As Lewis states, the virtues are most fatal to diabolical influence once they are embodied as habits in the will. Lewis shows us that the true will is not what we often mistake it for, "the conscious fume and fret of resolutions and clenched teeth,"[14] but what God would call the heart. Though we exert tremendous amounts of energy in the effort, we can never change another person. Lewis says we must work diligently to see ourselves as others see us and try never to think about their faults at all. Only there can we effect any change.

This unearths a major problem with the controlled imagination: it portrays a world too small and narrow. It is confined by its self-referentialism. In *A Grief Observed*, which Lewis wrote to process the death of his wife, Joy Davidman, he states, "All reality is iconoclastic. The earthly beloved, even in this life, incessantly triumphs over your mere idea of her. And you want her to; you want her with all her resistances, all her faults, all her unexpectedness. That is, in her foursquare and independent reality."[15] Lewis sees that our understanding of the world will need to be modified and nuanced lest it become projective and controlling.

This is also true in relation to one's ideas of God. Lewis declares, "My idea of God is not a divine idea. It has to be shattered time after time. He shatters it himself. He is the great iconoclast."[16] True reality is constantly breaking in on us in ways that we simply cannot expect, shattering the images and idols of the imagination. This reality offers a redemptive vision of the world as it really is rather than how one would imagine it. This is why it is so difficult to sustain the controlled imagination. It takes a great effort on our part to ignore reality and throw ourselves back into the pseudo-safety of our dreams or imaginings. Self-deception can have an air of deliberateness about it. It must force itself to deny reality.

Lewis portrays this idea of iconoclasm in *The Screwtape Letters* as well. Regardless of all their efforts, Screwtape and Wormwood lose the battle for the soul of the man. In their own delusion, they were unprepared for the ways reality constantly broke into the life of their subject, shattering their plans. They repeatedly adjusted their philosophy of hell in the hopes of crafting and creating tactics of diversion to enhance the controlled imagination. But reality itself was iconoclastic. These devils could not account for the ways of God. Their best efforts could not overpower the work of the great Iconoclast.

Another method of counterattack against the controlled imagination is Lewis's concept of the dialectic of desire. It enables us to engage in beneficial iconoclasm and prevents us from falling into idolatry. In speaking of his desire for joy and all the ways he had waited for it his whole life, he writes,

> All that such watching and waiting ever *could* find would be either an image (Asgard, the Western Garden, or what not) or a quiver in the diaphragm. I should never have to bother again about these images or sensations. I knew now that they were merely the mental track left by the passage of Joy—not the wave but the wave's imprint on the sand. The inherent dialectic of desire itself had

in a way already shown me this; for all images and sensations, if idolatrously mistaken for Joy itself, soon honestly confessed themselves inadequate. All said, in the last resort, "It is not I. I am only a reminder. Look! Look! What do I remind you of?"[17]

The dialectic of desire points us to the ultimate source of our longings—Christ, the ultimate reality—and enables us to see beyond all that we might be tempted to mistake for a pseudo-reality that does not point to God.[18] It allows us to avoid the denial of reality and self-deception that would entrap us in idolatry and fantasy and break our hearts. The idols can never be the longing itself; "they are only the scent of a flower we have not found, the echo of a tune we have not heard, news from a country we have never yet visited."[19]

Author Richard James writes, "He [Lewis] also affirmed that if this 'dialectic of desire' was followed to its end, it would in itself be a living ontological proof of God's existence."[20] Lewis explains that desire itself is the corrective for the longing to accept false objects or idols: "The dialectic of Desire, faithfully followed, would retrieve all mistakes, head you off from all false paths, and force you not to propound, but to live through, a sort of ontological proof."[21] The goal must be to see through the false idols that we pursue in searching for the object of our desires. We continue to do this until we arrive at the knowledge that the object of our longings is never fully given in this life. If we follow the dialectic of desire assiduously, we come to find the end to which all our desires point.

We invoke the dialectic of desire and thwart the abuses of the controlled imagination by cultivating the free activity of a healthy imagination. The free imagination allows itself the beneficial distraction of noticing the world, in all of its forms and expressions, as it is constantly breaking into the subconscious mind. This activity begins with something outside of self—as any good artist begins with a vision of something outside of self—and works with material independent of the self. The artist connects this vision of the outside world and these materials with his skill and craftsmanship to imaginatively embellish reality in a particular way that reveals its wider application. This embellishment unleashes an imaginative freedom that allows the materialization of what the artist imagined. It is inspired by fancy, freely at play with whatever was present to one's senses so that others might see and experience wonder.

To see the real and experience the true rekindles wonder. While any activity of the imagination can go wrong in a fallen and broken world, it is less likely to do so when the real story continues to break through all scrims of pretense. There is always another way to see things. The story of the world around us is told a multitude of times, yet is never fully told once. The controlled imagination balks at all that counts against its narrow, self-referential narrative. In the real world, one can always go deeper, and this encourages the perpetual awakening of wonder. As G. K. Chesterton rightly notes, "The world will never starve for want of wonders; but only for want of wonder."[22]

Chapter 12

Searching for the
Hidden Country

Absorbing Imagination in *Poems* and *Spirits in Bondage*

The absorbing imagination enlarges the self by establishing commonality of definition between multiple viewpoints or traditions and then synthesizing them to create a larger whole. Lewis cites seventeenth-century English poet John Milton as one whose imagination absorbed profoundly. Milton possessed a unique ability to combine disparate traditions in his work, particularly in *Paradise Lost*. For example, Lewis describes how Milton synthesized the old, medieval understanding of the universe as finite with the then new consciousness that it was infinite by hanging the cosmos in its own enclosed envelope from the floor of heaven. Outside of the envelope was infinity, the reality of outer space. In this ingenious way both realities could coexist.[1] Milton absorbed both understandings and then blended them.

The absorbing imagination also deflects the tendency to get stuck in our own particularity. The goal of absorbing various viewpoints and traditions is that we might enrich and widen our own imaginative landscapes. The absorbing imagination unifies imaginative or creative contributions from many sources that allow one to do one's own imaginative speculation. In this sense it is creative and expansive. It increases richness and understanding. It seeks to lead one on to fresh enjoyments and new modes of feeling and thinking as well as give one glimpses of the "hidden country" that we all seek. It ultimately reconciles reason and imagination by authenticating imagination as a source of truth. In both *Poems* and *Spirits in Bondage*, we will examine how Lewis imaginatively blends traditions to help extend our own vision.

Of Elephants and Blind Men: Looking Along the Beam

Establishing commonality of definition in order to absorb other viewpoints is the subject of a short essay by Lewis we've previously examined called "Meditation in a Toolshed." He states that there are two ways of looking at anything, "looking at" and "looking along." This means encountering a thing either from without or from within. From the outside, or "looking at," I can define pain as a certain type of neural activity. I have not thereby exhausted what pain means, because I have not "looked along" or experienced it. It is only in experiencing that I will have a fuller definition and common understanding of pain.[2] Similarly, we must begin our engagement of the absorbing imagination with commonality. We must be able to "look along" another's viewpoint; we must get right inside it and make that experience our own.

At this point we must differentiate between the absorbing imagination and the penetrating imagination. The two should not be confused. The penetrating imagination seeks to apprehend a thing more deeply by examining it from many angles (see chapter 6). On the other hand, the absorbing imagination takes differing points of view and then synthesizes them as an act of enlarging the self's own imaginative landscape. In short, it synthesizes dissimilar realities to enlarge one's own reality. This differs significantly from merely looking deeply from many angles into the reality of one thing.

We can quickly illustrate the basic ideas of the absorbing imagination by revisiting John Godfrey Saxe's amusing poem "The Blind Men and the Elephant." The poem describes how six blind men approached an elephant from six different angles. Thus, each developed his own definition of what an elephant was like. One grabbed the tail and thought it like a rope. Another grabbed the leg and thought it like a tree, and so on. None of them had the full picture, but each had a piece. If the poem had ended there, we would have a picture of the penetrating imagination. But the blind men's conflict was that each had a real, albeit limited, experience that discounted the experience of the others. Each man refused to believe that any other man's version of the elephant was correct. Each was trapped in his own particularity. How could they have resolved this? By empathizing with each other's views and absorbing them, they would have expanded their own world. In this way, each could have received a more complete understanding of the elephant. This willingness to empathize involves trust, and though others have imagined differently than we have, it doesn't mean they have imagined amiss.

The Harmony of Christian and Pagan: Absorbing Imagination in *Prince Caspian*

Lewis practiced the absorbing imagination on a large scale throughout the Chronicles of Narnia. We might even say that the Chronicles are themselves primarily a work of the absorbing imagination. Lewis, who loved all the old myths as well as the imaginative structure of the medieval worldview, freely blended pagan and Christian elements to create his own imaginative playground throughout the Chronicles. Though we could cite a host of examples from the books, this blending is perhaps most overtly evident in *Prince Caspian*.

In this tale, Aslan, who embodies the Christian element, is beginning the liberation of Narnia from the Telmarines, a people who have usurped the land from its true inhabitants. The narrative at this point is full of the rumor of the mythic and pagan past, imported into the midst of a Christian story; we are told of dryads, nymphs, naiads, and river gods. Or it might be more accurate to suggest that it is a pagan story into which a Christian element has been imported.

The Greco-Roman god Bacchus/Dionysius and his companion and tutor Silenus appear with their wild maenads in a retinue following Aslan and helping in the task of reclaiming Narnia from the usurping King Miraz. Bacchus and the Maenads arrive *because* Aslan allows them, not in spite of him. Though importing these pagan and Christian myths[3] into an imaginative world of his own creation, Lewis successfully synthesizes them by making each subservient to the other, all the while allowing them to fully function in their traditional roles.

We must not understand this synthesis as a synonym for syncretism, which compromises and thereby weakens a point of view. Rather, we should understand it as the bringing together of parts to form a more coherent whole. We don't get the feeling that the myths are out of place in this imaginative world, but that they are obedient to it, without losing their pagan or their Christian personality. In so doing, Lewis's Christianity is not becoming watered down but is increasing in richness. Though Lewis may intend other and deeper nuances of meaning, we will look at some of the more apparent nuances of the Bacchus myth to grasp his use of the absorbing imagination.

Bacchus, Silenus, and the maenads function as the source of joy, fun, and wild freedom that everyone experiences as the kingdom is reclaimed. This is a natural and normal response when a seemingly hopeless situation suddenly turns wildly hopeful. In Greek and Roman myth, Bacchus is traditionally the liberator, and his enchanted wine is what leads to romps and good times. And it is characteristic that his arrival is sudden and disorderly and full of living grapevines. But he also represents chaos, danger, and the unexpected, which prompts Lucy to say to Susan, "I wouldn't have felt safe with Bacchus and all his wild girls if we'd met them without Aslan," and Edmund to say, "There's a chap who might do anything—absolutely anything."[4]

In the pagan myth, the Maenads are the result of this cruel and unpredictable side of Bacchus. His wine enchants his female devotees into a frenzy of fierce ecstasy, wherein they are unstoppable and dangerous. Again, Lewis blends them into the narrative but makes them subservient to it while allowing them to possess all the characteristics that a Maenad would possess. Lewis seamlessly imports these pagan myths into his story because they are suitable as well as rich. Perhaps the most important function of importing any myth, Christian or otherwise, is that it brings a whole weight of historical connotation and richness to bear on the story. In this instance, it helps the reader to more fully imagine the joy and wild abandon that the characters must have experienced.

The fact that these myths function as a story within a story is significant. If Lewis had simply invented a character with a similar function to Bacchus, it wouldn't have the same impact as importing a character with an established history or reference. Not only are we getting the myth (with all its implications) mediated through our own understanding, we are getting the myth mediated through Lewis, who then transforms it into something new and fresh.

He has successfully absorbed and synthesized the pagan and Christian elements into an entirely new creative landscape that helps to broaden our own perspective as we see it through his eyes and absorb his vision. Not only does our understanding of the story deepen, but our understanding of the myths as well. Myths don't merely function as themselves, they also point to truths outside themselves. This was an important part of Tolkien's contribution to Lewis's understanding of myth.

The Delights of Paganism: The Blending or Fusing Imagination

The medieval and Elizabethan poets, whom Lewis revered, were masters of combining Christian and pagan elements in their work. He was captivated by the imaginative beauty of the medieval worldview, with all its complexity and intricacy and blending of traditions.[5] Author David Downing suggests that The Chronicles of Narnia include the amount of classical and medieval detail they do to enable the reader to experience the medieval vision of the world and the cosmos from within.[6] Lewis consistently wrote about the medieval worldview and its authors and artists because he found great pleasure in contemplating their model of the universe. So it would make sense that he would blend pagan and

Christian elements in The Chronicles to enable us to better grasp the richness of the medieval worldview.

Lewis gives us a beautiful vision of the world that, though false from a modern, scientific point of view, is still worth contemplating. This vision can expand our own vision by its sheer imaginative landscape and power to point to truths beyond it. Says Lewis, "I have made no serious effort to hide the fact that the old Model delights me as I believe it delighted our ancestors. Few constructions of the imagination seem to me to have combined splendour, sobriety, and coherence in the same degree." He adds, "The human imagination has seldom had before it an object so sublimely ordered as the medieval cosmos."[7]

These are strong statements about what Lewis feels to be imaginatively viable. He not only references this worldview constantly in his works, but also uses it as a springboard for creating his own imaginative worlds. If we are to value Lewis's use of the absorbing imagination, we must understand, value, and absorb, albeit with care, the medieval worldview. Lewis synthesizes these traditions to create what we might term "imaginative expansion" within his readers. If we value these traditions as Lewis does, then we will escape (to a certain extent) our own particularity and see what he sees and values. Consequently, we experience growth and expansion of the self.

In this sense, The Chronicles are a work of the absorbing imagination; indeed, they are doubly so. As the medieval scholastics blended traditions to create their own worldview, so Lewis blended traditions to create the Narnian world. It is a blended tradition within a blended tradition, just the sort of thing that would have delighted Lewis.

In attempting to set a precedent for his view that the Narnia books contain a great imaginative secret, author Michael Ward writes about Lewis's delight in *hiddenness* in his insightful book *Planet Narnia*. He speaks of Lewis's praise of the indirect approach to communication; of creating narratives or poems that suggest meanings rather than state them.[8] The Chronicles radiate this sense of hiddenness, as does Lewis's poetry. If Downing is correct, they are a work detailing the medieval worldview (itself a blended tradition), using multiple traditions that are themselves each self-contained stories prior to Lewis importing and blending them into the creation of his own story. This is like peeling an onion; every time you remove one layer, you discover another beneath it. But there is a richness of meaning in what is hidden.

In our attempt to define how and why Lewis used the absorbing imagination, we need to inspect this blending of Christian and pagan traditions, especially as he understood it. As discussed, commonality of definition between viewpoints or traditions is vital. It is the jumping-off point for practicing the absorbing imagination.

Lewis suggests that the pagans and Christians of the medieval age were not as unlike as we might suppose. He asserts that they were more like each other than either was like modern human beings. He elucidates four similarities: (1) Both were monotheists; (2) both believed in the existence of supernatural beings between God and humanity; (3) both were intellectual; and (4) both were superstitious.[9] The medieval scholastics had already absorbed both traditions. Now they used these similarities to blend the two into other imaginative narratives. According to Downing, Lewis believed paganism was the anticipation and Christianity the fulfillment. "[Lewis] associated paganism with myth and romance, and Christianity with the reality that myth and romance point to."[10] Lewis himself describes this in a letter to his childhood friend Arthur Greeves: "I think the thrill of Pagan stories and of romance may be due to the fact that they are mere beginnings—the first, faint whisper of the wind from beyond the world—while Christianity is the thing itself."[11]

As mentioned earlier, it was J. R. R. Tolkien who helped Lewis better understand myth. Though Tolkien strongly criticized Lewis for the "jumble of unrelated mythologies"[12] that he found and disliked in The Chronicles, he had something to say himself about this idea of a blending or fusing type of imagination in his essay "Beowulf: The Monsters and the Critics." He writes about the Beowulf author's ability to blend or fuse the Christian tradition with the pagan tradition, giving a Christian tint to the powers of darkness with which humans felt themselves to be surrounded, as represented by Grendel and the dragon.

Tolkien describes the imaginative milieu that was present before the writing of *Beowulf*. He depicts it as "the final defeat of the humane (and of the divine made in its image), and in the essential hostility of the gods and heroes on the one hand and the monsters on the other."[13] Now Tolkien describes how this pagan imagination intersected with the advent of Christianity and the scriptures to produce a change that made the old imagination seem dark and remote but also appealing. So at this critical juncture, the writer of *Beowulf* had available new faith and new learning as well as a whole body of native tradition with which to set his mind to work. He absorbed the Christian and pagan in order to enlarge his own vision and create the imaginative landscape that resulted in *Beowulf*.

Thistles and Donkey's Water: The Refusal of the Absorbing Imagination in *The Last Battle*

We can, however, resist the imaginative expansion that enlarges our vision. It is the way of the six blind men. What happens when we refuse to engage the absorbing imagination? Lewis's *The Last Battle* gives us great insight. In this tale, the ape, Shift, has convinced the creatures of Narnia that he is the mouthpiece of the lion Aslan, the Christ figure in the story. He has dressed the donkey, Puzzle, in a lion skin and kept him in a stable, only bringing him out occasionally for the creatures to see at a distance, so they might have proof that Aslan is indeed living in the stable and giving orders through Shift. Through this deception, Shift executes his selfish and destructive ends and controls the creatures of Narnia by using the fear of disobedience to Aslan's orders as an incentive. He also contracts a business deal with the Calormenes, a cruel people to whom Shift sells the inhabitants of Narnia into slavery.

Our example begins when the true king of Narnia, Tirian, in his quest to right these wrongs, stumbles on a number of dwarfs being led away to slavery in the mines of Calormen. After freeing them and showing them how they had been deceived by the donkey dressed in the lion's skin, Tirian expects the dwarfs to rejoice in their freedom. However, having been badly deceived once, the dwarfs refuse to be taken in again, even though this time they are being told the truth. They want no more of Aslan. "The Dwarfs for the dwarfs," they say.[14] They don't even believe that Tirian is the king, and they don't want kings anyway. Later, when the last battle of Narnia is being fought, they do not take sides but fight against both sides. And when we find them huddled in the stable at the end of the story, the stable that in reality is the door to Aslan's country, we understand more clearly where they fail to engage the absorbing imagination to expand their vision and see the reality around them.

In their determination not to be fooled again by anyone, the dwarfs become stuck in their own particularity; in the darkness of the stable, they cannot see the brightness of Aslan's country. And they are offered four different perspectives, four opportunities to see their surroundings through another's eyes. First, Queen Lucy (herself newly arrived in Aslan's country) attempts to convince them of the reality of the bright world by picking some violets and holding them under the dwarf Diggle's nose, but he mistakes it for stable litter and thistles. Second, King Tirian tries to pull a dwarf out of the stable, but the dwarf runs back as soon as he is set down, complaining that he has been thrown against the stable wall. Finally, Aslan twice attempts to show them with proofs of the existence of something real outside the stable. He growls, and then places a feast before them and fine wine in their hands, but they only think the noise of the growl is from some machine and that they are eating some rotten vegetables and drinking the donkey's water from the trough.

They rationalize every proof given to them with a conclusion based in their own particularity. They refuse to absorb the viewpoints of the others. Says Aslan to Lucy, "They have chosen cunning instead of belief. Their prison is only in their own minds, yet they are in that prison; and so afraid of being taken in that they cannot be taken out."[15] Elsewhere, Lewis reminds his readers that literature enormously enlarges the perspectives of those who read. Those who are not readers, who are content to be themselves, exist in what would be a prison too narrow for those who are readers. This principle applies to all of life; to expand our vision and our understanding of the world around us, we must engage the absorbing imagination. We must see the world, whenever possible by borrowing widely from the experiences of others. If we do not, we will inhabit a world of our own making. It will be no better than the world the dwarfs have chosen for themselves. Because they were trapped within their own minds, they could not see the wonderful country Aslan was calling them to, the country that we are all attempting to reach.

The Longing for the Hidden Country: *Poems* and *Spirits in Bondage*

Lewis's *Poems* and *Spirits in Bondage* are the perfect vehicles for examining how he engaged the absorbing imagination to great effect. Containing both pre- and postconversion poems, they wonderfully show Lewis's ability to combine traditions to help his readers taste rather than understand through imaginative expansion. We will limit our examination to several preconversion poems in *Spirits in Bondage*, and a number from the group in *Poems* that editor Walter Hooper has entitled "The Hidden Country."

Lewis was aware from an early age of the split or bifurcation between reason and imagination within himself and within the wider culture. "The two hemispheres of my mind were in the sharpest contrast," he writes. "On the one side a many-islanded sea of poetry and myth; on the other a glib and shallow 'rationalism.' Nearly all that I loved I believed to be imaginary; nearly all that I believed to be real I thought grim and meaningless."[16] Through our selection from *Poems*, an understanding of this contrast will emerge to give additional insight into Lewis's ability to manipulate the absorbing imagination. It will also enable us to see how bridging the gulf between reason and imagination is itself an act of the absorbing imagination. This bridging is vitally necessary in a culture that does not value imagination as a way of knowing and understanding truth.

This bifurcation is vividly apparent in Lewis's first collection of poetry, *Spirits in Bondage*. Lewis scholar Don King writes about how Lewis's experience as a young man in the trenches of World War I influenced these poems and helped to create a division in Lewis's mind that holds in tension the equation matter = nature = Satan on the one hand, and beauty on the other. King maintains that the Lewis of these poems is a frustrated dualist. He divides the poems into two categories. One is *sanguine*, showing Lewis's delight in beauty, mystery, and the world of faery, or fairyland. The other is *morose*, showing human inhumanity toward other humans and cursing a God he does not believe in, yet blames.[17] Lewis appears as yet unable to find a way to absorb and synthesize these opposing viewpoints or portions of his mind.

This bifurcation is seen clearly in the "Prologue," where Lewis sets forth the scope of the work.

> In my coracle of verses I will sing of lands unknown,
> Flying from the scarlet city where a Lord that knows
> > no pity
> Mocks the broken people praying round his iron
> > throne,
> —Sing about the Hidden Country fresh and full of
> > quiet green.
> Sailing over seas uncharted to a port that none has
> > seen.[18] (27–35)

The reality of war, life, and a pitiless God seems to jostle uneasily with imagination, longing, and beauty in this stanza. Indeed, Lewis seems to despair at times even of imagination, as seen in "French Nocturne":

> What call have I to dream of anything?
> I am a wolf. Back to the world again,
> And speech of fellow-brutes that once were men
> Our throats can bark for slaughter: cannot sing.[19] (17–20)

His hatred of God for the situation into which humanity has been thrust is the natural outcome of these thoughts. Thus, in "De Profundis," he curses the God in which he does not believe:

> Come let us curse our Master ere we die,
> For all our hopes in endless ruin lie.
> The good is dead. Let us curse God most high.
>
> Four thousand years of toil and hope and thought
> Wherein men laboured upward and still wrought
> New worlds and better, Thou hast made as naught.[20] (1–6)

The poem ends with a denunciatory stanza in which Lewis expresses a humanist belief that man is the measure of all things.

> Laugh then and slay. Shatter all things of worth,
> Heap torment still on torment for thy mirth—
> Thou art not Lord while there are men on earth.[21] (34–36)

And then the recognition and love of beauty and the imaginative impulse clamor to be expressed, despite the horrors of war and the world that Lewis thought grim and meaningless. "Song" expresses this upwelling of delight that is in stark contrast to the invective heaped upon God in the preceding poem:

> Fairies must be in the woods
> Or the satyrs' laughing broods—
> Tritons in the summer sea,
> Else how could the dead things be
> Half so lovely as they are?[22] (1–5)

He ends the poem thusly:

> Atoms dead could never thus
> Stir the human heart of us
> Unless the beauty that we see
> The veil of endless beauty be,
> Filled full of spirits that have trod
> Far hence along the heavenly sod
> And seen the bright footprints of God.[23] (19–25)

Even here, he is using the absorbing imagination to blend pagan and Christian, though at this point in his life he is a professed atheist. On the one hand, he clamors vociferously against God. On the other, he appears to acknowledge him as a source of beauty. The larger endeavor of the absorbing imagination, that is, the reconciliation of imagination with reason by something as of yet unidentified by Lewis, is still occluded by the dualism with which he was grappling. However, from a very young age, he was aware of the power of myth and poetry to transport the soul to regions of what he would later call joy. And he was always searching for this reconciliation of his seemingly unbridgeable divided nature.

Estranged Powers of the Soul and the Longing for Reconciliation

Lewis penned "Reason" to explore this essential division, this polarity, because he was aware of the chasm, not only in himself, but in the wider culture as well. The poem is worth quoting in its entirety.

Set on the soul's acropolis the reason stands
A virgin, arm'd, commercing with celestial light,
And he who sins against her has defiled his own
Virginity: no cleansing makes his garment white;
So clear is reason. But how dark imagining,
Warm, dark, obscure and infinite, daughter of Night:
Dark is her brow, the beauty of her eyes with sleep
Is loaded, and her pains are long, and her delight.
Tempt not Athene. Wound not in her fertile pains
Demeter, nor rebel against her mother-right.
Oh who will reconcile in me both maid and mother,
Who make in me a concord of the depth and height?
Who make imagination's dim exploring touch
Ever report the same as intellectual sight?
Then could I truly say, and not deceive,
Then wholly say, that I BELIEVE.[24] (1–16)

Poet Malcolm Guite understands this poem to be an extended metaphor of the soul as an inner Athens divided between two goddesses, Athene, who embodies reason, and Demeter, who embodies imagination. Here Lewis is clearly anticipating something that will bridge the gulf between the two. However, as this poem was written prior to Lewis's conversion to Christianity, we can only see in retrospect, as Lewis did, that Christ was the reconciler who would bring concord between the divided parts of his soul. Guite illumines the nature of this reconciliation through Christ: "On the one hand the story of his death and resurrection summons up the deepest imaginative and mythic response, but on the other the story of his incarnation brings imaginative myth and rational history together."[25] This response, as well as the bridge between the two, is a fundamental task of the absorbing imagination.

The problem, as Lewis writes, is that the imagination is not valued as an authentic source of truth the way reason is. It is not clear, but "warm, dark, obscure and infinite." The images of sleep and night further reinforce the dreamlike state of imagination. Perhaps the essential problem is that reason has long been associated with truth and imagination with make-believe. Therefore, we don't trust our imagination as a source of truth. Lewis asks in this poem how we can make "imagination's dim exploring touch / Ever report the same as intellectual sight?" Because for Lewis, as we've seen, it was a perpetual source of delight and life, the portion of his mind where he felt most at home. But despite this, perhaps he did not believe that imagination could ever play an important role in the finding and telling of truth.

We must strive to understand not only this gulf between reason and imagination but also how Lewis came to bridge it. We will also discover how it freed him to use this imagination in blending traditions within his fiction, a blending that would ultimately point to truths beyond themselves and give hints of the "hidden country." It contains implications for how the stories of our lives not only broaden our own imaginations, but those of others we come in contact with. As a result of this bridging, there is a fundamental increase in imaginative power that helps us to absorb others' imaginative viewpoints.

To get there, we eavesdrop on a conversation between Lewis, J. R. R. Tolkien, and Hugo Dyson, which took place on Addison's walk in Magdalene College, Oxford, on a September evening in 1931. Addison's walk is a magical, tree-lined place located in the heart of the Magdalene College grounds. Surrounded on all sides by the River Cherwell, it winds around a central meadow. On this particular night, the three friends were strolling and discussing metaphor and myth. Lewis made the comment that myths were simply lies breathed through silver. He understood their power but had never believed in them as a source of truth, as the poem "Reason" attests to.

Tolkien expounded a forceful argument that enabled Lewis to see how myths and the situations that kindle imagination are not lies. Though one can pervert thoughts into lies, the person comes from God and derives one's ultimate ideals from God. Therefore, not only abstract but also imaginative inventions must originate with God and must reflect something of eternal truth.

In mythmaking, or *mythopoeia*, a storyteller (what Tolkien calls a subcreator) is actually fulfilling God's purpose and reflecting splintered fragments of the true light. Therefore, pagan myths are not simply lies but must have something of the truth within them. Pagan myths are an example of God expressing himself through the minds of poets and using the images of myths to reflect fragments of his eternal truth.[26]

Although this is seemingly a paradox, Tolkien also helped Lewis to see Christianity as a true myth. The dying gods of pagan myth such as Balder and Adonis Lewis was already familiar with; in this case, however, the myth actually had happened. God was the poet who invented it, and the images in the myth were real men and actual history with historical consequences. Recall Lewis's definition of myth as a gleam of divine truth falling upon human imagination. He also understood reason to be the organ of truth and imagination the organ of meaning.[27] In treating Christianity as myth—a story from which you could come away with a definite taste and enjoyment without asking what it meant—you could receive from it things you could never receive from a list of abstract truths about it. Tolkien encouraged Lewis to transfer this same attitude that he adopted for other myths to the Christian story.[28]

This conversation was pivotal in Lewis's conversion to Christianity, and this idea of Christ as myth made history was later the subject of an essay in which he elaborates on Tolkien's idea that myth can only be true when it is approached without looking for meaning. In apprehending myth, you taste. This tasting is the vital channel through which we receive reality. On the abstract level, these realities lead to innumerable truths.[29] Myth is a way to experience abstract principles concretely, but again, the stress is on tasting and experiencing, not knowledge of what it is that comes to you. It is looking along the beam, not at it. The moment you begin thinking about it you are abstracting.

"We must not be ashamed of the mythical radiance resting on our theology," Lewis writes. "We must not be nervous about 'parallels' and 'Pagan Christs': they *ought* to be there—it would be a stumbling block if they weren't. We must not, in false spirituality, withhold our imaginative welcome."[30]

Here Lewis is fully embracing myth and the truths it contains that point to the true Myth, that is, Christ. We also understand more fully how and why he combines diverse myths in his work that we may taste realities that point to truths outside of and beyond the myth. "As myth transcends thought, so Incarnation transcends myth," he writes.[31] Lewis has reconciled reason and imagination through Christ, and both have now become sources of truth. But to do this he had to find the common ground, Christ, and absorb Christianity to enlarge his worldview and so provide the bridge between the two. This is achieved only by exercising the absorbing imagination. He goes so far as to say that in order to be truly Christian, we must acknowledge not only the historical fact of Christ but the myth of the dying god (even though fact) as well, according both with the same imaginative embrace we give to all myths.[32]

The Powers Reconciled: Myth as Bearer of Reality and Truth in *Poems*

A wonderful example of the absorbing imagination of Lewis, postconversion, is found in the poem "The Turn of the Tide." It begins with a simple description of the countryside surrounding Bethlehem on the night of Christ's birth. It then uses the analogy of a widening ripple to describe how "the deathly stillness spread from Bethlehem. It was shed / Wider each moment on the land" (5-6).[33] This stillness spreads into the taverns and out through the islands into the ocean to Caesar in his palace and all around the planet:

> From the Earth
> A signal, a warning went out
> And away behind the air. Her neighbors were aware
> Of change. They were troubled with a doubt.[34] (25–28)

We then see the effect as this ripple expands into the heavenly spheres where

> Ousiarchs divine
> Grew pale and questioned what it meant;
> Great Galactal lords stood back to back with swords
> Half-drawn, awaiting the event.[35] (33–36)

When the hush has stilled both earth and heaven with a paralyzing fear of death and annihilation, there returns with a rush a sense of life and equilibrium, a lightening of spirits. Then comes a small music that "swelled and drew nearer and held / All the worlds in the sharpness of its call" (55–56).[36] It shakes the heavens with music never before known.

> Heaven danced to it and burned. Such answer was returned
> To the hush, the *Favete*, the fear
> That Earth had sent out; revel, mirth and shout
> Descended to her, sphere below sphere.
> Saturn laughed and lost his latter age's frost,
> His beard, Niagara-like, unfroze;
> Monsters in the Sun rejoiced; the Inconstant One,
> The unwedded Moon, forgot her woes.
> A shiver of re-birth and deliverance on the Earth
> Went gliding. Her bonds were released.
> Into broken light a breeze rippled and woke the seas,
> In the forest it startled every beast.
> Capripods fell to dance from Taproban to France,
> Leprechauns from Down to Labrador,
> In his green Asian dell the Phoenix from his shell
> Burst forth and was the Phoenix once more.

So death lay in arrest. But at Bethlehem the bless'd
    Nothing greater could be heard
Than a dry wind in the thorn, the cry of the One new-born,
    And cattle in stall as they stirred.[37] (65–84)

Lewis has imported a number of myths as well as elements of the medieval cosmology to give us the sense of the vast import surrounding Christ's birth that reverberated through all the heavens and earth but made no sound in Bethlehem. We see great gods and celestial powers brought to a point of absolute stillness, then a shock wave of rejoicing and music that come with returning life. G. K. Chesterton has written similarly of the incarnation: "It might be suggested, in a somewhat violent image, that nothing had happened in that fold or crack in the great grey hills except that the whole universe had been turned inside out."[38] Lewis is asking us to taste, through the use of myth and story, a reality that we might not understand in any other way, the astounding ramifications of Christ's birth on the universe. The myths bring their own histories and associations to bear on our imaginations, widening our imaginative grasp of the incarnation, the birth of the true myth.

This is a vital aspect of the absorbing imagination; it allows us to taste without the distraction of needing to attach meaning to our experience. This atmosphere, for Lewis, was always the main value of any good story or myth, because, through it, we receive certain nourishment not available in any other way, especially not through trying to understand with our reason. And the resultant truths that pour into our minds are refractions of the divine.

For Lewis the absorbing imagination points to something beyond our knowledge, what we have previously referred to as "the hidden country," the place inside us that yearns for something we often cannot define. He attempts to define the nature of this awareness beyond knowledge. What is the "unnameable something, desire for which pierces us like a rapier at the smell of a bonfire, the sound of wild ducks flying overhead, the title of *The Well at the World's End*, the opening lines of *Kubla Khan*, the morning cobwebs in late summer, or the noise of falling waves?"[39]

It is a nebulous way of talking about the unknowable, approaching it obliquely. If we try to catch it by staring it in the face, it disappears. It has the feel of lightning; we catch glimpses of it, lambent across a storm-darkened sky. But when we turn our eyes to where it was, it's already gone. The question is how we talk about that longing. Lewis gives us a language; the absorbing imagination puts us in contact with it. This is where myth excels, and Lewis develops this idea further in his retelling of the Cupid and Psyche myth in *Till We Have Faces*.

Thus, the absorbing imagination absorbs for a purpose beyond mere widening of imaginative horizons: it absorbs in order to taste, in order to enter a climate or atmosphere suggested by the stimulus, not that it may understand, but simply that it may *bask*. In this way we attain a completely different form of knowing. Here we tap not into the *idea* of goodness, but goodness itself. It cannot be analyzed while we are experiencing it, as Lewis writes. Otherwise we cannot experience it and are only dealing with it as an abstraction. This is why Lewis calls reason the organ of truth and imagination the organ of meaning.

He examines this idea further in *The Weight of Glory*.

> In speaking of this desire for our own far off country, which we find in ourselves even now, I feel a certain shyness. I am almost committing an indecency. I am trying to rip open the inconsolable secret in each one of you—the secret which hurts so much that you take your revenge on it by calling it names like Nostalgia and Romanticism and Adolescence; the secret also which pierces with such sweetness that when, in very intimate conversation, the mention of it becomes imminent, we grow awkward and affect to laugh at ourselves; the secret we cannot hide and cannot tell, though we desire to do both. We cannot tell it because it is a desire for something that has never actually appeared in our experience. We cannot hide it because our experience is constantly suggesting it, and we betray ourselves like lovers at the mention of a name. Our commonest expedient is to call it beauty and behave as if that had settled the matter.[40]

Not only does the absorbing imagination help give us intelligence of the hidden country; it also validates the imagination as a source of truth about God. It dignifies the world of what we would call "make-believe" and enables us to see refractions of truth within it. Thus fairy stories, myths, and legends have value. They allow us to perceive truth. They give us glimpses of the unknowable, the unnamable, the inconsolable secret.

This longing is evident again in Lewis's poem "The Landing," which follows a group of questing sailors looking for the remote land of the Hesperides, nymphs who tend a garden in the far western corner of the world. The garden contains a tree of golden apples that gives immortality to those who eat. The narrator claims to have seen this land:

> Once before I'd seen it, but that was from Helicon,
> Clear and distinct in the circle of a lens,
> Peering on tip-toes, one-eyed, through a telescope
> —Goddesses' country, never men's.[41] (9–12)

At one point the sailors believe they have found the fabled place, only to land, climb to the top of a green hill and find a telescope through which the narrator again looks.

> There, once again, I beheld it, small and perilous,
> Distant beyond measure, in the circle of the lens
> —But this time, surely, the true one, the Hesperides'
> Country which is not men's.[42] (29–32)

When I (Mark) first read these words, "small and perilous / Distant beyond measure," I experienced the longing Lewis refers to. I, too, wished to be able to find the island; a sense of bittersweet sadness over the distance beyond measure came over me. I was tasting, not trying to analyze, and in so doing received the truth into my mind of the certainty that the objects of certain longings and desires cannot be accessed in this world, no matter how hard I strive. The difference is that the truth was in the feeling, the sensation, or the atmosphere, not in the words and abstraction I just wrote in trying to explain it. These are the truths that are suggested to us by the absorbing imagination. Lewis used Greek myth, but hidden within the myth was the atmosphere it triggered; this is Tolkien's refraction of the divine. It is God giving us the darkest glimpses into the hidden country.

The sailors resume their journey, where "Hope died—rose again—quivered, and increased in us / The strenuous longing" (33–34).[43] Again, Lewis is attempting through the telling of a story utilizing elements of Greek myth to give us a taste of that longing we all feel for the hidden country and the ways in which we search for, yet never find it. This is similar to John's search for the island in the sea in Lewis's *The Pilgrim's Regress*. But the myth, far from detracting from this truth, ennobles it and fleshes it out with its own set of associations that trigger our individual responses. Lewis's use of the absorbing imagination has helped to widen our imaginative landscapes.

In "The Last of the Wine," Lewis engages in mythmaking of his own to dignify and enrich the drinking of a last decanter of wine with a friend, to pull it from the common clay in which it resides, and imbue it with mythic significance. He imagines a man who, escaping the destruction of the legendary lost cities of Lemuria, Numinor, and Atlantis, sails across the ocean to lands unknown. Around his neck, a small phial hangs, "Holding the last of a golden cordial, subtle and sweet" (13).[44] He lands in ancient Europe, an untamed wilderness inhabited by dangerous beasts and peopled by barbarians who await him on the sand as he disembarks:

Horribly ridged are their foreheads. Weapons of bone,
Unhandy and blunt, they brandish in their clumsy grips.
Their females set up a screaming, their bagpipes drone;[45] (18–20)

Believing they will either kill him or fall down and worship him, the sailor
raises the flask to his lips. Instantly he is transported to the vanished court of
these ruined mythic cities from which he has fled. "It brings to mind the strings,
the flutes, the tabors, / How he drank with poets at the banquet, robed and
crowned" (22–23).[46] It reminds him of

The festal nights; the jest that flashed for a second
Light as a bubble, bright with a thousand years
Of nurture;[47] (26–28)

He recalls the ladies and their "Fearless and peerless beauty, flower-like hair,
/ Ruses and mockery, the music of grave dances" (31–32).[48] If we allow the myth
to work on us we may take away something of the poignancy of memory and the
longing it evokes in us via one of our senses, in this case, taste. We sense, with
the sailor, the sadness associated with remembrance of deeply treasured times in
the face of present troubles. We have absorbed Lewis's mythology and we now
see the drinking of a decanter of wine with a friend in a new light. There is an
atmosphere that rests upon and influences it. No amount of abstract thinking
can explain this. It ennobles the act of remembering, in which the absorbing
imagination ultimately calls us to participate.

The Legend of the Age of Trees: Memory and the Hidden Country

An examination of the ways Lewis's poem *The Future of Forestry* acts as a call
to action to engage the absorbing imagination and memory brings us to a fitting
conclusion. Though concerned with the erosion of nature, it details the losses of
a memory that has atrophied and darkened. It acts as a caution against excluding imagination and allowing reason to be the only source of truth. When the
situations through which we catch glimpses of the far-off country are forgotten
as sources of truth, the absorbing imagination comes to our aid. Lewis begins by
asking a series of questions.

How will the legend of the age of trees
Feel, when the last tree falls in England?
When the concrete spreads and the town conquers

The country's heart; when contraceptive
Tarmac's laid where farm has faded,
Tramline flows where slept a hamlet,
And shop-fronts, blazing without a stop from
Dover to Wrath, have glazed us over?[49] (1–8)

The first section details occurrences that dull imagination, the spreading of concrete that brings uniformity and utilitarianism; the conquering of the country by the town; the busyness that intrudes into silence and space; and the contraceptive tarmac that prevents anything from growing as well as placing a barrier between us and nature. It makes fecundity and the farm and land—the quintessence of open space, growth, and room to breathe—diminish. A tramline, denoting constant movement, operates in place of a small, quiet community. Shop-fronts feed impulses to consumerism and materialism, glazing us over in a sort of stupor and keeping our rational minds occupied in a manner that doesn't admit the imagination. Each of these erodes imagination and prevents remembering.

Through our reason, we may acknowledge these changes as necessary and even proper "advances." Certainly they are not negative. Roads allow us to travel from one place to another, shops to purchase what we need to live, cities and industry to work and be busy. But they exist at a cost. Importantly, Lewis uses the word *feel* in the second line. He isn't questioning what anyone will think about it or how it will be told. He is concerned with its atmosphere, what it will invoke in us when we hear it.

Simplest tales will then bewilder
The questioning children, "What was a chestnut?
Say what it means to climb a Beanstalk.
Tell me, grandfather, what an elm is.
What was Autumn? They never taught us."
Then, told by teachers how once from mould
Came growing creatures of lower nature
Able to live and die, though neither
Beast nor man, and around them wreathing
Excellent clothing, breathing sunlight—
Half understanding, their ill-acquainted
Fancy will tint their wonder-paintings
—Trees as men walking, wood-romances
Of goblins stalking in silky green,
Of milk-sheen froth upon the lace of hawthorn's
Collar, pallor on the face of birchgirl.

So shall a homeless time, though dimly
Catch from afar (for soul is watchful)
A sight of tree-delighted Eden.[50] (9–27)

Thus, the simplest knowledge about the nature of trees has been forgotten. However, the soul, what Lewis would at least partially equate with the imagination, that "warm, dark, obscure, and infinite" region, is watchful. It waits until we may pause long enough to remember. We are caught in a homeless time, because the hidden country, if we are honest, is where we long to be. Lewis writes, "If I find in myself a desire which no experience in this world can satisfy, the most probable explanation is that I was made for another world."[51] That other world, that far country, is our true home. It is Lewis's inconsolable wound, the idea of *sehnsucht*, or intense longing that we all experience. In order to catch that sight of tree-delighted Eden from afar, the ill-acquainted fancy (imagination that is not prized as a source of truth) must use myths, stories, and traditions to catch dim refractions of what we cannot remember but long to know, the hidden country.

The trees present to our imaginations the purity and splendor of an unsullied and freshly created world that must form the backdrop to the hidden country: the world God created when he made Eden. Thus, God is implicitly behind the imaginative response and has bridged the divide between reason and imagination.

We *must* imagine goblins and birch girls and trees as men walking. We must imagine the impact of Christ's birth on the universe, as Lewis has beautifully depicted in his poem. We must imagine how the drinking of a last decanter of wine in the company of friends is like a vial of memory around our necks conjuring up beautiful visions. We must imagine how impossible distances separate sailors from a far, hidden land and the ways in which this bears an affinity to our own hidden country. We must imagine so that we may remember. And ultimately, as Guite states, Christ summons up these imaginative and mythic responses within us to the story of himself and his action in the world and history, a story that we are in constant danger of forgetting and must attempt to recollect.

This is the imaginative response through the absorbing imagination that the poem encourages; it enables us to strengthen our weak imaginations by widening horizons through absorbing viewpoints. It discourages reason from being the sole source of truth. It allows for some mystery in life, mystery that points beyond itself, that somehow bears the truth. It shows us how knowledge once taken for granted may be lost. It helps to remythologize and reenchant our imaginations, even atrophied as they are through long disuse, because travels to fairyland inform our return to reality. It keeps us from being stuck in our own particularity, as the dwarfs were in *The Last Battle*.

After all, we must remember, as Lewis exhorts us, that we are under an enchantment. He writes, "We have need of the strongest spell that can be found to wake us from the evil enchantment of worldliness which has been laid upon us for nearly a hundred years. Almost our whole education has been devoted to silencing this shy, persistent, inner voice."[52] The shy, persistent voice is our knowledge of the far country, and Lewis is insistent that we wake up to it, that we keep its memory alive. Tramlines, concrete, cities, and shops will attempt to silence the voice. But the absorbing imagination invites us to pause and listen, though perilous and distant beyond measure, for a whisper of the wind that blows in tree-delighted Eden.

Conclusion

Illuminating the Path Ahead

T. S. Eliot wrote in *The Four Quartets*, "In my beginning is my end."[1] So too at the end of this exploration of Lewis's uses of the imagination we have come full circle. We end where we began. Lewis at the core of his being was an imaginative man. As was noted in the introduction, so we recount here that Lewis rightly said,

> The imaginative man in me is older, more continuously operative, and in that sense, more basic than either the religious writer or the critic. It was he who made me first attempt (with little success) to be a poet. It was he who, in response to the poetry of others, made me a critic, and in defense of that response, sometimes a critical controversialist. It was he who after my conversion led me to embody my religious beliefs in symbolical or mythopoeic forms, ranging from Screwtape to a kind of theologized science fiction. And it was of course he who has brought me, in the last few years to write the series of Narnian stories for children.[2]

We have seen, whether in his fiction or nonfiction, that Lewis is given to depictions, creating windows and images, inventing stories, developing metaphors, and crafting illustrations so his readers can see what he saw and more. He did these things that readers might better see and understand the real world.

It may seem incongruous for those who know the writings of Lewis and Eliot to hear them quoted in the same paragraph. These two men did not always see eye to eye at the beginning of their careers. It seems the offense was all on Lewis's side of the ledger. He failed to appreciate Eliot's poetic style. But in time they became acquainted, and were even collaborators as members of the archbishop's "Commission to Revise the Psalter" for the Church of England. Common things brought them together: a common faith, a common literary life, and eventually a shared endeavor working together. Walter Hooper even says of the relationship that "[Lewis] had come to love Eliot as a result of their companionship over a shared interest."[3]

So too, Lewis's use of the imagination makes it possible for us to enter into collaboration with things once outside of our vision of the world. Things we may have rejected due to misunderstanding, or impatience as the case may be, suddenly take on new light and fresh meaning. Lewis, by using his imagination, brings his readers into other worlds, much like Aslan brought children into his world. Joining those children, we receive access into places like Narnia. In encountering Aslan in the Chronicles we are enabled to hear what Lucy heard from the lion himself: "This was the very reason you were brought to Narnia, that by knowing me here for a little, you may know me better there."[4] Perhaps this is at the zenith of all imaginative endeavors. They afford us the possibility to see God and live. They are the cloak behind which the divine reveals itself in a way that seeing, we might believe.

We understand that Lewis's uses of the imagination are, at the end of the day, reconciling. They help his readers to reconcile themselves to a larger world. It may be a world full of complexities: a world of sorrows and triumphs, failure and redemption. But his worlds, depicted for his readers, are also worlds of the "happily ever after," full of hope. That is, they are like the real world. The idealism is there but it is idealism without illusion. Lewis brings his readers out of the cold vulgarity of daily life and helps them to see that "earth's crammed with heaven, / And every common bush afire with God."[5] It is with Lewis's full and fertile imagination that we his readers are able to see with sharper eyes.

Lewis also allows the reader to become more fully reconciled to the world in other ways, as well. We can learn to experience the world as it is rather than how we want it to be. For Lewis, the imagination helps us integrate faith and sight. The faith is undergirded by confidence in the love of God and his forgiveness. Such love allows us to receive what is delivered to us by the imagination. It is not seen as a final vision of reality but rather as a dynamic one. It is a doorway into a wider world where the imagination always will be employed, always providing illumination for every path that leads to greater understanding.

Lewis uses the imagination as a reconciler. He first wants his readers to find themselves reconciled to God and to embrace a constantly growing understanding of what that means. When he writes, "I want God not my idea of God," a sense of estrangement is implicit. How do we move from the present understanding into a more nuanced, more robust one if not by means of the imagination? Though God never grows (how could the immutable ever grow?), still we see him as bigger as *we* grow. How is this possible? How can we break out of the conventions of our past if we are not liberated by means of the imagination?

Lewis also says, I want my neighbor not my idea of my neighbor. How can we break free to see with new eyes the things we have missed in the past without the use of the imagination? Lewis helps us here, too. And how can we begin to see ourselves as we really are without some assistance? We are not Eustace, but Eustace-like; we may need to experience our own kind of undragoning.

In the story, the vicarious experience offered to us imaginatively may be far less painful and leave behind fewer scars for us and for others we may have hurt had our undragoning not occurred. We are not Ransom shanghaied to some strange planet, but Ransom-like we still have to understand the world. We are not ghosts on the threshold of heaven but people who are not yet fully made. We need to see, with the eyes of hope, that one day we may be mended and made solid and whole. Lewis helps us to be reconciled to new worlds of ideas. These may have been once out of reach or too opaque. Now, however, we are beginning to touch them and, in some cases, to see through into a growing transparency. Lewis has given us lenses through which we might look onto a wider world. We are being reconciled with ideas that once eluded us. We may see through a glass darkly, but, nevertheless, we are beginning to see.

Lewis teaches us to go where we have not been but need to go if we would understand. This kind of growth will always require the imagination. Lewis's confidence in the perfect love that casts out fear allowed him to take the torch of the imagination and illumine caverns yet to be explored. His depictions allow us to see better images of ourselves and others. Of course imaginative endeavors in a fallen, broken world can go two ways. Precisely because the world is fallen, and we ourselves are broken, abuses of the imagination do occur. The imagination can become the means to inflate and falsify, or the means to discover truths long eclipsed from view. We need the imagination so that whatever we learn can yet flourish and break forth into fresh applications.

Lewis, being unafraid to explore, encourages his readers to follow in his steps. He writes, "If our religion is something objective, then we must never avert our eyes from those elements in it which seem puzzling or repellent; for it is precisely the puzzling or the repellent which conceals what we do not yet know and need to know."[6] He is willing to look at the hard stuff. Such exploration begins with trust. He seems confident, even in the caverns of grief and despair, not to give up his quest to understand. Whether he is casting the pupil's metaphor to explore regions yet untrod, or crafting a master's metaphor from his rhetorical tool box, he seeks to lead his readers along paths now familiar to him but yet unknown to them.

Owen Barfield, Lewis's lifelong friend, once wrote, "If someone were to ask me at the point of a pistol, and with ten seconds to answer in: what was Lewis's relation to the imagination? I should reply (supposing I had my wits about me to meet the challenge): he was in love with it."[7] A man who knew Lewis so well saw that Lewis loved the life of the imagination. As it was obvious to those who knew him, so it becomes obvious to those who read him and have benefitted from his writing. And we can assume it will be equally true for generations to come. They, too, will benefit from Lewis's rich and fertile imagination. The stories, the word pictures, the metaphors that breathe life into some literary or theological proposition will never go out of fashion. Lewis is here to stay.

In our relatively brief study of Lewis's uses of the imagination, we have only scratched the surface. Lewis is like the Eskimos mentioned at the beginning of this book, whose daily, lifelong experience with snow and ice has allowed them to craft ways of describing the nuanced realities of their world. They can speak about snow with multiple numbers and combinations of words, creatively crafted with prefixes and suffixes, to refine and arrive at specific descriptions of reality. So too Lewis, who lived in a world he loved to describe, used refined imaginative depictions as he explored and clarified that world for his readers.

Whether it was the imagination that seeks, inappropriately, to transform reality and project upon it what it wants to find, or the baptized imagination that awakens and repents of those projections, Lewis helps his readers to see. He engages the baptized imagination to cultivate a regenerated grasp of the world as something different than our utilitarian interests. Further, he may employ the absorbing imagination that can absorb from many sources and create a patchwork quilt of understanding, or the material imagination ... the shared imagination ... the primary imagination ... and so forth.

These uses of the imagination become the canvas on which Lewis portrays his theological views. The practice has a long history. The medieval scholastic doctors of the church understood the difficulty and wrote about God using what they called the *way of analogy*. Lewis rightly observed that while reason may be the organ of truth, imagination remains the organ of meaning. Propositions can easily become as dry as the prophet Ezekiel's valley of bones, but story can bring them to life.

Where do we go from here? Barfield observed, "The use of the imagination is one thing; a theory of the imagination is another."[8] Lewis used the word *imagination* in so many ways that certainly his wide-ranging vocabulary must be considered were someone to attempt a theory of the imagination. This is just the beginning, of course. For those who want to go further into this world, we offer an appendix describing other uses of the imagination, cited by Lewis, yet untouched in this study. Do not think Lewis is the only one who can open a wardrobe door and say, "Look!" Remember that Lewis himself drew many of his categories of the imagination from Shakespeare, Dante, Milton, Marcus Aurelius, Sidney, Spenser, and others. So too, if we would be like Lewis, we must enter the garden where others have plowed, planted, and weeded before us, where there is still fruit ripe for the picking.

Ultimately, the imagination is a vital "organ of meaning" that we must cultivate if we desire to live well, if we are to grow and change and expand our understanding of the world that God has placed us in. God calls us to know it, and to know it well. But we can never get there on reason alone. Lewis recognized a bifurcation between reason and imagination early in his life. While he lived fully in his imagination, he didn't initially believe that it could be a source of truth. He finally found the reconciliation between the two in Christ, who allowed him to understand the nature of an imaginative life on a completely new plane. Thus, we hope that the reader takes away the understanding that the imagination functions as a vital source of truth and knowledge about the world and God. Knowledge gained through the imagination is equal to the knowledge received through reason alone.

The bifurcation that Lewis recognized in himself remains operative in culture today. We encourage you to fight the notion that the imagination is simply "make-believe" and therefore not to be trusted. Modern science certainly has not helped to foster the imagination as a source of truth. Reason, intellect, and method are prized above all else, while imagination is patted condescendingly on the head. We hope that this book enables you to see it as a means of enriching all of life, to add flesh on the framework provided by reason. The two should not be separated; they work together, completing, as it were, a marriage where the two become one in a way that is greater than each alone. We hope this glimpse into Lewis's own imaginative life has begun this process as well as encouraged you to continue your own explorations of the imagination "further up and further in."

Appendix

Additional Uses of the Imagination as Identified by C. S. Lewis

Following is a list of additional uses of the imagination as identified by Lewis. The work where each is found is referenced within each entry, along with footnoted bibliographic detail. If a work contains multiple uses of the imagination, the bibliographic data is given only the first time. It should be assumed that additional references to the same work are from the same edition. We hope this appendix will allow the reader to widen his or her explorations into the imagination of Lewis, and through Lewis, into an expansion of the self and a deeper understanding of reality.

Aroused

Lewis identifies two kinds of aroused imagination, one that is healthy, and one that is unhealthy. The first is "Flattery to the ego" and appeals to the lust for popularity, or the desire to be thought well of by others. "The pleasure consists in picturing oneself as the object of admiration." The second type of aroused imagination does not direct attention to oneself. It is awakened and its attention is directed elsewhere. It longs for other worlds. This imaginative longing "stirs and troubles him (to his lifelong enrichment) with the dim sense of something beyond his reach and, far from dulling or emptying the actual world, gives it a new dimension of depth." One imaginative use is diseased; the other is a spiritual exercise; for we can be aroused to positive as well as negative uses of the imagination.[1]

Cinematographic

Not so much an imagination of pictures but moving images (the dance compared with the sculpture). It creates a visual moving narrative. Lewis praises

Gower for this approach and notes of his *Confessio Amantis* that there is an "excellence in Gower's sea-pieces [that] has led some to suppose that he was familiar with sea travel—as he may well have been; but it is in fact only one manifestation of his devotion to movement and progression, his preoccupation with things that change as you watch them."[2]

Classical

It "loves to embrace its object completely, to take it in at a single glance, and see it as something harmonious, symmetrical, and self-explanatory." The benefits are that it sees with unity. Its liabilities are that it may miss the exceptions. It may over generalize.[3]

Common

Within any community or culture, those imaginative things that are recognized by all its members and that have persisted so long that they have achieved the status of fact.[4]

Compelled

Focuses attention on what can and must be talked about. It does not tell or suggest the type of response one should have. Rather, it awakens, focuses attention, and presents its material to the reader's senses: the smell, colors, sounds, textures, and tastes of the described world. The author has provided material for the reader—that is, given data to the reader—that compels a necessary response. In a sense the reader has entered into the artist's world full-bodied. This compelling is not one of coercion; it is a compelling made just by allowing the reader to render to the made-up or imagined world its proper due.[5]

Fertile

It "can build (in a moment) on the bare facts." It does not require embellishment in description. A simple phrase is often far more evocative than hackneyed phrases. The phrase "The moon shone clear" would act on the fertile imagination in a way that "the castle was bathed in a flood of silver moonlight" never could. It does not seek to evoke stereotypical reactions to a description, but requires close attention to the words one is reading.[6]

Formal

An ordered, balanced, and symmetrical imagination. The medieval cosmology is an example of it. It is aesthetically satisfying. It represents "unity through a harmonious plurality." Similar to the mythical imagination.[7]

Geographic

The creation of an imagined world or geography that sets the limits for what will develop in the story. Lewis accomplishes this in the Space Trilogy and in Narnia. It sets the scope of the imaginative development within the world created by the author. Lewis does not offer this use as the only way to write imaginatively, nor even as a preferred approach; it is simply a way and enables an author with particular imaginative interest to tell his or her story within certain parameters. On the other hand, and by contrast, Lewis also sees merit in a lack of specific geographic dimensions and situations for the telling of certain kinds of story. To make his point he turns to Spenser and writes,

> There is no situation in *The Faerie Queene*, no when nor where....A knight and lady ride across our field of vision. We do not know where they are, nor in what period; the poet's whole energy is devoted to telling us what they look like....Spenser begins like a man in a trance, or a man looking through a window, telling us what he sees. And however we dig in Spenser we shall never get to a situation, and never find a context in the objective world for the shapes he is going to show us. But this does not mean he is all surface....What lies below the surface of his poem will therefore be something subjective and immaterial.[8]

Historical

Seeks to reconstruct from available data what the conditions might have been like during some past period of time. This is an attempt to take the available data and imaginatively construct a worldview helpful to contextualize literature of a certain period. Certainly there are risks, not unlike those of historical anthropology; these are a result of the limits of available data and the lack of absolute epistemological verification. Nevertheless, the effort produces something better than the ignorance that occurs when no data is considered and no use of a plausible construction is attempted.[9]

Idealizing

A further development of the realizing imagination. In *The Allegory of Love*, Lewis describes the state of being "exercised about sex." This is in relation to the Love Allegory and the placing of the sexual act in adultery in a world where marriages were arranged and one did not necessarily marry his beloved. On the other hand, Spenser helped usher in a time where sex was idealized in marriage and the Christian ideal superseded the religion of love. Lewis notes, "Real changes in human sentiment are very rare—there are perhaps three or four on record—but I believe they occur, and this is one of them." Here he is referring to the Love Allegory and how in the Middle Ages it transformed from the projection onto one's beloved, who was most likely not one's spouse, to the gradual transformation mediated through Christianity and particular Christian poets, especially Edmund Spenser, to one's spouse. Lewis identifies similar idealized transformations relative to longing that occur over time. These he develops in *The Pilgrim's Regress*.[10]

Muscular

Describes movements of the body to convey feelings of a particular subject without the feelings being mentioned at all. In Christopher Marlowe's epyllion *Hero and Leander*, he allows this type of imagination to tell the story of Hero's misery over her love affair with Leander. "We see her tricked out again in her priestly garments and working with her needle. We are told little about what she felt during this period of false hope, but (we are made to feel it for ourselves because every picture her needle makes is truer than her conscious mind will confess." Her misery is not described by Marlowe, but rather communicated via her actions and movements.[11]

Mythical

Deals with a genial or animistic conception of the universe, inhabited by indwelling spirits, occult sympathies and antipathies, colors, smells, tastes. It is a very sensual, rich imagination. It is concerned with the beauty, order, harmony, delight, and repetition in the world. The medieval cosmology is an example.[12]

Obedient

An attentive imagination. It enables its user to "make use of full and precise description of a scene or an emotion."[13]

Pictorial

It paints a picture. It is similar to the visual imagination.[14]

Poetic

Invents—not *ex nihilo*—by working with existing images. A mathematician can use the symbols *a* and *b* as easily as *x* and *y*; but the poet must be selective with his or her material. The *Romance of the Rose* could not have been equally well written as what we might call, for example, the Romance of the Onion. Nevertheless, the poet invents the romance by drawing from what the reader already knows about roses and onions. This use of the imagination can be included as an example of the shared imagination.[15]

Romantic

The romantic imagination "loves to lose itself in a labyrinth, to surrender to the inextricable."[16] One example would be Dymer in the castle with all of the mirrors or in the Magician's house and the subjectivism of his dreams. Its benefits are that it is free (at least in one sense of the word *free*). It may wander where it will. Its liabilities are that the wandering may prove to be little more than imaginative projection if it is untethered. Lewis observes, "It is not at all plain that men's imaginations have always delighted in those pictures of the supernatural which they believed."[17] Lewis, a Christian, enjoyed Greek mythology more fully than the Christian story; he enjoyed Irish myth better still; and he liked Norse mythology best of all. Lewis also noted that Christian medieval Europe relished classical mythology.[18]

Surrendered

The refusal to use one's imagination; everything must be spelled out in order to hold the attention. It is unwilling to engage in imaginative speculation. Leech-like, it is surrendered to an author's imagination. We might liken this to what happens when we watch a film. Our imagination is suspended because all the work of imagining is done for us. This is a negative type of imagination.[19]

Visual

The ability to visualize details accurately and conjure vivid mental images. Lewis writes that this isn't imagination in a higher sense, but is rather a power that can serve true imagination from time to time. Often, however, it merely gets in the way. One benefit is that it is a help toward concentration, similar to the way that a well-designed church draws one's eyes to the altar. For Lewis, these images were of value in prayer when they were most elusive, when he couldn't fix his attention on them without them vanishing. But in their whole effect, they mediate something important, the qualitative experience that Lewis always prized.[20]

Notes

Introduction

1. C. S. Lewis, *Letters of C. S. Lewis* (New York: Harcourt, Brace & World, 1966), 260.

2. Evelyn Underhill, *The Letters of Evelyn Underhill* (London: Longmans, Green and Co., 1944), 268.

3. Ibid., 301.

4. Austin Farrer, *The Brink of Mystery*, ed. Charles Conti (London: SPCK, 1976), 46.

5. Pavel Hosek, *The Magic of Storytelling: Transforming Power of Narrative and the "Baptism of Imagination" in the Works of C. S. Lewis*, originally published in Czech as *Kouzlo vypraveni. Promenujici moc pribehu a "krest fantazie" v pojeti C. S. Lewise* (Navrat domu, Praha, 2013), 102. Pavel Hosek develops this notion also in his book *C. S. Lewis: Myth, Imagination and Truth*, originally published in Czech as *C. S. Lewis: Mytus, imaginace a pravda* (Navrat domu, Praha, 2004), 82–88; and in his recent book *Journey into the Center of Reality: The Heavenly Goal of Spiritual Pilgrimage in the Works of C. S. Lewis*, originally published in Czech as *Cesta do Stredu skutecnosti: Smerovani k nebeskemu cili duchovni pouti v mysleni a dile C. S. Lewise* (CDK, Brno, 2014), 102.

6. C. S. Lewis, *Surprised by Joy: The Shape of My Early Life* (New York: Harcourt Brace, 1955), 21.

7. George MacDonald, *Diary of an Old Soul: 366 Writings for Devotional Reflection* (Minneapolis: Augsburg, 1975), 113.

8. C. S. Lewis, *Studies in Words*, 2nd ed. (Cambridge: Cambridge University Press, 1967), 303.

9. C. S. Lewis, "Christianity and Culture" in *Christian Reflections*, ed. Walter Hooper (Grand Rapids: William B. Eerdmans, 1967), 22–23.

10. C. S. Lewis, *The Discarded Image: An Introduction to Medieval and Renaissance Literature* (Cambridge: Cambridge University Press, 1964), 145.

11. C. S. Lewis, "Dogma and the Universe" in *God in the Dock: Essays in Theology and Ethics*, ed. Walter Hooper (Grand Rapids: William B. Eerdmans, 1970), 44.

12. Ibid., 45.

1. The Book in the Bookstall

1. C. S. Lewis, *A Preface to Paradise Lost* (Oxford: Geoffrey Cumberlege, 1954), 3.

2. C. S. Lewis, *Of Other Worlds*, ed. Walter Hooper (London: Geoffrey Bles, 1966), 37.

3. Ibid., 67–73.

4. George Sayer, *Jack: C. S. Lewis and His Times* (San Fransciso: Harper & Row, 1988), 197.

5. Ibid., 198.

6. Ibid.

7. Alister McGrath, *The Intellectual World of C. S. Lewis* (Chichester: Wiley-Blackwell, 2014), 11.

8. C. S. Lewis, *Surprised by Joy: The Shape of My Early Life* (New York: Harcourt Brace, 1956), vii.

9. Norman Cantor, *Inventing the Middle Ages: Lives, Works, and Ideas of the Great Medievalists of the Twentieth Century* (Cambridge: The Lutterworth Press, 1991), 217.

10. McGrath, *Intellectual World of C. S. Lewis*, 15.

11. Lewis, *Surprised by Joy*, 190–91.

12. Ibid., 188–89.

13. C. S. Lewis, *The Discarded Image: An Introduction to Medieval and Renaissance Literature* (Cambridge: The University Press, 1964), 14.

14. Terry Eagleton, *After Theory* (London: Penguin, 2004), 47.

15. C. S. Lewis, *Letters to Malcolm: Chiefly on Prayer* (London: Geoffrey Bles, 1964), 100–101.

16. C. S. Lewis, *Selected Literary Essays*, ed. Walter Hooper (Cambridge: Cambridge University Press, 1969), 265.

17. Lewis, *Surprised by Joy*, 7.

18. Ibid., 16.

19. Ibid.

20. Ibid., 17.

21. Ibid.

22. Ibid., 170.

23. George MacDonald, *Phantastes and Lilith* (Grand Rapids: William B. Eerdmans, 1971).

24. George MacDonald, *Diary of an Old Soul* (Minneapolis: Augsburg, 1975), 113.

25. C. S. Lewis, *The Abolition of Man* (San Francisco: Harper Collins, 2001), 104–5.

26. See Lewis's *Reflections on the Psalms*.

2. Hunting the Woolly Mammoth

1. C. S. Lewis, *Of Other Worlds* (London: Geoffrey Bles, 1966), 34.

2. C. S. Lewis, *The Collected Letters of C. S. Lewis*, ed. Walter Hooper, vol. 2, *Books, Broadcasts, and the War 1931–1949* (San Francisco: Harper, 2004), 766.

3. Anthony Trollope, *Barchester Towers* (New York: Washington Square Press, 1963), 50.

4. Plato, *Gorgias*, trans. Benjamin Jowett, *The Great Books of the Western World* (Chicago: Encyclopedia Britannica, 1952).

5. C. S. Lewis, "De Futilitate," in *Christian Reflections*, ed. Walter Hooper (Grand Rapids: William B. Eerdmans, 1967), 65–66.

6. C. S. Lewis, *Mere Christianity* (London: Geoffrey Bles, 1953), 6.

7. C. S. Lewis, *The Abolition of Man* (New York: The Macmillan Company, 1947), 12.

8. Lewis, *Mere Christianity*, 29.

9. Ibid., 29.

10. Ibid., 42.

11. Ibid., 43.

12. Ibid., 55.

13. Ibid., 56.

14. Ibid.

15. Blaise Pascal, *Pensees*, trans. W. F. Trotter, Great Books of the Western World, vol. 33 (Chicago: Encyclopedia Britannica, 1952), 484.

16. Lewis, *Mere Christianity*, 106.

17. Ibid., 108.

18. C. S. Lewis, "Membership," in *The Weight of Glory: And Other Addresses*, ed. Walter Hooper (New York: Touchstone, 1996), 125.

19. Lewis, *Mere Christianity*, 138.

20. Ibid., 122.

3. The Smell of Deity

1. C. S. Lewis, *The Discarded Image: An Introduction to Medieval and Renaissance Literature* (London: Cambridge University Press, 1974), 202–3.

2. C. S. Lewis, *Studies in Medieval and Renaissance Literature* (New York: Cambridge University Press, 2007), 44–45.

3. Ibid., 45–46.

4. Ibid., 45.

5. Ibid., 49–50.

6. Ibid., 51.

7. Ibid., 53–54.

8. Ibid., 58.

9. Ibid., 54–55.

10. Ibid., 52.

11. C. S. Lewis, *Out of the Silent Planet* (New York: Scribner, 1996), 31–32.

12. Ibid., 32.

13. Lewis, *Studies in Medieval and Renaissance Literature*, 59.

14. Ibid., 59.

15. Ibid., 60.

16. C. S. Lewis, *Spenser's Images of Life*, ed. Alastair Fowler (London: Cambridge University Press, 1967), 3–4.

17. G. K. Chesterton, *Tremendous Trifles* (Mineola, NY: Dover Publications, 2007), 6.

18. C. S. Lewis, *Letters to Malcolm: Chiefly on Prayer* (New York: Harcourt, Brace & World, Inc., 1964), 75.

19. Ibid., 79–80.

20. Ibid., 81–82.

21. Ibid., 90.

22. Gerard Manley Hopkins, "God's Grandeur," 1918.

23. Lewis, *Letters to Malcolm*, 88.

24. Ibid., 88–89.

25. Ibid., 90.

26. Ibid.

27. Ibid., 91.

28. Ibid.

29. George MacDonald, *An Anthology: 365 Readings,* ed. C. S. Lewis (New York: HarperSanFrancisco, 2001), xxxviii.

30. Lewis, *Letters to Malcolm*, 90.

31. Lewis, *Discarded Image*, 203–4.

32. Lewis, *Letters to Malcolm*, 93.

4. Breaking Out of the Dungeon

1. C. S. Lewis, "Dogma and the Universe," in *God in the Dock: Essays on Theology and Ethics,* ed. Walter Hooper (Grand Rapids: William B. Eerdmans, 1970), 38.

2. Ibid., 44.

3. C. S. Lewis, *The Allegory of Love: A Study in Medieval Tradition* (London: Oxford University Press, 1973), 1.

4. Lewis, "Dogma and the Universe," 45.

5. Mortimer Adler, *The Great Books of the Western World,* vol. 1, *The Great Conversation* (Chicago: Encyclopedia Britanica, 1952).

6. C. S. Lewis, "Dogma and the Universe," 45.

7. C. S. Lewis, *The Problem of Pain* (London: Bles, 1940).

8. C. S. Lewis, "The Vision of John Bunyan," in *Selected Literary Essays,* ed. Walter Hooper (Cambridge: Cambridge University Press, 1969), 147.

9. Lewis, *Allegory of Love*, 205.

10. Ibid., 206–7.

11. C. S. Lewis, *An Experiment in Criticism* (Cambridge: Cambridge University Press, 1961).

12. Ibid., 72

13. Ibid., 19.

14. Ibid., 24.

15. Ibid., 41.

16. Ibid., 43.

17. Ibid., 44.

18. Ibid., 45.

19. Ibid., 50.

20. Ibid., 53.

21. Ibid.

22. Ibid., 56.

23. Ibid., 57.

24. Ibid., 59.

25. Ibid., 62.

26. Ibid., 72.

27. Ibid., 73.

28. Ibid., 112.

29. Ibid., 82.

30. Ibid., 82–83.

31. Ibid., 85.

32. Ibid.

33. C. S. Lewis, "De Futilitate" in *Christian Reflections*, ed. Walter Hooper (Grand Rapids: William B. Eerdmans, 1977), 65–66.

34. Benjamin Jowett, *Select Passages from the Introductions to Plato*, ed. Lewis Campbell (London: John Murray, Albemarle Street, 1902), 57.

35. Ibid., 221.

36. C. S. Lewis, *The Pilgrim's Regress* (Grand Rapids: William B. Eerdmans, 1981), 146.

37. Owen Barfield, *Owen Barfield on C. S. Lewis*, ed. G. B. Tennyson and Jane Hipolito (Middletown: Wesleyan University Press, 1989), 46.

38. Jowett, *Select Passages from the Introductions to Plato*, 227.

39. Lewis, *Experiment in Criticism*, 8.

40. C. S. Lewis, *Perelandra* (New York: Macmillan, 1975), 81.

41. Lewis, *Experiment in Criticism*, 138.

42. Ibid., 140–41.

43. Ibid., 138.

5. On the Shoulders of Giants

1. C. S. Lewis, "Is Theology Poetry?" in *The Weight of Glory: And Other Addresses*, ed. Walter Hooper (New York: Touchstone, 1996).

2. Basil Mitchell, *Faith and Criticism* (Oxford: Oxford University Press, 1994), 27.

3. C. S. Lewis, [N. W. Clerk, pseud.], *A Grief Observed* (London: Faber & Faber, 1961), 52. See also Lewis's *Letters to Malcolm: Chiefly on Prayer* (London: Geoffrey Bles, 1964), 114. This idea, "reality is iconoclastic," is the biggest idea in all of Lewis's writing, both preconversion and postconversion. Evidence of it can be found in all of his books expressed in a variety of ways.

4. C. S. Lewis, *Surprised by Joy: The Shape of My Early Life* (New York: Harcourt Brace and Company, 1956), 167.

5. C. S. Lewis, *Letters to Malcolm: Chiefly on Prayer* (Vancouver: Regent College Publishing, 1998), 109.

6. C. S. Lewis, *Prince Caspian* (New York: Macmillan, 1951), 117.

7. Hab 3:4.

8. Baron Friedrich Von Hügel, *Letters to a Niece*, ed. Gwendolyn Greene (Vancouver: Regent Publishing, 1998), 62.

9. Robert Browning, "Rabbi ben Ezra," in *Tennyson and Browning*, by Guy Boas (London: Thomas Nelson & Sons, 1936), 230.

10. Walter Hooper, *C. S. Lewis: A Companion Guide* (London: Harper Collins Publishers, 1996), 61.

11. C. S. Lewis, *The Discarded Image* (Cambridge: Cambridge University Press, 1964), 1.

12. Ibid., 5.

13. Ibid., 11.

14. Ibid., 10.

15. Ibid., 12.

16. C. S. Lewis, *Studies in Medieval and Renaissance Literature*, ed. Walter Hooper (London: Oxford University Press, 1966), 43.

17. Ibid., 44.

18. Ibid.

19. Ibid., 44–45.

20. Ibid., 45.

21. G. K. Chesterton, *Tremendous Trifles* (New York: Sheed and Ward, 1955), 6.

22. See Lewis's "The Genesis of a Medieval Book" and "Imagination and Thought" in *Studies in Medieval and Renaissance Literature*; "What Chaucer Really Did to 'Il Filostrato'" in *Selected Literary Essays*, ed. Walter Hooper (London: Cambridge University Press, 1969). Lewis also notes this characteristic of embellishment in medieval literature in *Discarded Image*.

23. Lewis, *Discarded Image*, 14. Later Lewis notes again, "The model was recognized as provisional," 18.

24. Ibid., 93.

25. Ibid., 15.

26. Ibid., 17.

27. Ibid., 185.

28. Charles Williams, *The Descent of the Dove: A Short History of the Holy Spirit in the Church* (Grand Rapids: William B. Eerdmans, 1974), 112.

29. Lewis, *Discarded Image*, 22.

30. Ibid., 22–34.

31. Ibid., 34.

32. Ibid., 35–36.

33. Ibid., 36.

34. Ibid., 37.

35. Ibid.

36. Ibid., 38.

37. Ibid., 39.

38. Ibid., 85.

39. Ibid., 42. When Lewis speaks of "that great movement of internalization" he is referring to what he believed was a developing disregard for the objective by means of a swelling sense of subjectivism. It is a matter to which he gives further attention on p. 215 and also in the essay, "The Poison of Subjectivism" in *Christian Reflections*, ed. Walter Hooper (Grand Rapids: William B. Eerdmans, 1967).

40. Lewis, *Discarded Image*, 75–91.

41. Ibid., 75.

42. Ibid., 81.

43. Ibid., 88.

44. Ibid., 89.

45. Ibid.

46. Ibid., 92.

47. Ibid., 102.

48. Ibid., 113.

49. Ibid. Discussed in chapter 6.

50. Ibid., 146.

51. Ibid., 152

52. Ibid., 155.

53. Ibid., 154.

54. Ibid., 113.

55. Mitchell, *Faith and Criticism*, 25.

56. C. S. Lewis, *The Four Loves* (London: Geoffrey Bles, 1960), 11.

57. Lewis, *Discarded Image*, 113–14.

58. Ibid., 185.

59. Ibid., 216.

60. Ibid.

61. Ibid., 222.

6. Narnia and the North

1. C. S. Lewis, *The Discarded Image* (London: Cambridge University Press, 1974), 14–15. See also Owen Barfield's *Saving the Appearances*.

2. Ibid., 14–15.

3. Ibid.

4. C. S. Lewis, "Variation in Shakespeare," in *Selected Literary Essays*, ed. Walter Hooper (London: Cambridge University Press, 1969), 75.

5. William Shakespeare, *Macbeth*, act 2, scene 2.

6. Richard Weaver, *The Ethics of Rhetoric* (Chicago: Henry Regnery Company, 1953), 56–57.

7. C. S. Lewis, *The Great Divorce* (New York: Touchstone, 1996), 122.

8. C. S. Lewis, *Studies in Medieval and Renaissance Literature* (New York: Cambridge University Press, 2007), 77.

9. Ibid., 73–74.

10. Ibid., 74.

11. Ibid., 76–77.

12. Ibid., 76.

13. E. M. W. Tillyard and C. S. Lewis, *The Personal Heresy* (London: Oxford University Press, 1939), 27.

14. C. S. Lewis, *Spenser's Images of Life*, ed. Alastair Fowler (London: Cambridge University Press, 1967), 115.

15. Michael Ward, *Planet Narnia* (New York: Oxford University Press, 2008), 75.

16. Ibid., 76.

17. Ibid., 152.

18. Ibid., 160.

19. C. S. Lewis, *The Horse and His Boy* (New York: HarperTrophy, 1994), 140.

20. Ibid., 236.

21. Ibid., 215.

22. C. S. Lewis, *The Silver Chair* (New York: HarperTrophy, 1994), 17.

23. Lewis, *Horse and His Boy*, 176.

24. Ward, *Planet Narnia*, 158.

25. Further discussed in chapter 12, the absorbing imagination.

26. Lewis, *Horse and His Boy*, 20.

27. Ibid., 60–61.

28. Ibid., 66.

29. Ibid., 142.

30. Ibid., 155.

7. A Passionate Sanity

1. C. S. Lewis, *English Literature in the Sixteenth Century Excluding Drama* (London: Oxford University Press, 1954), 486.

2. Ibid., 486–87.

3. C. S. Lewis, "Hero and Leander," in *Selected Literary Essays*, ed. Walter Hooper (London: Cambridge University Press, 1969), 61.

4. Ibid., 62.

5. Lewis, *English Literature in the Sixteenth Century*, 488.

6. Christopher Marlowe, "Hero and Leander," 1598.

7. Charles Williams and C. S. Lewis, *Arthurian Torso* (Grand Rapids: William B. Eerdmans Publishing Company, 1980), 331.

8. C. S. Lewis, *A Preface to Paradise Lost* (London: Oxford University Press, 1942), 3.

9. C. S. Lewis, *An Experiment in Criticism* (Cambridge: Cambridge University Press, 2008), 57.

10. Ibid., 60.

11. Gideon O. Burton, "Progymnasmata," *Silva Rhetoricae,* http://rhetoric.byu .edu/Pedagogy/Progymnasmata/Progymnasmata.htm.

12. Gideon O. Burton, "Figures of Description," *Silva Rhetoricae,* http://rheto ric.byu.edu/Figures/Groupings/of%20Description.htm.

13. Craig Gibson, trans. *Libanius's progymnasmata: Model Exercises In Greek Prose Composition and Rhetoric* (Atlanta: Society of Biblical Literature, 2008), 444–45.

14. William Blake, *The Complete Poetry and Prose of William Blake*, ed. David V. Erdman (New York: Anchor Books, 1988), 550.

15. C. S. Lewis, *The Voyage of the Dawn Treader* (New York: HarperTrophy, 1994), 100.

16. Ibid., 92.

17. Ibid., 163.

18. Ibid., 249–50.

19. Ibid., 258.

20. Michael Ward, *Planet Narnia* (New York: Oxford University Press, 2008), 112.

21. Lewis, *Experiment in Criticism*, 82.

22. Scott Cairns, "What Now?" *Image* 80 (Winter/Spring 2014): 105–6.

23. C. S. Lewis, *Spenser's Images of Life*, ed. Alastair Fowler (London: Cambridge University Press, 1967), 115.

24. Lewis, *Experiment in Criticism*, 82–83.

25. Ibid., 85.

26. Ibid., 80.

27. Ibid.

28. Ibid., 86.

29. E. M. W. Tillyard and C. S. Lewis, *The Personal Heresy* (London: Oxford University Press, 1939), 12.

30. Allison Coudert, *Alchemy: The Philosopher's Stone* (Boulder: Shambhala Publications, Inc., 1980), 11–13.

31. Philip Yancey, ed., *Reality and the Vision* (Dallas: Word Publishing, 1990), xi.

8. Discovering New Worlds

1. C. S. Lewis, *The Discarded Image* (Cambridge: Cambridge University Press, 1964), 164–65.

2. William James, *Principles of Psychology*, The Great Books of the Western World, vol. 53, ed. Robert Maynard Hutchins (Chicago: Encyclopedia Britannica, 1952), 260.

3. John Locke, *An Essay Concerning Human Understanding,* The Great Books of the Western World, vol. 35, ed. Robert Maynard Hutchins (Chicago: Encyclopedia Britannica, 1952), 121. Locke does not actually call the mind a blank slate but says, instead it is "as white paper" and that experience writes upon it.

4. C. S. Lewis, *Miracles* (London: Geoffrey Bles, 1947), 50.

5. Something along these lines is also developed in Lewis's essay, "Meditations in a Tool Shed," in *God in the Dock: Essays in Theology and Ethics,* ed. Walter Hooper (Grand Rapids: William B. Eerdmans, 1970).

6. Blaise Pascal, *Pensees*, The Great Books of the Western World, vol. 33, ed. Robert Maynard Hutchins (Chicago: Encyclopedia Britannica, 1952), section 2, no. 72.

7. Benjamin Jowett, *Selected Passages from the Introductions to Plato by Benjamin Jowett*, ed. Lewis Campbell (London: John Murray, 1902), 94.

8. George MacDonald, *Annals of a Quiet Neighbourhood* (White Thorne, CA: Johannesen, 1995; a reproduction of the 1867 Hurst & Blackett edition), 480–81.

9. Aristotle, *Ethics*, The Great Books of the Western World, vol. 8, ed. Robert Maynard Hutchins (Chicago: Encyclopedia Britannica, 1952), book 2, section 4–11.

10. Ibid., book 7, section 8.

11. C. S. Lewis, *A Preface to Paradise Lost* (London: Oxford University Press, 1942), 10.

12. C. S. Lewis, "Transposition," in *The Weight of Glory: And Other Addresses*, ed. Walter Hooper (New York: Touchstone, 1996), 88.

13. John Polkinghorne, in *The Narnia Code*, BBC documentary, directed and produced by Norman Stone (1A Productions, Ltd., 2009), DVD.

14. C. S. Lewis, *Out of the Silent Planet* (New York: Macmillan, 1965), 40.

15. Ibid., 42

16. Ibid., 41–42.

17. Ibid., 51.

18. Ibid., 45.

19. Ibid., 55.

20. Ibid.

21. Ibid., 62–65.

22. Ibid., 68.

23. Ibid., 69.

24. Ibid., 71.

25. Ibid., 72.

26. Ibid., 73ff.

27. Ibid., 73.

28. Ibid., 74.

29. Ibid., 81.

30. Ibid., 83–84.

31. Ibid., 93.

32. Ibid., 95.

33. Ibid., 101.

34. Ibid., 102.

35. Ibid., 115.

36. Ibid., 110.

37. Ibid., 121.

9. The Magician's Bargain

1. C. S. Lewis, *Studies in Words*, 2nd ed. (London: Cambridge University Press, 1967), 282–83.

2. Ibid., 294.

3. Ibid., 294–95

4. Ibid., 300.

5. Ibid., 301.

6. Ibid., 302.

7. Ibid., 303.

8. Richard Weaver, *The Ethics of Rhetoric* (Chicago: Henry Regnery Company, 1953), 23.

9. Ibid., 25.

10. Ibid., 213–18.

11. Ibid., 227.

12. Ibid., 229–31.

13. C. S. Lewis, *The Abolition of Man* (New York: Harper One, 2001), 29.

14. Ibid., 15–18.

15. Ibid., 21.

16. Ibid., 24.

17. Ibid., 31–32.

18. Ibid., 44.

19. Ibid., 65.

20. Ibid., 71–73.

21. Ibid., 74.

22. See chapter 12, on the absorbing imagination.

23. C. S. Lewis, *Out of the Silent Planet* (New York: Scribner Paperback Fiction, 1996), 138–39.

24. Lewis, *Abolition of Man*, 44.

25. C. S. Lewis, *That Hideous Strength* (New York: Scribner Paperback Fiction, 1996), 38.

26. Lewis, *Abolition of Man*, 60.

27. Ibid., 65.

28. Lewis, *That Hideous Strength*, 296.

29. Ibid., 177.

30. Lewis, *Abolition of Man*, 61.

31. Lewis, *That Hideous Strength*, 351.

32. Ibid., 24–25.

33. Lewis, *Abolition of Man*, 14.

34. Benjamin Jowett, trans., *Plato: The Republic, Book 2*, in *Five Great Dialogues* (Roslyn, NY: Walter J. Black, Inc., 1942), 256–57.

35. C. S. Lewis, "The Trouble with X," in *God in the Dock*, ed. Walter Hooper (Grand Rapids: William B. Eerdmans, 1970), 151–55.

36. Lewis, *Studies in Words*, 284.

37. Lewis, *That Hideous Strength*, 299.

38. Lewis, *Abolition of Man*, 77.

10. The Hellish Nature of Projection

1. C. S. Lewis, *Prince Caspian: The Return to Narnia* (New York: Macmillan, 1951), 182.

2. C. S. Lewis, *The Discarded Image: An Introduction to Medieval and Renaissance Literature* (Cambridge: Cambridge University Press, 1964), 206.

3. C. S. Lewis, "Talking about Bicycles," in *Present Concerns* (San Diego: Harcourt Brace Jovanovich, 1986), 68.

4. C. S. Lewis, *Dymer* (London: J. M. Dent & Sons LTD, 1950), xii.

5. C. S. Lewis, *Mere Christianity* (London: Geoffrey Bles, 1953 [reprint]), 108.

6. C. S. Lewis, "Historicism," in *Christian Reflections*, ed. Walter Hooper (Grand Rapids: William B. Eerdmans, 1967), 100.

7. Ibid., 106.

8. Lewis, "The Funeral of the Great Myth," in *Christian Reflections*, 83.

9. Ibid., 84–85.

10. Ibid., 85.

11. C. S. Lewis, *English Literature in the Sixteenth Century Excluding Drama* (Oxford: Oxford University Press, 1954), 30.

12. C. S. Lewis, "Bulverism," in *God in the Dock: Essays in Theology and Ethics*, ed. Walter Hooper (Grand Rapids: William B. Eerdmans), 273.

13. Ibid.

14. Ibid., 274.

15. Ibid., 277.

16. C. S. Lewis, *Studies in Medieval and Renaissance Literature*, ed. Walter Hooper (Cambridge: Cambridge University Press. 1966), 62.

17. C. S. Lewis, *The Great Divorce* (New York: Macmillan, 1946), 1.

18. Ibid., 19.

19. Ibid., 18.

20. Ibid., 21.

21. Ibid., 65.

22. Ibid., 66.

23. Ibid., 69.

24. Lewis, *Problem of Pain*, 115.

25. Ibid., 113.

26. Lewis, *Great Divorce*, 26.

27. Ibid., 27.

28. Ibid., 27–28.

29. Ibid., 26.

30. Ibid., 28.

31. Ibid., 32.

32. Ibid., 33.

33. Ibid.

34. Ibid.

35. Ibid., 37–38.

36. Ibid., 39.

37. Ibid., 85.

38. Ibid., 86.

39. Ibid., 88.

40. Ibid., 87.

41. Ibid.

42. Ibid.

43. Ibid., 90.

44. Ibid., 91.

45. Ibid.

46. Ibid.

47. Ibid., 97.

48. Lewis, *Problem of Pain*, 111.

49. Lewis, *Great Divorce*, 110–11.

50. Ibid., 126.

11. The Grey Town

1. C. S. Lewis, *Reflections on the Psalms* (New York: Harcourt, Inc., 1986), 41.

2. C. S. Lewis, "On Three Ways of Writing for Children," in *Of Other Worlds*, ed. Walter Hooper (San Diego: Harcourt Brace Jovanovich Publishers, 1966), 29.

3. C. S. Lewis, "Psycho-Analysis and Literary Criticism," in *Selected Literary Essays*, ed. Walter Hooper (London: Cambridge University Press, 1969), 290.

4. Lewis, *Of Other Worlds*, 30.

5. George MacDonald, *Unspoken Sermons, Third Series* (Eureka, CA: Sunrise Books Publishers, 1996), 102–3.

6. C. S. Lewis, *The Magician's Nephew* (New York: HarperTrophy, 1994), 71.

7. C. S. Lewis, "The Shoddy Lands," in *Of Other Worlds* (New York: Harcourt, Inc., 1994), 106.

8. C. S. Lewis, *The Screwtape Letters* (New York: The Macmillan Company, 1964), 45.

9. Ibid., 46.

10. Ibid., from the preface.

11. Ibid., 92.

12. Ibid., 160.

13. Ibid., 37.

14. Ibid., 37.

15. C. S. Lewis, *A Grief Observed* (New York: HarperSanFrancisco, 1961), 52.

16. Ibid.

17. C. S. Lewis, *Surprised by Joy* (New York: Harcourt, Brace & World, Inc., 1955), 219–20.

18. See chapter 12 on the absorbing imagination for a more in-depth analysis of a desire for the hidden country.

19. C. S. Lewis, *The Weight of Glory* (New York: The Macmillan Company, 1949), 29.

20. Richard V. James, "C. S. Lewis's Belfast Childhood," in *C. S. Lewis: An Examined Life*, ed. Bruce L. Edwards, vol. 1 (Westport: Praeger Publishers, 2007), 35.

21. C. S. Lewis, *The Pilgrim's Regress* (Grand Rapids, MI: William B. Eerdmans, 1981), 204–5.

22. G. K. Chesterton, *Tremendous Trifles* (Mineola, NY: Dover Publications, 2007), 7.

12. Searching for the Hidden Country

1. C. S. Lewis, *The Discarded Image* (London: Cambridge University Press, 1974), 100.

2. C. S. Lewis, "Meditation in a Toolshed," in *God in the Dock: Essays in Theology and Ethics*, ed. Walter Hooper (Grand Rapids: William B. Eerdmans, 1970), 212–14.

3. When we employ the term *Christian myth* we are subscribing to Lewis's definition of myth: "A real though unfocussed gleam of divine truth falling upon human imagination." Lewis believed that faith isn't just facts but the mythic elements that give meaning to those facts. C. S. Lewis, *Miracles* (New York: The Macmillan Company, 1955), 161 footnote.

4. C. S. Lewis, *Prince Caspian* (New York: HarperTrophy, 1994), 167, 169.

5. C. S. Lewis, *Selected Literary Essays*, ed. Walter Hooper (London: Cambridge University Press, 1969), 65.

6. David Downing, *Into the Wardrobe: C. S. Lewis and the Narnia Chronicles* (San Francisco: Jossey-Bass, 2005), 111.

7. Lewis, *Discarded Image*, 121, 216.

8. Michael Ward, *Planet Narnia* (New York: Oxford University Press, 2008), 21.

9. Lewis, *Discarded Image*, 46.

10. Downing, *Into the Wardrobe*, 109.

11. C. S. Lewis, *The Collected Letters of C. S. Lewis,* ed. Walter Hooper, vol. 2, *Books, Broadcasts, and the War 1931–1949* (New York: HarperSanFrancisco, 2004), 12–13.

12. George Sayer, *Jack: C. S. Lewis and His Times* (London: Macmillan London, Limited, 1988), 189.

13. J. R. R. Tolkien: "Beowulf: The Monsters and the Critics," in *The Monsters and the Critics: And Other Essays*, ed. Christopher Tolkien (Boston: Houghton Mifflin Company, 1984), 21.

14. C. S. Lewis, *The Last Battle* (New York: HarperTrophy, 1994), 91.

15. Ibid., 186.

16. C. S. Lewis, *Surprised by Joy* (New York: Harcourt, Brace & World, Inc., 1955), 170.

17. Don King, *C. S. Lewis, Poet* (Kent, OH: The Kent State University Press, 2001), 52, 58.

18. C. S. Lewis, *Spirits in Bondage* (San Diego: Harcourt Brace Jovanovich, 1984), xlii.

19. Ibid., 4.

20. Ibid., 20.

21. Ibid., 21.

22. Ibid., 50.

23. Ibid.

24. C. S. Lewis, *Poems* (San Diego: Harcourt Brace Jovanovich, 1964), 81.

25. Malcolm Guite, *C. S. Lewis: Apologetics and the Poetic Imagination*, available from http://www.thetablet.co.uk/UserFiles/Files/GUITE_-_CSLewis_and_the_poet ic_imagination.docx.

26. Humphrey Carpenter, *The Inklings* (Boston: Houghton Mifflin Company, 1979), 43.

27. C. S. Lewis, "Bluspels and Flalansferes," in *Selected Literary Essays* (London: Cambridge University Press, 1969), 265.

28. Humphrey Carpenter, *The Inklings* (Boston: Houghton Mifflin Company, 1979), 44.

29. Lewis, *God in the Dock*, 67.

30. Ibid., 66.

31. Ibid.

32. Ibid., 67.

33. Lewis, *Poems*, 49.

34. Ibid.

35. Ibid., 50.

36. Ibid.

37. Ibid., 51.

38. G. K. Chesterton, *The Everlasting Man* (San Francisco: Ignatius Press, 1993), 171–72.

39. C. S. Lewis, *The Pilgrim's Regress* (Grand Rapids: William B. Eerdmans, 1981), 204.

40. C. S. Lewis, *The Weight of Glory* (New York: The Macmillan Company, 1949), 4.

41. Lewis, *Poems*, 27.

42. Ibid., 28.

43. Ibid.

44. Ibid., 40.

45. Ibid.

46. Ibid.

47. Ibid., 41.

48. Ibid.

49. Ibid., 61.

50. Ibid.

51. C. S. Lewis, *Mere Christianity* (New York: Touchstone, 1996), 121.

52. Lewis, *Weight of Glory*, 5.

Conclusion

1. T. S. Eliot, "Four Quartets," part 2: East Coker, I (Orlando: Harcourt, Inc.), 23.

2. C. S. Lewis, *Letters of C. S. Lewis* (New York: Harcourt, Brace & World, 1966), 260.

3. Walter Hooper, *C. S. Lewis: Companion & Guide* (London: Harper Collins Publishers), 654.

4. C. S. Lewis, *The Voyage of the Dawn Treader* (New York: The Macmillan Company), 209.

5. Elizabeth Barrett Browning, "Aurora Leigh," retrieved from http://www.bartleby.com/236/86.html.

6. C. S. Lewis, "The Weight of Glory," in *They Asked for a Paper: Papers and Addresses* (London: Geoffrey Bles, 1962), 202.

7. Owen Barfield, *Owen Barfield on C. S. Lewis* (Oxford: Barfield Press, 2011), 101–2.

8. Ibid., 100.

Appendix

1. C. S. Lewis, *Of Other Worlds: Essays and Stories*, ed. Walter Hooper (San Diego: Harcourt Brace Jovanovich Publishers, 1966), 29.

2. C. S. Lewis, *The Allegory of Love* (London: Oxford University Press, 1973), 206–7.

3. C. S. Lewis, *The Weight of Glory* (New York: The Macmillan Company, 1949), 2.

4. C. S. Lewis, *The Discarded Image* (London: Cambridge University Press, 1974), 181.

5. C. S. Lewis, *English Literature in the Sixteenth Century Excluding Drama* (London: Oxford University Press, 1954), 329.

6. C. S. Lewis, *An Experiment in Criticism* (Cambridge: Cambridge University Press, 2008), 33–34.

7. C. S. Lewis, *Studies in Medieval and Renaissance Literature* (New York: Cambridge University Press, 2007), 49.

8. Lewis, *Allegory of Love*, 260, 310.

9. Ibid., 1. See also: C. S. Lewis, *A Preface to Paradise Lost* (London: Oxford University Press, 1954), 70.

10. Ibid., 10–11.

11. C. S. Lewis, *Selected Literary Essays*, ed. Walter Hooper (London: Cambridge University Press, 1969), 72.

12. C. S. Lewis, *English Literature in the Sixteenth Century Excluding Drama* (London: Oxford University Press, 1954), 4.

13. Lewis, *Experiment in Criticism*, 34.

14. Lewis, *Allegory of Love*, 205.

15. Lewis, *Studies in Medieval and Renaissance Literature*, 42.

16. Lewis, "Is Theology Poetry?" in *The Weight of Glory*, 92.

17. Ibid.

18. Ibid.

19. Lewis, *Experiment in Criticism*, 47.

20. Ibid., 94; Lewis, *Letters to Malcolm: Chiefly on Prayer* (London: Geoffrey Bles, 1964), 84–85; *Selected Literary Essays*, 72.

Bibliography

Primary Sources

Lewis, C. S. *The Abolition of Man: Or, Reflections on Education, with Special Reference to the Teaching of English in the Upper Forms of Schools*. New York: Macmillan, 1947.

———. *The Allegory of Love: A Study in Medieval Tradition*. Oxford: Oxford University Press, 1936.

———. *All My Road before Me: The Diary of C. S. Lewis, 1922–1927*. Edited by Walter Hooper. New York: Harcourt, 1991.

———. *Arthurian Torso: Containing the Posthumous Fragment "The Figure of Arthur" by Charles Williams and a Commentary on the Arthur Poems of Charles Williams by C. S. Lewis*. London: Oxford University Press, 1948.

———. *Boxen: The Imaginary World of the Young C. S. Lewis*. Edited by Walter Hooper. New York: Harcourt, 1985.

———. *Christian Reflections*. Edited by Walter Hooper. Grand Rapids: William B. Eerdmans, 1967.

———. *C. S. Lewis: Letters to Children*. Edited by Lyle Dorsett and Marjorie Lamp Mead. New York: Macmillan, 1985.

———. *C. S. Lewis's Lost Aeneid: Arms and the Exile*. Edited with an introduction by A. T. Reyes. New Haven: Yale University Press, 2011.

———. *The Collected Letters of C. S. Lewis*. Vol. 1, *Family Letters 1905–1931*. Edited by Walter Hooper. San Francisco: Harper, 2004.

———. The *Collected Letters of C. S. Lewis.* Vol. 2, *Books, Broadcasts, and the War 1931–1949.* Edited by Walter Hooper. San Francisco: Harper, 2004.

———. The *Collected Letters of C. S. Lewis.* Vol. 3, *Narnia, Cambridge, and Joy 1950–1963.* Edited by Walter Hooper. San Francisco: Harper, 2004.

———. *The Collected Poems of C. S. Lewis.* Edited by Walter Hooper. London: Fount Paperbacks, 1994.

———. *The Dark Tower and Other Stories.* Edited by Walter Hooper. New York: Harcourt, 1977.

———. *The Discarded Image: An Introduction to Medieval and Renaissance Literature.* Cambridge: Cambridge University Press, 1964.

———[Clive Hamilton, pseud.]. *Dymer.* London: Dent, 1926.

———. *English Literature in the Sixteenth Century, Excluding Drama. The Oxford History of English Literature.* Vol. 3. Oxford: Oxford University Press, 1954.

———, ed. *Essays Presented to Charles Williams.* Grand Rapids: William B. Eerdmans, 1974.

———. *An Experiment in Criticism.* Cambridge: Cambridge University Press, 1961.

———. *The Four Loves.* New York: Harcourt, 1960.

———. *God in the Dock: Essays on Theology and Ethics.* Edited by Walter Hooper. Grand Rapids: William B. Eerdmans, 1970.

———. *The Great Divorce: A Dream.* London: Bles, 1945.

——— [N. W. Clerk, pseud.]. *A Grief Observed.* New York: Faber, 1961.

———. *Hamlet: The Prince or the Poem?* Norwood, PA: Norwood editions, 1978.

———. *The Horse and His Boy.* New York: Macmillan, 1954.

———. *Image and Imagination: Essays and Reviews.* Edited by Walter Hooper. Cambridge: Cambridge University Press, 2013.

———. *The Last Battle: A Story for Children.* New York: Harcourt, 1956.

———. *Letters, C. S. Lewis—Don Giovanni Calabria: A Study in Friendship.* Translated and edited by Martin Moynihan. Ann Arbor: Servant, 1988.

———. *Letters of C. S. Lewis.* Edited and with a memoir by W. H. Lewis. New York: Harcourt, 1966.

———. *Letters to an American Lady.* Edited by Clyde Kilby. Grand Rapids: William B. Eerdmans, 1967.

———. *Letters to Malcolm: Chiefly on Prayer.* London: Bles, 1964.

———. *The Lion, the Witch and the Wardrobe: A Story for Children.* New York: Macmillan, 1950.

———. *The Magician's Nephew.* New York: Macmillan, 1955.

———. *Mere Christianity: A Revised and Amplified Edition with a New Introduction of the Three Books; Broadcast Talks, Christian Behavior and Beyond Personality.* New York: Macmillan, 1952.

———. *Miracles: A Preliminary Study.* London: Bles, 1945.

———. *Narrative Poems.* Edited by Walter Hooper. London: Bles, 1969.

———. *Of Other Worlds.* Edited by Walter Hooper. New York: Harcourt, 1966.

———. *Out of the Silent Planet.* Oxford: John Lane, 1938.

———. *Perelandra.* Oxford: John Lane, 1943.

———. *The Pilgrim's Regress: An Allegorical Apology for Christianity, Reason and Romanticism.* London: Dent, 1933.

———. *Poems.* Edited by Walter Hooper. New York: Harcourt, 1965.

———. *A Preface to Paradise Lost.* Oxford: Oxford University Press, 1942.

———. *Present Concerns: Essays by C. S. Lewis.* Edited by Walter Hooper. New York: Harcourt, 1986.

———. *Prince Caspian.* New York: Macmillan, 1951.

———. *The Problem of Pain.* London: Bles, 1940.

———. *Reflections on the Psalms.* New York: Harcourt, 1958.

———. *Rehabilitations and Other Essays.* London: Oxford University Press, 1939.

———. *The Screwtape Letters.* London: Bles, 1942.

———. *Screwtape Proposes a Toast and Other Pieces.* Edited by Walter Hooper. London: Fontana Books, 1965.

———. *Selected Literary Essays.* Edited by Walter Hooper. Cambridge: Cambridge University Press, 1969.

—. *The Silver Chair*. New York: Macmillan, 1954.

—. *Spenser's Images of Life*. Edited by Alistair Fowler. Cambridge: Cambridge University Press, 1967.

— [Clive Hamilton, pseud.). *Spirits in Bondage: A Cycle of Lyrics*. London: Heinemann, 1919.

—. *Studies in Medieval and Renaissance Literature*. Edited by Walter Hooper. Cambridge: Cambridge University Press, 1966.

—. *Studies in Words*. 2nd ed. Cambridge: Cambridge University Press, 1967.

—. *Surprised by Joy: The Shape of My Early Life*. London: Bles, 1955.

—. *That Hideous Strength: A Modern Fairytale for Grownups*. Oxford: John Lane, 1945.

—. *They Asked for a Paper: Papers and Addresses*. London: Bles, 1962.

—. *They Stand Together: The Letters of C. S. Lewis to Arthur Greeves, 1914–1963*. Edited by Walter Hooper. London: William Collins Sons & Co, Ltd, 1979.

—. *Till We Have Faces: A Myth Retold*. New York: Harcourt, 1957.

—. *The Voyage of the Dawn Treader*. New York: Macmillan, 1952.

—. *The Weight of Glory and Other Addresses*. New York: Macmillan, 1949.

—. *The World's Last Night and Other Essays*. New York: Harcourt, 1960.

—. *Yours, Jack: Spiritual Direction from C. S. Lewis*. Edited by Paul Ford. New York: HarperCollins Publishers, 2008.

Lewis, C. S., and E. M. W. Tillyard. *The Personal Heresy: A Controversy*. Oxford: Oxford University Press, 1939.

Books Edited or with a Preface by C. S. Lewis

Athanasius. *The Incarnation of the Word of God: Being the Treatise of St. Athanasius "De Incarnatione Verbi Dei."* Translated by a religious of C. S. M. V. S. Th. Introduction by C. S. Lewis. London: Geoffrey Bles, 1944.

Bentley, Eric. *The Cult of the Superman: A Study in the Idea of Heroism in Carlyle and Nietzsche, with Notes on Other Hero-Worshippers of Modern Times*. With an appreciation by C. S. Lewis. New York: The Macmillan Company, 1954.

Brook, G. L., ed. *Selections from Layamon's Brut.* Introduction by C. S. Lewis. Oxford: Oxford University Press, 1963.

Davidman, Joy. *Smoke on the Mountain: An Interpretation of the Ten Commandments.* Foreword by C. S. Lewis. Philadelphia: The Westminster Press, 1954.

Farrer, Austin. *A Faith of Our Own.* Preface by C. S. Lewis. Cleveland: The World Publishing Company, 1960.

Harding, D. E. *The Hierarchy of Heaven and Earth: A New Diagram of Man in the Universe.* Preface by C. S. Lewis. New York: Harper Brothers, 1952.

MacDonald, George. *George MacDonald: An Anthology.* Edited by C. S. Lewis. London: Geoffrey Bles, 1946.

Phillips, J. B. *Letters to Young Churches: A Translation of the New Testament Epistles.* Introduction by C. S. Lewis. New York: The Macmillan Company, 1954.

Sandhurst, B. G. *How Heathen Is Britain?* Preface by C. S. Lewis. London: Collins, 1946.

Secondary Sources

Abanes, Richard. *Harry Potter, Narnia, and the Lord of the Rings: What You Need to Know about Fantasy Books and Movies.* Eugene, OR: Harvest House Publishers, 2005.

Adey, Lionel. *C. S. Lewis: Writer, Dreamer, and Mentor.* Grand Rapids: William B. Eerdmans, 1998.

———. *C. S. Lewis's "Great War" with Owen Barfield.* University of Victoria, British Colombia: ELS Monographs, 1978.

Aeschliman, Michael D. *The Restitution of Man: C. S. Lewis and the Case against Scientism.* Grand Rapids: William B. Eerdmans, 1983.

Arnott, Anne. *The Secret Country of C. S. Lewis.* London: Hodder and Stoughton, 1974.

Arthur, Sarah. *Walking through the Wardrobe: A Devotional Quest into The Lion, the Witch and the Wardrobe.* Wheaton, IL: Tyndale House Publishers, 2005.

Barfield, Owen. *Owen Barfield on C. S. Lewis.* Edited by G. B. Tennyson and Jane Hipolito. Middletown: Wesleyan University Press, 1989.

Barkman, Adam. *C. S. Lewis & Philosophy as a Way of Life: A Comprehensive Historical Examination of His Philosophical Thoughts*. Allentown, PA: Zossima Press, 2009.

Bassham, Gregory, and Jerry L. Walls. *The Chronicles of Narnia and Philosophy: The Lion, the Witch and the Worldview*. Chicago and La Salle, IL: Open Court, 2005.

Batstone, Patricia. *In Debt to C. S. Lewis*. Dunkeswell, Devon: A Cottage Books, 1999.

Bell, James Stuart, Carrie Pyykkonen, and Linda Washington. *Inside the Lion, the Witch and the Wardrobe: Myths, Mysteries, and Magic from The Chronicles of Narnia*. New York: St. Martin's Griffin, 2005.

Beversluis, John. *C. S. Lewis and the Search for Rational Religion*. Grand Rapids: William B. Eerdmans, 1985.

Billy, Dennis J. *C. S. Lewis on the Fullness of Life: Longing for Deep Heaven*. New York: Paulist Press, 2009.

Bingham, Derick. *A Shiver of Wonder*. Greenville, SC: Ambassador International, 2004.

Bleakley, David. *C. S. Lewis at Home in Ireland*. Bangor, Ireland: Strandtown Press, 1998.

Bowen, John P. *The Spirituality of Narnia: The Deeper Magic of C. S. Lewis*. Vancouver, British Columbia: Regent College Publishing, 2007.

Bramlette, Perry. *C. S. Lewis: Life at the Center*. Macon, GA: Peake Road, 1996.

Bramlette, Perry C., and Higdon, Ronald W. *Touring C. S. Lewis' Ireland and England*. Macon, GA: Smyth & Helways, 1998.

Brennan, Herbie, ed. *Through the Wardrobe: Your Favorite Authors on C. S. Lewis's Chronicles of Narnia*. Dallas: BenBella Books, 2010.

Brown, Devin. *Inside Narnia: A Guide to Exploring the Lion, the Witch and the Wardrobe*. Grand Rapids: Baker Books, 2005.

———. *Inside Prince Caspian: A Guide to Exploring the Return to Narnia*. Grand Rapids: Baker Books, 2008.

———. *Inside the Voyage of the Dawn Treader: A Guide to Exploring the Journey beyond Narnia*. Grand Rapids: Baker Books, 2010.

————. *A Life Observed: A Spiritual Biography of C. S. Lewis.* Grand Rapids: Brazos Press, 2013.

Bruner, Kurt, and Jim Ware. *Finding God in the Land of Narnia.* Carol Stream, IL: Tyndale House Publishers, 2005.

Burson, Scott R., and Jerry L. Walls. *C. S. Lewis and Francis Schaeffer: Lessons for a New Century from the Most Influential Apologists of Our Time.* Downers Grove, IL: InterVarsity Press, 1998.

Cantor, Norman F. *Inventing the Middle Ages: The Lives, Works, and Ideas of the Great Medievalists of the Twentieth Century.* Cambridge: The Lutterworth Press, 1992.

Carnell, Corbin Scott. *Bright Shadow of Reality: C. S. Lewis and the Feeling Intellect.* Grand Rapids: William B. Eerdmans, 1974.

Carpenter, Humphrey. *The Inklings: C. S. Lewis, J. R. R. Tolkien, Charles Williams, and Their Friends.* Boston: Houghton Mifflin Company, 1979.

Caughey, Shanna, ed. *Revisiting Narnia: Fantasy, Myth and Religion in C. S. Lewis' Chronicles.* Dallas: Benbella Books, 2005.

Christensen, Michael J. *C. S. Lewis on Scripture: His Thoughts on the Nature of Biblical Inspiration, the Role of Revelation and the Question of Inerrancy.* Waco, TX: Word Books, 1979.

Christopher, Joe R. *C. S. Lewis.* Boston: Twayne Publishers, 1987.

Christopher, Joe R., and Joan Ostling. *C. S. Lewis: An Annotated Checklist of Writings about Him and His Works.* Kent, OH: Kent State University Press, 1973.

Clark, David G. *C. S. Lewis Goes to Heaven: A Reader's Guide to the Great Divorce.* Hamden, CT: Winged Lion Press, 2012.

Colbert, David. *The Magical Worlds of Narnia: A Treasury of Myths, Legends, and Fascinating Facts behind the Chronicles.* New York: Berkley Books, 2005.

Como, James. *Branches to Heaven: The Geniuses of C. S. Lewis.* Dallas: Spence Publishing Company, 1998.

————. *C. S. Lewis at the Breakfast Table and Other Reminiscences.* New York: Macmillan Publishing Co., Inc., 1979.

————. *Why I Believe in Narnia: 33 Reviews and Essays on the Life & Work of C. S. Lewis.* Allentown, PA: Zossima Press, 2008.

Connolly, Sean. *Inklings of Heaven: C. S. Lewis and Eschatology.* Leominster, UK: Gracewing, 2007.

Cording, Robert. *The Lion and the Land of Narnia: Our Adventures in Aslan's World.* Eugene, OR: Harvest House Publishers, 2008.

Cording, Ruth James. *C. S. Lewis: A Celebration of His Early Life.* Nashville: Broadman & Holman, 2000.

Coren, Michael. *The Man Who Created Narnia: The Story of C. S. Lewis.* Grand Rapids: William B. Eerdmans, 1994.

Cunningham, Richard B. *C. S. Lewis: Defender of the Faith.* Philadelphia: The Westminster Press, 1967.

Davidman, Joy. *Out of My Bone: The Letters of Joy Davidman.* Edited by Don King. Grand Rapids: William B. Eerdmans, 2009.

Derrick, Christopher. *C. S. Lewis and the Church of Rome.* San Francisco: Ignatius Press, 1981.

Derrick, Christopher et al. *G. K. Chesterton and C. S. Lewis: The Riddle of Joy.* Grand Rapids: William B. Eerdmans, 1989.

Dickerson, Matthew, and David O'Hara. *Narnia and the Fields of Arbol: The Environmental Vision of C. S. Lewis.* Lexington, KY: University Press of Kentucky, 2009.

Ditchfield, Christin. *A Family Guide to the Lion, the Witch and the Wardrobe.* Wheaton, IL: Crossway Books, 2005.

———. *A Family Guide to Narnia: Biblical Truths in C. S. Lewis's The Chronicles of Narnia.* Wheaton, IL: Crossway Books, 2003.

———. *A Family Guide to Prince Caspian.* Wheaton, IL: Crossway Books, 2008.

Dorsett, Lyle W. *And God Came In: The Extraordinary Story of Joy Davidman, Her Life and Marriage to C. S. Lewis.* New York: Macmillan Publishing Company, 1983.

———. *Seeking the Secret Place: The Spiritual Formation of C. S. Lewis.* Grand Rapids: Brazos Press, 2004.

Downing, David C. *Into the Region of Awe: Mysticism in C. S. Lewis.* Downers Grove, IL: InterVarsity, 2005.

———. *Into the Wardrobe: C. S. Lewis and the Narnia Chronicles.* San Francisco: Jossey-Bass, 2005.

————. *Planets in Peril: A Critical Study of C. S. Lewis's Ransom Trilogy.* Amherst, MA: The University of Massachusetts Press, 1992.

Duncan, John Ryan. *The Magic Never Ends: The Life and Work of C. S. Lewis.* Nashville: W. Publishing Group, 2001.

Duriez, Colin. *C. S. Lewis: A Biography of Friendship.* Oxford: Lion, 2013.

————. *The C. S. Lewis Handbook: A Comprehensive Guide to His Life, Thought, and Writings.* Grand Rapids: Baker Book House, 1990.

————. *Tolkien and C. S. Lewis: The Gift of Friendship.* Mahwah, NJ: Hidden Spring, 2003.

Edwards, Bruce, ed. *C. S. Lewis: Life, Works and Legacy.* 4 vols. Westport: Praeger Publishers, 2007.

————. *Further Up & Further In: Understanding C. S. Lewis's The Lion, the Witch and the Wardrobe.* Nashville: Broadman & Holman Publishers, 2005.

————. *Not a Tame Lion: Unveil Narnia Through the Eyes of Lucy, Peter, and Other Characters Created by C. S. Lewis.* Wheaton, IL: Tyndale House Publishers, 2005.

————. *A Rhetoric of Reading: C. S. Lewis's Defense of Western Literacy.* Provo, UT: Center for the Study of Christian Values in Literature, 1986.

————, ed. *The Taste of the Pineapple: Essays on C. S. Lewis As Reader, Critic, and Imaginative Writer.* Bowling Green, KY: Bowling Green State University Popular Press, 1988.

Ferrier, Jordan C. *Calvin & C. S. Lewis: Solving the Riddle of the Reformation.* Self-published, 2010.

Filmer, Kath. *The Fiction of C. S. Lewis: Mask and Mirror.* New York: St. Martin's Press, Inc, 1993.

Filmer-Davies, Kath. *Towards a "Good Death": The Fantasy Fiction of C. S. Lewis and the Experience of Reading.* New Lambton, Australia: Nimrod Publications, 1998.

Fleischer, Leonore. *Shadowlands: A Novel.* New York: Signet Publishing, 1993.

Ford, Paul F. *Companion to Narnia.* New York: Macmillan, 1986.

Fuller, Edmund, Clyde S. Kilby, Russell Kirk, John W. Montgomery, and Chad Walsh. *Myth Allegory and the Gospel: An Interpretation of J. R. R. Tolkien,*

C. S. Lewis, G. K. Chesterton, Charles Williams. Minneapolis: Bethany Fellowship, Inc., 1974.

Gibb, Jocelyn, ed. *Light on C. S. Lewis*. New York: Harcourt, Brace, and World, 1965.

Gibson, Evan K. *C. S. Lewis: Spinner of Tales: A Guide to His Fiction*. Washington, DC: Christian University Press, 1980.

Gilbert, Douglas, and Clyde Kilby. *C. S. Lewis: Images of His World*. Grand Rapids: William B. Eerdmans, 1973.

Gilchrist, K. J. *A Morning after War: C. S. Lewis and WW I*. New York: Peter Lang Publishing, 2005.

Gillespie, Natalie. *Believing in Narnia: A Kid's Guide to Unlocking Secret Symbols of Faith in C. S. Lewis's The Chronicles of Narnia*. Nashville: Thomas Nelson, 2008.

Glaspey, Terry W. *Not a Tame Lion: The Spiritual Legacy of C. S. Lewis*. Nashville: Cumberland House Publishing, Inc., 1996.

Glover, Donald E. *C. S. Lewis and the Art of Enchantment*. Athens, OH: Ohio University Press, 1981.

Glyer, Diana Pavlac. *The Company They Keep: C. S. Lewis and J. R. R. Tolkien as Writers in Community*. Kent, OH: Kent State University Press, 2007.

Goffar, Janine. *C. S. Lewis Index: Rumours from the Sculptor's Mill*. Riverside, CA: La Sierra University Press, 1995.

Gormley, Beatrice. *C. S. Lewis: Christian and Storyteller*. Grand Rapids: William B. Eerdmans, 1998.

Gray, William. *C. S. Lewis*. Plymouth, UK: Northcote House, 1998.

Green, Roger Lancelyn. *Into Other Worlds: Space-Flight in Fiction, from Lucian to Lewis*. Grand Rapids: William B. Eerdmans, 1973.

Green, Roger Lancelyn, and Walter Hooper. *C. S. Lewis: A Biography*. New York: Harcourt, Brace & Jovanovich, 1974.

Gresham, Douglas H. *Jack's Life: The Life Story of C. S. Lewis*. Nashville: Broadman & Holman Publishers, 2005.

———. *Lenten Lands: My Childhood with Joy Davidman and C. S. Lewis*. New York: Macmillan Publishing Company, 1988.

Griffin, William. *C. S. Lewis: Spirituality for Mere Christians*. New York: The Crossroad Publishing Company, 1998.

———. *Clive Staples Lewis: A Dramatic Life*. San Francisco: Harper & Row, Publishers, 1986.

Hajek, Matej. *Imaginace: Imaginace v Pojeti Owena Barfielda v Rozhovorou s Clivem S. Lewisem*. Bratislava, Slovakia: Dingir, 2014.

Hamilton, Janet. *C. S. Lewis: Twentieth Century Pilgrim*. Greensboro, NC: Morgan Reynolds Publishing, 2011.

Hannay, Margaret Patterson. *C. S. Lewis*. New York: Frederick Ungar Publishing Co, 1981.

Harries, Richard. *C. S. Lewis: The Man and His God*. Wilton, CT: Morehouse-Barlow, 1987.

Hart, Dabney Adams. *Through the Open Door: A New Look at C. S. Lewis*. Nashville: Express Media, 1994.

Harwood, Lawrence. *C. S. Lewis, My Godfather*. Downers Grove, IL: InterVarsity Press, 2007.

Heck, Joel, D. *Irrigating Deserts: C. S. Lewis on Education*. Saint Louis: Concordia Academic Press, 2005.

Hillegas, Mark R., ed. *Shadows of Imagination: The Fantasies of C. S. Lewis, J. R. R. Tolkien, and Charles Williams*. Carbondale, IL: Southern Illinois University Press, 1979.

Himes, Jonathan B., with Joe R. Christopher and Salwa Khoddam. *Truths Breathed through Silver: The Inklings' Moral and Mythopoeic Legacy*. Newcastle, UK: Cambridge Scholars Publishing, 2008.

Hinten, Marvin D. *The Keys to the Chronicles: Unlocking the Symbols of C. S. Lewis's Narnia*. Nashville: Broadman & Holman Publishers, 2005.

Holmer, Paul L. *C. S. Lewis: The Shape of His Faith and Thought*. New York: Harper & Row Publishers, 1976.

Hooper, Walter. *C. S. Lewis: A Companion & Guide*. London: HarperCollins Publishers, 1996.

———. *Past Watchful Dragons: The Narnian Chronicles of C. S. Lewis*. New York: Collier Books, 1979.

Hosek, Pavel. *C. S. Lewis: Mytus, Imaginace a Pravda*. Praha, Czech Republic: Navrat domu, 2004.

———. *Louzlo Vypraveni: Promenujici moc Pribehu a "Krest Fantazie" v Pojeti C. S. Lewis*. Praha, Czech Republic: Navrat domu, 2013.

Howard, Thomas. *The Achievement of C. S. Lewis: A Reading of His Fiction*. Wheaton, IL: Harold Shaw Publishers, 1980.

———. *C. S. Lewis Man of Letters: A Reading of His Fiction*. San Francisco: Ignatius Press, 1987.

———. *Narnia and Beyond: A Guide to the Fiction of C. S. Lewis*. San Francisco: Ignatius Press, 2006.

Joeckel, Samuel. *The C. S. Lewis Phenomenon: Christianity and the Public Sphere*. Macon, GA: Mercer University Press, 2013.

Karkainen, Paul A. *Narnia Explored*. Old Tappan, NJ: Revell, 1979.

Karlson III, Henry C. Anthony. *Thinking with the Inklings: A Contemplative Engagement with the Oxford Fellowship*. Silver Spring, MD: CreateSpace, 2010.

Keefe, Carolyn, ed. *C. S. Lewis: Speaker & Teacher*. Grand Rapids: Zondervan Publishing House, 1971.

Khoddam, Salwa. *Mythopoeic Narnia: Memory, Metaphor, and Metamorphoses in the Chronicles of Narnia*. Hamden, CT: Winged Lion Press, 2011.

Kilby, Clyde S. *The Christian World of C. S. Lewis*. Grand Rapids: William B. Eerdmans, 1964.

———. *Images of Salvation in the Fiction of C. S. Lewis*. Wheaton, IL: Harold Shaw Publishers, 1978.

Kilby, Clyde S., and Marjorie Lamp Mead. *Brothers and Friends: The Diaries of Major Warren Hamilton Lewis*. San Francisco: Harper and Row, 1988.

King, Don. *C. S. Lewis, Poet: The Legacy of His Poetic Impulse*. Kent, OH: The Kent State University Press, 2001.

Knight, Gareth. *The Magical World of the Inklings: J. R. R. Tolkien, C. S. Lewis, Charles Williams, Owen Barfield*. Longmead, UK: Element Books, 1990.

Kort, Wesley A. *C. S. Lewis: Then and Now*. Oxford: Oxford University Press, 2001.

Kreeft, Peter. *Between Heaven and Hell: A Dialog Somewhere beyond Death with John*

F. Kennedy, *C. S. Lewis & Aldous Huxley.* Downers Grove, IL: Inter Varsity Press, 1982.

———. *C. S. Lewis: A Critical Essay.* Grand Rapids: William B. Eerdmans, 1969.

———. *C. S. Lewis for the Third Millennium: Six Essays on the Abolition of Man.* San Francisco: Ignatius Press, 1994.

———. *The Shadow-Lands of C. S. Lewis: The Man behind the Movie.* San Francisco: Ignatius Press, 1994.

Lawlor, John. *C. S. Lewis: Memories and Reflections.* Dallas: Spence Publishing Company, 1998

———, ed. *Patterns of Love and Courtesy: Essays in Memory of C. S. Lewis.* London: Edward Arnold (Publishers) Ltd, 1966.

Lindskoog, Kathryn Ann. *C. S. Lewis: Mere Christian.* Glendale: Gospel Light Publishers, 1973.

———. *The C. S. Lewis Hoax.* Portland: Multnomah Press, 1988.

———. *Finding the Landlord: A Guidebook to C. S. Lewis's Pilgrim's Regress.* Chicago: Cornerstone Press, 1995.

———. *Journey into Narnia.* Pasadena, CA: Hope Publishing House, 1998.

———. *Light in the Shadowlands: Protecting the Real C. S. Lewis.* Pasadena, CA: Questar Publishers, Inc., 1994.

———. *The Lion of Judah in Never Never Land: The Theology of C. S. Lewis Expressed in His Fantasies for Children.* Grand Rapids: William B. Eerdmans, 1973.

Lindvall, Terry. *Surprised by Laughter: The Comic World of C. S. Lewis.* Nashville: Thomas Nelson Publishers, 1996.

Loomis, Steven R., and Jacob P. Rodriguez. *C. S. Lewis: A Philosophy of Education.* New York: Palgrave Macmillan, 2009.

Lowenberg, Susan. *C. S. Lewis: A Reference Guide, 1972–1978.* Grand Rapids: William B. Eerdmans, 1993.

MacSwain, Robert, and Michael Ward. *The Cambridge Companion to C. S. Lewis.* Cambridge: Cambridge University Press, 2010.

Manlove, C. N. *C. S. Lewis: His Literary Achievement.* New York: St. Martin's Press, 1987.

Markos, Louis. *Lewis Agonistes: How C. S. Lewis Can Train Us to Wrestle with the Modern and Postmodern World*. Nashville: Broadman & Holman Publishers, 2003.

————. *Restoring Beauty: The Good, the True, and the Beautiful in the Writings of C. S. Lewis*. Colorado Springs: Biblica, 2010.

Martin, Thomas L., ed. *Reading the Classics with C. S. Lewis*. Grand Rapids: Baker Book House Company, 2000.

Martindale, Wayne, and Jerry Root, eds. *The Quotable Lewis*. Wheaton, IL: Tyndale House Publishers, Inc., 1989.

Martindale, Wayne, Jerry Root, and Linda Washington. *The Soul of C. S. Lewis*. Wheaton, IL: Tyndale House Publishers, Inc., 2010.

Mastrolia, Arthur. *C. S. Lewis and the Blessed Virgin Mary: Uncovering a "Marian Attitude."* Lima, OH: Fairway Press, 2000.

McColman, Carl. *The Lion, the Mouse and the Dawn Treader: Spiritual Lessons from C. S. Lewis's Narnia*. Brewster, MA: Paraclete Press, 2011.

McGrath, Alister E. *C. S. Lewis: Eccentric Genius. Reluctant Prophet*. Carol Stream, IL: Tyndale House Publishers, Inc., 2013.

————. *If I Had Lunch with C. S. Lewis: Exploring the Ideas of C. S. Lewis on the Meaning of Life*. Carol Stream, IL: Tyndale House Publishers, Inc., 2014.

————. *The Intellectual World of C. S. Lewis*. Chichester, UK: Wiley-Blackwell, 2014.

McInnis, Jeff. *Shadows and Chivalry: C. S. Lewis and George Mac Donald on Suffering, Evil and Goodness*. Hamden, CT: Winged Lion Press, 2012.

Meilaender, Gilbert. *The Taste for the Other: The Social and Ethical Thought of C. S. Lewis*. Grand Rapids: William B. Eerdmans, 1978.

Menuge, Angus, ed. *C. S. Lewis: Lightbearer in the Shadowlands*. Wheaton, IL: Crossway Books, 1997.

Miller, Rod, ed. *C. S. Lewis and the Arts: Creativity in the Shadowlands*. Baltimore, MD: Square Halo Books, 2013.

Miller, Ryder W. *From Narnia to a Space Odyssey: The War of Ideas between Arthur C. Clarke and C. S. Lewis*. New York: ibooks, 2003.

Mills, David, ed. *The Pilgrim's Guide: C. S. Lewis and the Art of Witness*. Grand Rapids: William B. Eerdmans, 1998.

Milward, Peter. *A Challenge to C. S. Lewis.* Madison, NJ: Fairleigh Dickinson University Press, 1995.

Moynihan, Martin. *The Latin Letters of C. S. Lewis: To Don Giovanni Calabria of Verona and to Members of His Congregation, 1947 to 1961.* Wheaton, IL: Crossway Books, 1987.

Mueller, Steven P. *Not a Tame God: Christ in the Writings of C. S. Lewis.* Saint Louis: Concordia Publishing House, 2002.

Myers, Doris T. *Bareface: A Guide to C. S. Lewis's Last Novel.* Columbia: University of Missouri Press, 2004.

———. *C. S. Lewis in Context.* Kent, OH: Kent State University Press, 1994.

Musacchio, George. *C. S. Lewis: Man & Writer; Essays and Reviews.* Belton, TX: University of Mary Hardin-Baylor, 1994.

Newsom, William Chad. *Talking of Dragons: The Children's Books of J. R. R. Tolkien and C. S. Lewis.* Geanies House, UK: Christian Focus Publications, 2005.

Nicholson, William. *Shadowlands.* New York: Plume, 1991.

Patrick, James. *The Magdalen Metaphysicals: Idealism and Orthodoxy at Oxford, 1901–1925.* Macon, GA: Mercer University Press, 1985.

Payne, Leanne. *Real Presence: The Christian World View of C. S. Lewis as Incarnational Reality.* Wheaton, IL: Crossway Books, 1988.

Pearce, Joseph. *C. S. Lewis and the Catholic Church.* San Francisco: Ignatius Press, 2003.

Peters, John. *C. S. Lewis: The Man and His Achievement.* Exeter: The Paternoster Press, 1985.

Peters, Thomas C. *Simply C. S. Lewis: A Beginner's Guide to His Life and Works.* Wheaton, IL: Crossway Books, 1997.

Poe, Harry Lee, and Rebecca Whitten Poe, eds. *C. S. Lewis Remembered.* Grand Rapids: Zondervan, 2006.

Purtill, Richard L. *C. S. Lewis's Case for the Christian Faith.* San Francisco: Harper & Row, Publishers, 1981.

Reed, Gerard. *C. S. Lewis and the Bright Shadow of Holiness.* Kansas City, MO: Beacon Hill Press of Kansas City, 1999.

Reilly, R. J. *Romantic Religion: A Study of Barfield, Lewis, Williams, and Tolkien.* Athens, GA: University of Georgia Press, 1971.

Reppert, Victor. *C. S. Lewis's Dangerous Idea: A Philosophical Defense of Lewis's Argument from Reason.* Downers Grove, IL: Inter Varsity Press, 2003.

Richardson, Marianna Edwards and Christine Edwards Thackeray. *C. S. Lewis: Latter-Day Truths in Narnia.* Springfield, UT: CFI, 2008.

Rigney, Joe. *Live Like a Narnian: Christian Discipleship in Lewis's Chronicles.* Minneapolis: Eyes & Pen Press, 2013.

Rogers, Jonathan. *The World according to Narnia: Christian Meaning in C. S. Lewis's Beloved Chronicles.* New York: Warner Faith, 2005.

Root, Jerry. *C. S. Lewis and a Problem of Evil: An Investigation of a Pervasive Theme.* Princeton Theological Monograph Series 96. Eugene, OR: Pickwick Publications, 2010.

———, ed. *The C. S. Lewis Bible.* San Francisco: Harper Collins, 2009.

Ryken, Leland, and Marjorie Lamp Mead. *A Reader's Guide through the Wardrobe: Exploring C. S. Lewis's Classic Story.* Downers Grove, IL: InterVarsity Press, 2005.

———. *A Reader's Guide to Caspian: A Journey into C. S. Lewis's Narnia.* Downers Grove, IL: InterVarsity Press, 2008.

Sammons, Martha C. *A Guide through C. S. Lewis' Space Trilogy.* Westchester, IL: Cornerstone Books, 1980.

———. *A Guide through Narnia.* Wheaton, IL: Harold Shaw, 1979.

Sayer, George. *Jack: C. S. Lewis and His Times.* London: Macmillan, 1988.

Schakel, Peter J. *Is Your Lord Large Enough? How C. S. Lewis Expands Our View of God.* Downers Grove, IL: InterVarsity Press, 2008.

———, ed. *The Longing for a Form: Essays on the Fiction of C. S. Lewis.* Grand Rapids: Baker Book House, 1979.

———. *Reason and Imagination in C. S. Lewis: A Study of Till We Have Faces.* Grand Rapids: William B. Eerdmans, 1984.

———. *The Way into Narnia: A Reader's Guide.* Grand Rapids: William B. Eerdmans, 2005.

Schakel, Peter J., and Charles A. Huttar, eds. *Word and Story in C. S. Lewis.* Columbia, MO: University of Missouri Press, 1991.

Schofield, Stephen, ed. *In Search of C. S. Lewis.* South Plainfield, NJ: Bridge Publishing, Inc., 1983.

Schriftman, Jacob. *The C. S. Lewis Book on the Bible: What the Greatest Christian Writer Thought about the Greatest Book.* n.p.: Moonrise, 2008.

Schwartz, Sanford. *C. S. Lewis on the Final Frontier: Science and the Supernatural in the Space Trilogy.* Oxford: Oxford University Press, 2009.

Sellers, J. T. *Reasoning beyond Reason: Imagination as a Theological Source in the Works of C. S. Lewis.* Eugene, OR: Pickwick Publications, 2011.

Sibley, Brian. *C. S. Lewis Through the Shadowlands.* Old Tappen, NJ: Fleming H. Revell Company, 1994.

————. *The Land of Narnia: Brian Sibley Explores the World of C. S. Lewis.* New York: HarperCollins Juvenile Books, 1990.

————. *Shadowlands: The Story of C. S. Lewis and Joy Davidman.* London: Hodder and Stoughton, 1985.

Sims, John A. *Missionaries to the Skeptics. Christian Apologists for the Twentieth Century: C. S. Lewis, Edward John Carnell, and Reinhold Niebuhr.* Macon, GA: Mercer University Press, 1995.

Smith, Mark Eddy. *Aslan's Call: Finding Our Way to Narnia.* Downers Grove, IL: InterVarsity, 2005.

Smith, Robert Houston. *Patches of Godlight: The Pattern of Thought of C. S. Lewis.* Athens, GA: University of Georgia Press, 1981.

Smith, Sandy. *C. S. Lewis and the Island of His Birth: The Places, the Stories, the Inspiration.* Derry-Londonderry, Ireland: Lagan Press, 2013.

Starr, Charlie W. *Light: C. S. Lewis's First and Final Short Story.* Hamden, CT: Winged Lion Press, 2012.

Stauffer, Douglas, and Larry Spargimino. *The Chronicles of Narnia: Wholesome Entertainment or Gateway to Paganism? Trading Biblical Absolutes for Pagan Myths.* Bethany, OK: Bible Belt Publishing, 2006.

Sturgis, Amy H. *Past Watchful Dragons: Fantasy and Faith in the World of C. S. Lewis.* Altadena, CA: The Mythopoeic Press, 2007.

Swift, Catherine. *C. S. Lewis*. Minneapolis: Bethany House Publishers, 1989.

Tadie, Andrew A., and Michael H. MacDonald, eds. *Permanent Things: Toward the Recovery of a More Human Scale at the End of the Twentieth Century.* Grand Rapids: William B. Eerdmans, 1995.

Tandy, Gary L. *The Rhetoric of Certitude: C. S. Lewis's Nonfiction Prose*. Kent, OH: The Kent State University Press, 2009.

Turner, Charles, ed. *Chosen Vessels: Portraits of Ten Outstanding Men*. Ann Arbor, MI: Servant Publications, 1985.

Urang, Gunnar. *Shadows of Heaven: Religion and Fantasy in the Writing of C. S. Lewis, Charles Williams, and J. R. R. Tolkien*. Philadelphia: Pilgrim Press, 1971.

Vanauken, Sheldon. *A Severe Mercy*. New York: Harper and Row, 1977.

Vander Elst, Philip. *Thinkers of Our Time: C. S. Lewis*. London: The Claridge Press, 1996.

Vaus, Will. *The Hidden Story of Narnia: A Book-by-Book Guide to C. S. Lewis' Spiritual Themes*. Cheshire, CT: Winged Lion Press, 2010.

———. *Mere Theology: A Guide to the Thought of C. S. Lewis*. Downers Grove, IL: InterVarsity Press, 2004.

———. *The Professor of Narnia: The C. S. Lewis Story*. Washington, DC: Believe Books, 2008.

———. *Speaking of Jack: A C. S. Lewis Discussion Guide*. Hamden, CT: Winged Lion Press, 2011.

Van Leeuwen, Mary Stewart. *A Sword between the Sexes? C. S. Lewis and the Gender Debates*. Grand Rapids: Brazos Press, 2010.

Velarde, Robert. *Conversations with C. S. Lewis: Imaginative Discussions about Life, Christianity and God*. Downers Grove, IL: InterVarsity Press, 2008.

———. *The Heart of Narnia: Wisdom, Virtue, and Life Lessons from the Classic Chronicles*. Colorado Springs, CO: NavPress, 2008.

———. *The Lion, the Witch, and the Bible: Good and Evil in the Classic Tales of C. S. Lewis*. Colorado Springs, CO: NavPress, 2005.

Vieth, Gene. *The Soul of Prince Caspian: Exploring Spiritual Truth in the Land of Narnia*. Colorado Springs, CO: David C. Cook, 2008.

Walker, Andrew, and James Patrick, eds. *A Christian for All Christians: Essays in Honor of C. S. Lewis*. London: Hodder & Stoughton, 1990.

Walsh, Chad. *C. S. Lewis: Apostle to the Skeptics*. New York: The Macmillan Company, 1949.

———. *Chad Walsh Reviews C. S. Lewis: With a Memoir by Damaris Walsh McGuire*. Altadena, CA: Mythopoeic Press, 1998.

———. *The Literary Legacy of C. S. Lewis*. New York: Harcourt Brace Jovanovich, 1979.

———. *The Visionary Christian*. Touchstone Books, 1996.

Walsh, Milton. *Second Friends: C. S. Lewis and Ronald Knox in Conversation*. San Francisco: Ignatius Press, 2008.

Ward, Michael. *The Narnia Code: C. S. Lewis and the Secret of the Seven Heavens*. Carol Stream, IL: Tyndale House Publishers, 2010.

———. *Planet Narnia: The Seven Heavens in the Imagination of C. S. Lewis*. New York: Oxford University Press, 2008.

Watson, George, ed. *Critical Thought Series: 1. Critical Essays on C. S. Lewis*. Aldershot, UK: Scolar Press, 1992.

Wellman, Sam. *C. S. Lewis: Author of Mere Christianity*. Philadelphia: Chelsea House Publishers, 1999.

West, John G., ed. *The Magician's Twin: C. S. Lewis on Science, Scientism, and Society*. Seattle: Discovery Institute Press, 2012.

White, Michael. *C. S. Lewis: A Life*. New York: Carroll & Graf Publishers, 2004.

White, William Luther. *The Image of Man in C. S. Lewis*. Nashville: Abingdon Press, 1969.

Wielenberg, Erik J. *God and the Reach of Reason: C. S. Lewis, David Hume, and Bertrand Russell*. Cambridge: Cambridge University Press, 2008.

Williams, Donald T. *Inklings of Reality: Essays toward a Christian Philosophy of Letters*. Toccoa Falls, GA: Toccoa Falls College Press, 1996.

———. *Mere Humanity: G. K. Chesterton, C. S. Lewis, and J. R. R. Tolkien on the Human Condition*. Nashville: Broadman & Holman Publishers, 2006.

Williams, Peter S. *C. S. Lewis vs. the New Atheists*. Milton Keynes, UK: Paternoster, 2013.

Williams, Rowan. *The Lion's World: A Journey into the Heart of Narnia*. London: SPCK, 2012.

Williams, Thomas. *The Heart of the Chronicles of Narnia: Knowing God Here by Finding Him There*. Nashville: W. Publishing Group, 2005.

———. *Knowing Aslan: An Encounter with the Lion of Narnia*. Nashville: W. Publishing Group, 2005.

Willis, John Randolph. *Pleasures Forevermore: The Theology of C. S. Lewis*. Chicago: Loyola University Press, 1983.

Wilson, A. N. *C. S. Lewis: A Biography*. London: Collins, 1991.

Wilson, Douglas. *What I Learned in Narnia*. Moscow, ID: Canon Press, 2010.

Wolfe, Judith, and Brendan N. Wolfe, eds. *C. S. Lewis and the Church: Essays in Honor of Walter Hooper*. London: Bloomsbury, 2011.

Journal Articles and Other Articles

Atkinson, Bruce E. "From Facelessness to Divine Identity: An Analysis of C. S. Lewis's 'Till We Have Faces.'" *The Lamp-Post of the Southern California C. S. Lewis Society: A Journal for Lewis Studies* 15, no. 1 (1991): 21–30.

Barfield, Owen. "A Visit to Beatrice." *Seven: An Anglo American Literary Review* 9 (1988): 15–18.

Bechtel, Paul. "C. S. Lewis Apostle of Joy." *The Christian Reader* 16, no. 4 (July/August 1978): 3–8.

Benson, Bruce Ellis. "The End of the Fantastic Dream: Testifying to the Truth in the 'Post' Condition." *Christian Scholar's Review* 30, no. 2 (2000): 145–61.

Blamires, Harry. "Against the Stream: C. S. Lewis and the Literary Scene (The Inaugural C. S. Lewis Memorial Lecture, 8th October 1982)." *Journal of the Irish Christian Study Center* 1 (1983): 11–22.

Brew, Kelli. "Facing the Truth on the Road to Salvation: An Analysis of 'That Hideous Strength' and 'Till We Have Faces.'" *The Lamp-Post of the Southern California C. S. Lewis Society: A Literary Review of Lewis Studies* 22, no. 1 (1998): 10–12.

Charles, J. Daryl. "Permanent Things." In "Inklings of Glory." Special issue, *Christian Reflections: A Series in Faith and Ethics* (2004): 54–58.

Dearborn, Kerry L. "The Baptized Imagination." In "Inklings of Glory." Special issue, *Christian Reflections: A Series in Faith and Ethics* (2004): 11–20.

Dorsett, Lyle W. "C. S. Lewis and Evangelism: A Survey of Useful Books." *Evangelism* 1, no. 4 (August 1987): 3–8.

Duriez, Colin. "C.S. Lewis and the Evangelicals." *Christian Librarian: The Journal and Yearbook of the Librarians' Christian Fellowship* 22 (1998): 11–31.

Edwards, Michael. "C. S. Lewis: Imagining Heaven (The Eighth C. S. Lewis Memorial Lecture, 15th February, 1991)." *Journal of the Irish Christian Study Centre* 5 (1994): 16–33.

Fetherston, Patience. "C. S. Lewis on Rationalism: (Unpublished Notes)." *Seven: An Anglo-American Literary Review* 9 (1988): 87–89.

Filmer, Kath. "The Polemic Image: The Role of Metaphor and Symbol in the Fiction of C. S. Lewis." *Seven: An Anglo-American Literary Review* 7 (1986): 61–76.

Gardner, Helen. "Clive Staples Lewis, 1898–1963." *Proceedings of the British Academy* 51 (1965): 417–28.

Gilchrist, K. James. "Second Lieutenant Lewis." *Seven: An Anglo-American Literary Review* 17 (2000): 61–78.

Gilley, Sheridan. "A Prophet Neither in Ireland Nor in England. (The Third C. S. Lewis Memorial Lecture, 25th October, 1985)." *Journal of the Irish Christian Study Centre* 3 (1985).

Hannay, Margaret P. "Provocative Generalizations: 'The Allegory of Love' in Retrospect." *Seven: An Anglo-American Literary Review* 7 (1986): 41–60.

Hilder, Monika B. "The Foolish Weakness in C. S. Lewis's Cosmic Trilogy: A Feminine Heroic." *Seven: An Anglo-American Literary Review* 19 (2002): 77–90.

Jacobs, Alan. "The Values of Literary Study: Deconstruction and Other Developments." *Christian Scholar's Review* 16, no. 4 (1987): 373–83.

Jeffrey, David Lyle. "Structuralism, Deconstructionism, and Ideology." *Christian Scholar's Review* 17, no. 4 (1988): 436–48.

Kreeft, Peter. "Lewis and the Two Roads to God." In *The World and I*. Washington DC: The Washington Times Corporation, 1987.

Lessel, Thomas M. "The Legacy of C. S. Lewis and the Prospect of Religious Rhetoric." *The Journal of Communication and Religion* 27, no. 1 (2004): 117–37.

Lindskoog, Kathryn. "The Poetic Finale of the Pilgrim's Regress." *The Lamp-Post of the Southern California C. S. Lewis Society: A Literary Review of Lewis Studies* 22, no. 1 (1998): 6–9.

Macky, Peter W. "Appeasing the Gods in C. S. Lewis's 'Till We Have Faces'." *Seven: An Anglo-American Literary Review* 7 (1986): 77–90.

Manlove, Colin. "'The Lion' at 50." *Seven: An Anglo-American Literary Review* 17 (2000): 19–26.

Moynihan, Martin. "C. S. Lewis and T. D. Weldon." *Seven: An Anglo-American Literary Review* 5 (1984): 101–5.

———. "The Latin Letters of C. S. Lewis to Don Giovanni Calabria." *Seven: An Anglo-American Literary Review* 6 (1985): 7–22.

Mulia, Hendra G. "C. S. Lewis's Concept of Myth: An Answer to Linguistic Philosophers." *Stulos Theological Journal* 1, no. 1 (1993): 49–65.

Murrin, Michael. "The Dialectic of Multiple Worlds: An Analysis of C. S. Lewis's Narnia Stories." *Seven: An Anglo-American Literary Review* 3 (1982): 93–112.

Musacchio, George. "Fiction in 'A Grief Observed.'" *Seven: An Anglo-American Literary Review* 8 (1987): 73–83.

Myers, Doris T. "Browsing the Glome Library." *Seven: An Anglo-American Literary Review* 19 (2002): 63–76.

Noll, Mark A. "C. S. Lewis's 'Mere Christianity' (the Book and the Ideal) at the Start of the Twenty-First Century." *Seven: An Anglo-American Literary Review* 19 (2002): 31–44.

Nuttall, A. D. "Jack the Giant-Killer." *Seven: An Anglo-American Literary Review* 5 (1984): 84–100.

Okiyama, Steve. Review of *Till We Have Faces* by C. S. Lewis. *The Lamp-Post of the Southern California C. S. Lewis Society: A Journal for Lewis Studies* 15, no. 1 (1991): 15–20.

Pittenger, W. Norman. "A Critique of C. S. Lewis." *Christian Century*, October 1, 1958, 1104–7.

Price, Geoffrey. "Review Article: Scientism and the Flight from Reality." *Seven: An Anglo-American Literary Review* 7 (1986): 117–26.

Prothero, James. "On Lewis Worship and Lewis Bashing: Text and Subtext in A.N. Wilson's 'C.S. Lewis: A Biography.'" *The Lamp-Post of the Southern California C.S. Lewis Society: A Journal for Lewis Studies* 15, no. 4 (1991): 8–17.

———. "What are We to Make of C. S. Lewis? C. S. Lewis and the Literary Landscape of the 20th Century." *The Lamp-Post of the Southern California C. S. Lewis Society: A Journal for Lewis Studies* 15, no. 1 (1991): 3–14.

Root, Jerry. "Following That Bright Blur." *Christian History Magazine* 4, no. 3 (1985): 27, 35.

———. "Lewis, Clive Staples (1898–1963)." In *Evangelical Dictionary of Christian Education*, edited by Michael Anthony, 425–26. Grand Rapids: Baker Academic.

———. "The Man Who Created Narnia." *Focus on the Family* 22, no. 12 (December 1998): 2–3.

———. "Narnia: What Must God Be Like?" *Focus on the Family* 22, no. 12 (December 1998): 4.

———. "Tools Inadequate and Incomplete: C. S. Lewis and the Great Religions." *Mission and Ministry: The Magazine of Trinity Episcopal School for Ministry* 11, no. 4 and 12, no. 1(1998): 50–53.

Sayer, George. "C. S. Lewis's 'Dymer'." *Seven: An Anglo-American Literary Review* 1 (1980): 94-116.

Schakel, Peter J. "Irrigating Deserts with Moral Imagination." In "Inklings of Glory." Special issue, *Christian Reflections: A Series in Faith and Ethics* (2004): 21–29.

———. "Seeing and Knowing: The Epistemology of C. S. Lewis's 'Till We Have Faces.'" *Seven: An Anglo-American Literary Review* 4 (1983): 84–97.

Sykes, John D., Jr. "The Gospel in Tolkien, Lewis, and Sayers." In "Inklings of Glory." Special issue, *Christian Reflections: A Series in Faith and Ethics* (2004): 88–93.

Talbott, Thomas. "C. S. Lewis and the Problem of Evil." *Christian Scholar's Review* 17, no. 1 (1987): 36–51.

Taliaferro, Charles. "The Co-Inherence." *Christian Scholar's Review* 18, no. 4 (1989): 333–45.

———. "A Hundred Years with the Giants and the Gods: Christians and Twentieth Century Philosophy." *Christian Scholar's Review* 29, no. 4 (2000): 695–712.

Taylor, D. J. "What Is Truth?: An Open Letter to Kathleen Nott." *Seven: An Anglo-American Literary Review* 4 (1983): 10–13.

Thorson, Stephen. "'Knowledge' in C. S. Lewis's Post-Conversion Thought: His Epistemological Method." *Seven: An Anglo-American Literary Review* 9 (1988): 91–116.

Trueblood, D. Elton. "Intellectual Integrity." *Faculty Dialogue: Journal of the Institute for Christian Leadership* 2 (Winter 1984–85): 45–60.

Walsh, Chad. "C. S. Lewis: Critic, Creator and Cult Figure." *Seven: An Anglo-American Literary Review* 2 (1981): 60–80.

Ward, Patricia A. "Worldly Readers and Writerly Texts." *Christian Scholar's Review* 17, no. 4 (1988): 425–35.

Yandell, Keith E. "Evangelical Thought." *Christian Scholar's Review* 14, no. 4 (June 1988): 341–46.

Other Sources

Anscombe, G. E. M. *The Collected Papers of G. E. M. Anscombe.* Vol. 2. *Metaphysics and the Philosophy of Mind.* Minneapolis: University of Minnesota Press, 1981.

Barfield, Owen. *Saving the Appearances: A Study in Idolatry.* New York: Harcourt Brace Jovanovich, 1965.

Carpenter, Humphrey. *Tolkien: A Biography.* Boston: Houghton Mifflin Company, 1977.

Chesterton, G. K. *The Everlasting Man.* London: Hodder and Stoughton, 1947.

———. *Heretics.* In *The Collected Works of G. K. Chesterton,* edited by David Dooley, vol. 1. San Francisco: Ignatius Press, 1986.

———. *Orthodoxy.* In *The Collected Works of G. K. Chesterton,* edited by David Dooley, vol. 1. San Francisco: Ignatius Press, 1986.

———. *Tremendous Trifles.* New York: Sheed and Ward, 1955.

Dante. *The Divine Comedy.* Translated by Charles Eliot Norton. Great Books of the Western World. Vol. 21. Chicago: Encyclopedia Britannica, 1952.

Farrer, Austin. *The Brink of Mystery.* Edited by Charles Conti. London: SPCK, 1976.

———. *Finite and Infinite: A Philosophical Essay.* Westminster: Dacre Press, 1943.

————. *The Glass of Vision.* Westminster: Dacre Press, 1958.

Grahame, Kenneth. *The Wind in the Willows.* London: Methuen & Co. Ltd, 1940.

Hastings, Adrian. *A History of English Christianity 1920–1990.* London: SCM Press, 2001.

Helm, Paul, ed. *Objective Knowledge: A Christian Perspective.* Leicester: Inter-Varsity Press, 1987.

Hutchins, Robert M., and Mortimer Adler, eds. *The Great Ideas Today.* Chicago: Encyclopedia Britannica, 1968.

Julian of Norwich. *A Revelation of Divine Love.* Edited by Marion Glasscoe. Rev. ed. Exeter: University of Exeter Press, 1996.

MacDonald, George. *Phantastes: A Faerie Romance for Men and Women.* London: Arthur C. Fifield, 1905.

Mitchell, Basil. *Faith and Criticism.* Oxford: Clarendon, 1994.

————. *How to Play Theological Ping Pong: Essays on Faith and Reason.* Edited by William J. Abraham and Robert W. Prevost. Grand Rapids: William B. Eerdmans, 1990.

————. *The Justification of Religious Belief.* London: Macmillan, 1978.

Montgomery, John Warwick. *History & Christianity.* Downers Grove, IL: InterVarsity Press, 1974.

Otto, Rudolph. *The Idea of the Holy: An Inquiry into the Non-Rational Factor in the Idea of the Divine and Its Relation to the Rational.* Translated by John W. Harvey. London: Oxford University Press, 1925.

Pascal, Blaise. *Pensees.* Translated by W. F. Trotter. Great Books of the Western World. Vol. 33. Chicago: Encyclopedia Britannica, 1952.

Phillips, J. B. *The Ring of Truth: A Translator's Testimony.* New York: Macmillan Company, 1967.

Plato. *The Dialogues of Plato.* Translated by Benjamin Jowett. Great Books of the Western World. Vol. 7. Chicago: Encyclopedia Britannica, 1957.

————. *The Seventh Letter.* Translated by J. Harward. Great Books of the Western World. Vol. 7. Chicago: Encyclopedia Britannica, 1957.

Polkinghorne, John. *Science and Theology: An Introduction.* London: SPCK, 1998.

Sayers, Dorothy L. *Creed or Chaos?* Manchester: Sophia Institute Press, 1974.

Shakespeare, William. *MacBeth.* New York: Penguin Books, 1971.

Soper, David Wesley. *These Found the Way: Thirteen Converts to Protestant Christianity.* Philadelphia: The Westminster Press, 1951.

Tolkien, J. R. R. *Farmer Giles of Ham.* Boston: Houghton Mifflin Co., 1978.

———. *The Fellowship of the Ring: Being the First Part of the Lord of the Rings.* New York: Ballantine Books, 1974.

———. *The Hobbit, or, There and Back Again.* Boston: Houghton Mifflin Company, 1966.

———. *The Letters of J. R. R. Tolkien.* Selected and edited by Humphrey Carpenter. Assisted by Christopher Tolkien. Boston: Houghton Mifflin Company, 1981.

———. *The Return of the King: Being the Third Part of the Lord of the Rings.* New York: Ballantine Books, 1973.

———. *Smith of Wootton Major.* London: George Allen & Unwin Ltd., 1967.

———. *The Two Towers: Being the Second Part of the Lord of the Rings.* New York: Ballantine Books, 1974.

———. *Tree and Leaf.* London: Unwin Books, 1964.

Underhill, Evelyn. *The Letters of Evelyn Underhill.* Edited by Charles Williams. London: Longmans, Green and Co., 1956.

Von Hügel, Baron Friedrich. *Selected Letters 1896–1924.* Edited with a memoir by Bernard Holland. London: J. M. Dent & Sons, 1928.

Williams, Charles. *The Descent of the Dove.* Grand Rapids: William B. Eerdmans, 1974.

———. *The Image of the City: Essays by Charles Williams.* Edited by Anne Ridler. London: Oxford University Press, 1958.

Specific Bibliographical Works and Editions Cited within the Text

(especially with reference to C. S. Lewis books where the citation may have come from a printing different than those cited above)

Aristotle. *Ethics*. The Great Books of the Western World. Vol. 8. Edited by Robert Maynard Hutchins. Chicago: Encyclopedia Britannica, 1952.

Barfield, Owen. *Owen Barfield on C. S. Lewis*. Edited by G. B. Tennyson and Jane Hipolito. Oxford: Barfield Press, 2011.

Blake, William. *The Complete Poetry and Prose of William Blake*. Edited by David V. Erdman. New York: Anchor Books, 1988.

Burton, Gideon O. "Figures of Description." *Silva Rhetoricae*, http://rhetoric.byu .edu/Figures/Groupings/of%20Description.htm.

———. "Progymnasmata." *Silva Rhetoricae*, http://rhetoric.byu.edu/Pedagogy/ Progymnasmata/Progymnasmata.htm

Cairns, Scott. "What Now?" *Image* 80 (2014).

Cantor, Norman. *Inventing the Middle Ages: Lives, Works, and Ideas of the Great Medievalists of the Twentieth Century.* Cambridge: The Lutterworth Press, 1991.

Carpenter, Humphrey. *The Inklings*. Boston: Houghton Mifflin Company, 1979.

Chesterton, G. K. *The Everlasting Man*. San Francisco: Ignatius Press, 1993.

———. *Tremendous Trifles*. Mineola, NY: Dover Publications, 2007.

———. *Tremendous Trifles*. London: Sheed and Ward, 1955.

Coudert, Allison. *Alchemy: The Philosopher's Stone*. Boulder: Shambhala Publications, Inc., 1980.

Downing, David. *Intro the Wardrobe: C. S. Lewis and the Narnia Chronicles*. San Francisco: Jossey-Bass, 2005.

Eagleton, Terry. *After Theory*. Penguin: London, 2004.

Farrer, Austin. *The Brink of Mystery*. Edited by Charles Conti. London: SPCK, 1976.

Gibson, Craig, trans. *Libanius's Progymnasmata: Model Exercises in Greek Prose Composition and Rhetoric*. Atlanta: Society of Biblical Literature, 2008.

Guite, Malcolm. *C. S. Lewis: Apologetics and the Poetic Imagination*. 2014. Available from http://www.thetablet.co.uk/UserFiles/Files/GUITE_-_CSLewis_and _the_poetic_imagination.docx.

Hopkins, Gerard Manley. *The Major Works*. Edited by Catherine Phillips. New York: Oxford University Press, 2009.

James, Richard V. "C. S. Lewis's Belfast Childhood." In *C. S. Lewis: An Examined Life*. Vol. 1. Edited by Bruce L. Edwards. Westport: Praeger Publishers, 2007.

James, William. *Principles of Psychology*. The Great Books of the Western World. Vol. 53. Edited by Robert Maynard Hutchins. Chicago: Encyclopedia Britannica, 1952.

Jowett, Benjamin. *Selected Passages from the Introductions to Plato by Benjamin Jowett*. Edited by Lewis Campbell. London: John Murray, 1902.

King, Don. *C. S. Lewis, Poet*. Kent, OH: The Kent State University Press, 2001.

Lewis, C. S. *The Abolition of Man*. San Francisco: Harper Collins, 2001.

————. *Out of the Silent Planet*. New York: Macmillan, 1965.

————. *Perelandra*. New York: Macmillan, 1975.

————. *Reflections on the Psalms*. San Diego: Harcourt, 1986.

————. *Selected Literary Essays*. Edited by Walter Hooper. Cambridge: Cambridge University Press, 1979.

————. *The Weight of Glory: And Other Addresses*. Edited by Walter Hooper. New York: Touchstone, 1996.

Locke, John. *An Essay Concerning Human Understanding*. The Great Books of the Western World. Vol. 35. Edited by Robert Maynard Hutchins. Chicago: Encyclopedia Britannica, 1952.

MacDonald, George. *Annals of a Quiet Neighbourhood*. Translated by W. F. Trotter. White Thorne, CA: Johannesen, 1995.

————. *Diary of an Old Soul: 366 Writings for Devotional Reflection*. Minneapolis: Augsburg Publishing House, 1975.

————. *Unspoken Sermons, Third Series*. Eureka, CA: Sunrise Books Publishers, 1996.

MacSwain, Robert, and Michael Ward, eds. *The Cambridge Companion to C. S. Lewis*. New York: Cambridge University Press, 2010.

Marlowe, Christopher. "Hero and Leander." In *The Plays of Christopher Marlowe*. London: J.M Dent & Sons Ltd., 1914.

Pascal, Blaise. *Pensees*. Translated by W. F. Trotter. Great Books of the Western World. Vol. 33. Chicago: Encyclopedia Britannica, 1952.

Plato. *Gorgias.* Translated by Benjamin Jowett. Great Books of the Western World. Vol. 7. Chicago: Encyclopedia Britannica, 1952.

———. *The Republic.* In *Five Great Dialogues.* Roslyn, NY: Walter J. Black, Inc., 1942.

Sayer, George. *Jack: C. S. Lewis and His Times.* London: Macmillan London, Limited, 1988.

Tillyard, E. M. W., and C. S. Lewis. *The Personal Heresy.* London: Oxford University Press, 1939.

Tolkien, J. R. R. *The Monsters and the Critics and Other Essays.* Edited by Christopher Tolkien. Boston: Houghton Mifflin Company, 1984.

Trollope, Anthony. *Barchester Towers.* New York: Washington Square Press, 1963.

Underhill, Evelyn. *The Letters of Evelyn Underhill.* Edited by Charles Williams. London: Longmans, Green and Co., 1947.

Ward, Michael. *Planet Narnia.* New York: Oxford University Press, 2008.

Weaver, Richard. *The Ethics of Rhetoric.* Chicago: Henry Regnery Company, 1953.

Williams, Charles. *The Descent of the Dove: A Short History of the Holy Spirit in the Church.* Grand Rapids: William B. Eerdmans, 1974.

Williams, Charles, and C. S. Lewis. *Arthurian Torso.* Grand Rapids: William B. Eerdmans, 1980.

Yancey, Philip, ed. *Reality and the Vision.* Dallas: Word Publishing, 1990.

Index

CPSIA information can be obtained at www.ICGtesting.com
Printed in the USA
LVOW06s0255180915

454593LV00015B/946/P